THE MAKERS HANDBOOK

THE CASE FOR INTELLIGENT DESIGN

BY

JOHN W.T. QUINN

First Edition 2008

Published by Lulu

ISBN 978-1-4092-0167-0

CONTENTS

FOREWORD

The memory is dimmed by time, and sharpness of the images is lost: most are fact but some are just imaginings or dreams that peopled sleep and seem more real in retrospect than that that really was. Ghosts are summoned up to speak again the wisdom that they spoke before, and those who're yet to come are called upon to lift a corner of the curtain that divides the future from the past.

In anonymity is hid the teller of the tale, who in real time speaks of what he sees, as events unfold before his eyes: he hears the views expressed by others which may not accord with his.

In the second part one meets that most eccentric man the Atom King, who, being unnaturally conceived, believes that he's not formed of human cells, instead retaining likeness to the individual inorganic atoms whose temperament and character he shares, anthropomorphic representative of these the elementary basic bits from which all in the Universe is made.

BOOK ONE

THE ATOMIC GARDEN

And I will give thee the treasures of darkness, and hidden riches of secret places

One The Sacred Peak

Is there a supernatural force, a providence or hand of fate, that oversees the lives of women and of men? Or does all by chance occur, circumstances unforeseen that come into conjunction as if by throw of dice? The problem posed by life is this: at each attempt to rise in self-esteem, it seems the self is driven back by Power unseen.

Here is told the tale of how this Power is sought, and how the knowledge of the Truth's acquired whilst working for the boss of BioMech, the one who, aided by sagacious priest, seeks to synthesise things made by hand of man which are with life endowed, that live and breathe, utensils made of flesh instead of plates of steel and bits of wire. But first, what leads the train of thought to think of matters so profound, what unpremeditated chance results in revelation of this information sought also by these men of science and of cloth?

Truth lies in the heart of every man, obscured by daily cares and worried fears, by pleasures sought to feed the hunger of an idle mind, and boredom to allay. There must be followed path on which events unfold, displaying way in which blind Chance decides the destiny of men.

If universe the laws of Nature does obey, (and who would dare to doubt this well-known fact?), where then does Nature dwell, from whence dispense this governance? It is supposed it is beyond this lofty cliff, sheer face of rock, it lives, on mountain top perpetually lost in mist and noctilucent cloud.

The cliff rears up a dizzy height; from rock-strewn base it can't be seen, what lies beyond, one can but guess. Some try to climb the trail that's cut in face by constant drip of moisture from above, but, driven back by steepness of the way and harshness of the cold, they mostly fail; a few there are who scale the heights and disappear, searching for eternal life in some strange distant land that's hid in cloud, where the throne of Nature's found, from whence are handed down the scientific laws. None come back, and yet it's said there's those who dwell in some far place beyond the crest who pass this way sometimes and mingle unobserved in streets of towns below, the cities of the plain through which great rivers flow.

Barren is the land beneath that lies all day in sunless shadow of this rock, on which are heaped the boulders and the stones, broken from the face by centuries of heat and cold. Far above the ravens fly, circling over ledges where they nest; on the ground the serpent slithers in the dust, and lizards hidden lie in cracks and crannies where they can't be seen by buzzards, or by owls that shriek at night, eking out a living in this lonely place where satyrs dance.

Apart from pilgrims come to climb the rocky heights in search of everlasting life by path both strait and steep, the road of no return, there come the archaeologists who seek among the rubble of the fallen rocks the stones engraved with Nature's Laws, rediscovered recently and named by Fahrenheit and Boyle, and many other clever men beside. All other tissue's been destroyed by steady drip of rain, by heat and cold, by nagging wind and rabbit's tooth and peck of bird: only rock remains of former things, and artefacts of stone, substance at the lowest state that by degradation can be reached. In some far future time there will be found the Cenotaph, a single sign of Empire long forgot, and scientists will say "See here, those Ancient Brits, they knew not how to write with pen and ink, their names they've cut with chisel on the stone, and listed sites of battles where they fell."

Geologists join in the search, tapping tentatively with tiny hammers at the multi-coloured strata where they lie exposed. Thus they hope to solve the mysteries of the universe before astronomers can prise from constellations the secret of the origin of Life as it is lived on Earth.

Carefree youths on cycles come to court adventure in this scary place, they too explore the caves at foot of cliff, seeking treasure non-existent under crags guano-covered by the birds of prey.

Returning home across the fields, meadows lush and green when once beyond sepulchral shadow of the mountain range, a clump of elms is reached, tall and gaunt against the sky, and in their tops there sway the herons' nests.

A challenge this, to climb so high and claim for prize a clutch of eggs. First must be procured some ropes with which to reach the lower branch, weighted with a stone and thrown across the lowest limb. It's getting late, the sun is setting in the west, assault must wait another day.

Swiftly passes time, another day has come and is half gone, as freedom's gained and school is left behind. Ropes are bundled onto bicycles, and way is made back to the field in which the elms still silent stand, untidy nests of sticks and twigs still grace their tops; it's most unlikely that they can be reached, they're far too high for those who cannot fly.

However, all is not as was before: a bull now stands alone in field, pawing ground and tossing head. From time to time he charges trees and scars the trunks with pointed horns, as if to warn against approach to this his sacred grove; he is the guardian of the nests, protector of the birds!

It seems the project must abandoned be, for who would dare to cross the field to reach the tree while this mad beast that stamps and snorts is circling round the spot from which the climb should start? No sooner asked than answered is this query that expected no reply, for over on the other side is seen a man who enters meadow, ducking under strand of wire. A pole in hand with hook in end, a stockman he must surely be, come to grapple with the surly beast.

The great black brute, he turns and stares with lowered head, then charges at this man who's come to take him to the stall where he may brood in solitude. The man his ground he stands in corner by the fence, close by the wire from which hang strands of hair caught on the barbs; the pole he points at beast that paws the ground, and feels its breath upon his face.

What now to do? To dare to enter field, to save this man from gory death upon the horns, to cause diversion, attract attention of this proud animal whose heart's inflamed with fear and hatred for this man who dares to try to subjugate his free and independent mind, and lead him by the nose? All drained away is courage through the feet, hearts are left in boots that turn and unseen leave the scene, for there is none to see this cowardly retreat: the stockman's eyes hold fast to those of bull in trial of strength of will.

No word is ever spoke of this ignominious episode. Nothing's heard of how the farmer fared, of how he must have overpowered the stubborn pride of leader of the cows and led him, fuming, to the byre.

The college block stands on a little knoll, a building painted creamy white, constructed in a classic style, becoming for an institution dedicated to the study of the Romans and the Greeks.

The Head's a man of slender build, his blondish hair is rather sparse, his pale blue eyes are shielded by a pair of spectacles of rimless glass. As is becoming to a man of his exalted rank, he's rarely seen to laugh: his humour's either wry, or else it's very dry. No one would ever dare to risk his wrath, he dominates by hidden strength of character's charisma. He teaches science to the senior class, and leads the morning prayers: although well versed in scientific lore, he also yearns to be ordained and enter Church.

With distinction did he serve in war, survivor of the horror of the trenches, the blood that mingled with the mud. Now he has to train the callow youths, inspire them with a nationalistic pride with tales of Crecy and of Agincourt, omitting the reality of English Archers' cold brutality, for soon they'll follow in the footsteps of their fathers, treading on that foreign soil.

As well as academic subjects and the manly sports, he would instil a little something of the social graces in these awkward in-betweenies that he has to teach. To this end the first-year entrants to this school are entertained, two at a time, to tea by wife of Head, to whom they have not yet been introduced.

Dressed in best the pair advance across the quad and past the college block, continue on until they reach the house that respite offers to the Head from constant chatter and the clatter of a hundred pairs of shoes. The door is opened by the maid all trimly dressed in black and white: they're ushered in to lacy parlour, where, behind the dainty china cups, the chatelaine she sits. Before they came they feared they'd know not what to say, now they're here they speechless are - Headmaster's wife a bobby-dazzler blonde is she!

Autumn's here, and shorter grow the afternoons, and after soccer on the playing field the classroom lights are needed when the studies are resumed. It is the hour when will be read the literature of France, when mind shall dwell on Frankish land, transported by the beauty of the tongue of kings, and be inspired with wish to cross the sea and see this territory of which so much is told, ambition soon to be fulfilled in circumstances unforeseen, which will with time unfold.

The class next moves to science block, and sits in lecture hall before the chemist who's abandoned commerce, seeking peace in Academe, free from the pressures of the business world. Here is acquaintance made with substances who heretofore were merely names and nothing more: Chlorine, Bromine, Actinium and Fluorine, Potash, Sulphur, Antimony and Tin; their use in industry's described at length and how is manufactured H_2SO_4: but boring is recounting of the method used, telling of production plants, immense in size, embellished with tall stacks that smoke and stinking fumes emit both day and night. Physics is preferred, explaining stress and strain, and how it stays up in the air, the aeroplane.

Skill in titration is achieved, and ability acquired in analysing common compounds by their colour and their taste and the temperature of point at which they melt. But now at last is left behind the talk of process plants where nitro-glycerine's produced and petrol is refined and acids gush from massive pipes. It turns to matters on a smaller scale, the facts more intimate that form the basis of the atoms' lives. Atoms are the least in size of parts of which all matter may be split, the basic building blocks of which all things are made that can be touched or held in hand; and yet solidity they do not have: each is a system like the planets and the sun, electrons circling round the nuclei who hold them by attractive force. Short the course that they must run, so very small they are; they haven't far to go, and so it seems as if they form a shell as round and round they race.

The lecturer he holds in air the wooden balls with which he demonstrates the unions made to form the molecules, and then commences peroration in these terms:

"Atoms form the basis of all matter, strangely structured so that complete contentment they can never find: when configuration is complete and correct the compliment of every shell, their attractive charge is out of step, they're left with feeling of revulsion or a great desire. They do not die, they find no rest, electrons never cease to circulate: when their energy's at lowest state, they by their natural urges suffer still. Only when bombarded by a barrage, from the sun or other star, composed of photons raising orbits, breaking bonds, or by particles impacted, carried on the cosmic wind, only then are they destroyed by flames of everlasting fire.

"The atoms of one element are all alike, loosely joined as siblings are, satisfied to live together till seduced by strong attraction of a passing atom of another clan.

"The atoms they find happiness in marriage, but forced to share a pair of orbiting electrons, their independence they forego; with regret they tend to fret when freedom's lost. By marriage molecules are formed, families composed of elements of various sorts, and progeny produced.

"Confirmed bachelors and old maids, these are the inert elements, their shells complete and charges balanced, by emotions quite unmoved, living quietly with their kin, showing neither joy nor anger. What a lucky lot one thinks, never swept into ecstatic state, never downcast in despair.

"Gold stands aloof, a noble metal cold and proud; his heart is hidden deep beneath electrons' layers, unmoved by what is seen by yellow eye's unblinking stare.

"Oxygen, on other hand, the great seducer is, moving in on other unsuspecting elements when opportunity itself presents, to infiltrate their molecules and oxidise them one by one: the sire of rust it is.

"To quench the fire of strong desire, most atoms seek to wed, to find an atom of another kind, compatible, possessing strong attractive force. By polarity of charge is known the sex of each, positive or negative they are: poles that are alike repel, opposites attract. Hermaphroditic are the members of Group Four, uncertain of their sex, sometimes positively dressed, at other times in drag.

"There exist two sorts of marriage, the civil and the church. Electro-valence represents the first, participants of which are greatly given to loose living when in water they're dispersed. More stable is the second, the partners living in co-valent clasp, embracing one another within electrons' grasp.

"As one would expect, these happy unions oft give rise to offspring, who must go and seek their fortune on their own. Water's one of these, frequently it's found among the progeny resulting from reactions taking place, electrons being exchanged as are the wedding vows and golden rings; in dissolution does it flirt with ions till with age they dehydrate and crystalline become: seized by stiffness of the limbs and hardness of the skin, these crystals cease participation in an active life.

"Of course divorce occurs. Some unions undertaken with unseemly haste and insufficient thought lack the energy that's needed to maintain a stable state; some are split by intervention of an atom more mature, possessed of powerful personality and of independent means.

"Each family of molecules its likes and dislikes has, its character and way of life. Each is choosey as to what it does, and with whom it interacts; class-conscious are they all, each is valued by its valence. Injudicious is the pairing of atoms of unequal worth, a marriage doomed to failure fairly soon. A suitor who is suitable will come to take up all the bonds unsatisfied before."

This concept of atomic life will dormant lie for many years, as other matters more material to the day will fill the mind, until the memory will reawakened be by need to understand the workings of the biosphere.

The bonfire has been built on edge of field, sticks and planks of wood piled high, a massive heap it is. Firework night is here again, every year it comes exactly at this time, a wild and pagan feast that nothing owes to Master Fawkes, a celebration of the shorter days, and of the evil which can stalk the Earth unseen in absence of the light.

The tinder is ignited by the teacher at the base, the flames take hold and lick the timber heaped above; leaping up, they light with reddish glow the faces of the watching youths who stand around on every side - as redskin warriors they appear, gathered for their tribal rites, and this is how it actually is.

The sparks are carried up as is the smoke by heat below; now the fireworks are ignited by the staff, and briefly brightened is the sky by a thousand stars released from rockets cleaving darkness as they, whistling, rise, and having reached their apogee explode with loud report. The set-piece with reluctance lights, strung between two poles. Fountains spout their golden sparks, the Catherine wheels rotate: the whole enwreathed in coloured smoke - then fizzles out, remaining pieces glowing red whilst swinging on the wire.

The fire's burnt down, a red-hot heap of smouldering ash is all that now is left. The mood is changing, there's a menace in the air. Some have departed, Sam is gone, aware that mischief is afoot. The crowd of students, intelligent and well behaved, have suddenly become a mob, swept by savagery primeval. The fire is left and ring reforms about the pit dug long ago for purpose long forgot, as chanting starts. "The sump! the sump!" the cry is heard, as now unfolds the annual ritual, symbolic sacrifice exuberant youth must make this time of year to whatever god it is that youths may fear, the god that rules examination room maybe. How the sacrificial victim's chosen is not clear, some tacit understanding must have moved the mutual leaders of the mob to pick on one who is least liked, a loner solitary by nature, living on the social circle's edge. Carried off is he, accompanied by frenzied shouts of milling crowd, who throw him in the dank damp pit below.

It seems he has not suffered hurt, except to dignity and pride, for tomorrow he'll be there, indifferent to his comrades as he always is, and to all the world around. The hurt lies in the hearts of those who come to realise, as they wander back to bed, that they lost their self-control, carried off by passion primitive and base, preying on the weakest like the hyena and the jackal do.

Winter has arrived, and with it frost that freezes fields of which the flood-plain is composed, the water-meadows parted by the renes that carry surplus rain back to the slowly flowing river as it wends its tortuous way to coast, seeping through the shingle-bank that blocks the entrance to the sea; ice now joins these fields that water separates at other times of year, a state of rigor mortis grips the land. The years of childhood too are dead: rebirth awaits the rising sun and longer days. The lane winds round the meadows' edge: the elms, now bare of leaves, still stand in paddock next the road;

deserted nests remain inviolate in upper boughs, the birds have flown to warmer waters by the shore; and now content to wait in comfort for the year's rebirth the bull chews straw in farmyard stall. Brilliant shines the sun on this the frosty scene, though never rising very high, and setting early in the afternoon.

Thus peacefully do pass the days of youth in simple games and harmless pranks, precursors of the spring of manhood and the sterner years that lie ahead as stormclouds threatening war are seen to gather on horizon on the other side of sea that separates the land; and ever present in the distance, as if suspended in the sky (for round it swirl the clouds, and oft the top is hid in mist) is mighty rock that rises from the earth and reaches up to heaven above. If one could climb, ascending path that leads past waterfalls of ice and vertiginous crevasse to summit covered by the cloud, what sort of country would one find? Is it really Nature's home, a land beyond the gravitational force that drags men down when they aspire to higher things, where air's so thin that rust does not occur for lack of oxygen and absence of ozone? Or is it, as the cynics say, just rocky boulders frozen to the earth, or endless wastes of snow and ice?

Today, as students jostle on their way to class, a foreign aircraft passes down the coast, strafing gun-emplacements as it goes.

Two A Foreign Field

Disembarked upon the sands, the convoy moves along the dry and dusty lanes, moves inland from the sea until the little city's reached, set amongst the fields of this bucolic province, this 'lost land' that modernity has missed; in its centre stands cathedral church that here has stood since Conqueror's reign, the lightish whitish local stone from which it's built untouched by time. Passing through the narrow streets, loaded with machines that will be used to build a road more suited to the unexpected traffic of the army trucks that take supplies to soldiers in the battle-line, the lorries leave the highroad on the outskirts of the town and enter field where tents are pitched while troops await the order to proceed to destination prearranged.

The tents are set up in a line on either side of field. Apathy hangs in the hot and humid air. The bundled tents are dropped from back of truck, they fall on grass with muffled thud, and with haste they are put up by those who'll call them home for months to come; at least some shade they give, protection from the burning sun.

No relief as yet there is, the sergeant passes down the lines, "Trenches must be dug" he says, "a slit by every tent in which a man may stand." The sun beats down on shirtless backs as with reluctance the swaddies strike the solid earth with pick, and shovel out the dislodged soil; rather would they lie in shade, victims of a listless lassitude induced by heavy sultry air.

The task is done: the soil is heaped, the slit is deep, deep enough for man to stand, his helmet level with the ground.

The sun has gone, mid-night's past, when distant drone of lonely aircraft can be heard, a foreign flier dropping bombs at random so it seems: for sure he cannot see a target on unlighted ground where all are wrapped in slumber, bar the guard who leans on rifle, fearful lest his throat be cut by special agent lurking in the dark, sent by foe to sabotage the fresh supplies sent up from vessels stranded on the sandy shore. Wakened by the sound of aeroplane now overhead, the young men do not stir, their trenches dug at cost of so much sweat are now ignored; lazily they turn and, fearless, fall fast asleep again.

These bombs no danger pose, falling on the farmland round about: it is the shards of shells from ack-ack guns, two feet in length with jagged pointed ends that lie between the tents, revealed by rising sun reflected on the twisted broken iron, that was the unknown menace in the night.

It is a different danger that disturbs their sleep, that causes palpitations of their hearts. The threat comes not from fearsome foe but from a friendly force, an armoured column, tanks with clanking tracks and noisy roar, that approaches in the blackness of the night, that can't be seen but only heard. Now close at hand the ghostly horde comes rattling o'er the sward that lies between the lines of tents, guided so it seems by unseen hand. In a moment are they past, their metallic clatter soon subsides, dwindling in the distance as is their path pursued across the sleeping fields to point from which they'll launch attack before the dawn breaks in the east, led on by some sixth sense.

Lounging on the side of road whilst waiting for the word to move to final destination, marching men are seen to come in sight, a mighty column long in length and four men deep, prisoners captured at the front, composed of men both young and old, some mere boys who, captives now, are thankful to be free of constant fear of death when in defence. By their side a single swaddie walks, his rifle slung across his back, no risk is there that any make escape when food and rest and safety lie ahead.

After noon, another column comes in sight, bedraggled peasants dragging carts, refugees that flee the fighting, their homes destroyed by mortar-fire: conflicting forces have reduced to rubble the villages in which they lived. Pitiful they do appear in their distress, and yet the soldiers watching from the verge are filled with hatred and contempt at sight of these whose fellow countrymen have bombed the cities of the Kingdom, killing in their turn the soldiers' kith and kin.

Now the little children come from neighbouring town to see the army camp. With great delight the soldiers play with these, the boys and girls and little mites they dandle on the knee; they feed them chocolate from their meagre store, minded of the families they've left behind on further shore. Naught but love there is that can be felt for these, these innocents who nothing know of hatred fuelled by cruelty of war.

The time drags by, a week has passed, at last the convoy's on the move again; woolly hats are donned and eye-shields cover face of those who ride on rear of trucks, half-hidden by the clouds of dust the lorrys raise from rutted dried-up mud that serves the peasants for a road.

The officer, he rides on motor-bike, he sweeps from end to end of line, the Matadors and trailers and the Diamond T's that groan beneath their heavy loads; in their cabs the drivers, some of whom have never learnt to drive, wrestle with the wheels and fumble with the screeching gears. When he gives the signal the trucks turn in to meadow at one side, and further on but not far off there can be seen the rocky cliff from which there will be quarried stone to build a by-pass fit for frequent usage by an army on the move.

On three sides are hazel hedges interspersed with blackberry brambles, the berries ripening now. On the fourth a cider orchard hides the farmhouse half a mile away; the little apples have a rosy blush that does belie their bitter taste when bitten, and mouth is moistened by acidic juice to give relief from torrid heat. Once more the tents are pitched around the edge along the hedge, the trucks are resting in the centre ground. The crushers and the screeners have been put in place beneath the face of cliff from top of which the rocks will fall from dumpers' skips, fall in to the crusher's maw; finely ground, the chippings pass along the screener's belt for sorting into size.

Behind the tents, beyond the hedge, the cattle graze, each tethered to a peg. The grass is cropped in semi-circles stretching straight across the field. Each morning early, when the night gives way to day, there comes the farmer's wife, her figure bent by life of toil and aged before her time; she's dressed in black, her skirt sweeps to the grass, her head's protected by a scarf of this same sober hue. She looks not at the rows of tents: the men who their ablutions make in shelter of the hedge she does ignore, briskly going about her business, moving stakes to which the cows are tied, so that each day the kine may have fresh grass to chew.

In each tent six men find rest, their loaded rifles stacked around the pole supporting roof. They sleep upon the hard unyielding ground. Those with energy and enterprise have for themselves made mattresses of wire, woven from the phone lines that festoon the hedges bordering on the lanes, placed there by the Signal Corps; the rest, rendered lazy and lethargic by the humid heat, rise stiffly from earth's bosom at first sign of light, with no desire to linger longer in her harsh embrace once dawn has spread across the sky.

The cooks prepare their greasy fare on makeshift fire that's fuelled by diesel oil; a canopy of canvas gives protection from the rain. No bread there is, but tins of biscuits hard as iron to dunk in cups of compo tea.

The blast-hole borers sit on planks of wood against the face of rock, their feet press on jack-hammers' handles as the bits bite through the stone. When blasting's done and all around the boulders lie, the digger comes to load the dumpers, massive RB twenty-four. The hungry crusher's fed all day and through the night (the lights stay on without regard for air attack), and stock-pile quickly grows beneath conveyor-belt.

A few weeks more and road's complete; silent falls the site. The constant roar of these machines, the hum from two-stroke Allis-Chalmers, the clatter of the screener, the foreman's horn he blows when blasting is begun, all have ceased and stillness supersedes. The men, released from urgent work that's now complete, slip back in to that apathetic state induced by idleness and summer heat. They laze about or wander through the lanes, and seeds of mischief start to grow as they must do in hearts of some when too heavy hangs the time.

Taffy is a Welshman, that is no surprise. Slightly older than the others, but not by very much, for authority he little cares: and yet no trouble does he court, he is so circumspect that no suspicion is aroused. Today he comes back into camp, beneath his coat is hid a bird whose head hangs limply down: one less layer does the farmer have to scratch the farmyard's dusty earth. "Tonight we'll feast on fowl instead of tins of stew".

Alas, the bird is very old and much too tough to eat: cooked over petrol fire the taste's high octane too. Another prank of greater scope the Welshman must conceive.

Across the land the farms are scattered far and wide. At fall of night the watchdogs may be heard to bark, chained outside each farmhouse to a kennel made of wood; their baying echoes in the emptiness, over fields and shrubby scrub where cattle munch the cud and now and then are heard to give low cough, should there be anyone to hear. These hounds are big and fierce and black, kept to frighten off marauders, bands of ne'erdowells who would break down the door and rob the farmer and his wife. Well known it is that, trusting not the bank that tradesmen use, they keep their cash stashed in the mattress of their beds, or buried in the earthen floor.

Not far beyond the camp, along a narrow lane that twists between high hedges, one comes upon a little house, a cottage standing all alone, half hidden in the scrubby trees. No dog there is that barks when strangers pass this way, it is supposed some hermit therein dwells, a miser guarding fortune of which he dare not tell.

The Welshman now proposes that a visit should be made to this unguarded dwelling by the six who share his tent, comrades drawn together just by chance, to seek the treasure therein hid. All are welded in a bond of trust that never can be broke, freely can each speak within the tent as discussion now ensues: some are for this desperate act, and some against. It seems at first just empty talk to while away another hour, an escapade that could in fact be never carried out; thinking that it's all a bit of foolish fun, loud support is given to the scam, the others pressed to undertake this sordid crime. What horror fills the heart when action is approved, decision swayed by need of some adventure to relieve monotony of service life here in this wilderness with no more work to do: the plan is put in hand to carry out the robbery tonight before it's dark. Youngest of the band and reticent by nature, fearing ridicule if changing stance and speaking of the wrongness of this venture, remonstration is not made, shameful silence takes the place of former unintended exhortation.

In this forward camp the discipline is lax, no guardroom guards the gate, only in the night the sentry watches while his comrades sleep, himself a prey to fear of imagined figures lurking in the shadows as he keeps his lonely vigil, hours going by on leaden feet until he is relieved, and he can snatch some sleep before cold dawn lights eastern sky. The men may wander where they please, they may go missing for a day or more, unnoticed by the subaltern entrusted to command these unruly carefree conscripts, himself no older than these men he oversees.

The dusk begins to fall, long shadows of the trees have disappeared and mist is forming on the meadows where the cattle go on grazing as diminishes the light. The little party moves along the lane, no need to muffle tread for there is none to hear, no need to hide the face for there is none to see them go. Far behind fall camp and farmhouse, nearer now the ancient cottage, humble home of unsuspecting victim of these foolish men.

As they circle round the lonely dwelling, the light is nearly gone, the cloak of warm September night is spread across the landscape, no wind disturbs the leaves; no sound there is but distant bark of dog a mile away across the fields. Feeble yellow rays of oil-lamp light a window at the rear.

Now Taffy strides up to the door. Grasping latch he flings it open, steps inside. The others closely follow, crowding into cluttered parlour now in darkness. The inner door is standing half ajar, light filters through from further room, from which the sound of movement can be overheard.

Opening wide the inner door, the six stand dumbstruck by the sight that meets their eyes. No miser sits before the table, skull-cap on his head, counting out his golden hoard. No old peasant puffs his pipe in quiet contentment, thinking of the fortune hid beneath the bed that stands one side against the wall, savings scraped together over many years of backbreak toil and careful living. No, it's three old crones that there they see, three sisters of great age who live in direst poverty, dressed in wretched rags, remains of those black dresses all the older peasant women wear. Their hair is sparse, their skin is wrinkled on their bony faces, and deep sunken eyes stare at the bold intruders, filled with fear. They sit around the table, holding in their claw-like hands the chicken bones at which they presently are gnawing; in the centre on a china dish, the remnants of the carcass, like them just skin and bone.

No treasure here for sure, only dirt and squalor as the three old maids eke out their latter years. The little band of men is filled with shame; they mutter some apologetic words, "a grave mistake, misunderstanding of the way that we should take; we thought..." Hastily they do withdraw, and firmly closing door they silently retrace their steps, and quickly pass along the lane now plunged in total darkness, hidden from the afterglow by the hedges' height.

Dawn breaks once more, and stiffly rise the soldiers from their beds of earth, creeping out to greet the sun whose rays reflect on dewy grass the spectrum's iridescent shades, revealing silken threads of spiders' webs strung out across the hedges and the trees. The fiasco of the night before has by sleep been swept from simple minds of swaddies living for the present hour, without regard for what is past or what the future holds in store. The mind more sensitive with sad regret is filled, regret at failure to speak up and stop the wicked prank that might have had a tragic end: shame still haunts the contrite heart. It was not thought these simple souls would stoop to reckless crime; it would not have done to stay behind because of what they would have said, to have become an outcast living in their midst. These thoughts are put away, put in the back of mind, from whence in future times perhaps they'll reappear, undermining self-esteem.

From the farmyard far away the call of chanticleer is clearly heard, carried on the morning air.

Three The Gardener's Apprentice

The conscript soldier ever dreams of dawning of the day when he's 'demobbed', when he'll be free again from army discipline, the marching and the rifle drill and the sergeant's shouted orders and commands. When it comes at last as it must do, reality is rather different from the dream. No more the company of true and trusty friends bound by the bond of loyalty forged in the fire of hardship and adversity; when whistle blows at end of day each goes his own way home, the single man is left bereft of mates: the lodging house lacks warmth of comradeship so evident in bleakly furnished barrack hut.

Neglected during years of conflict when so many men were absent from their homes, when normal life was in abeyance held, the garage workshop now is showing signs of lack of care: the whitewash on the walls has taken on a greyish hue, blackened lower down by carbon fumes and splashed by grease and oil, the two that seem to seep from cans and drums and cover all the benches and the floor as well. The wiring hangs from ceiling in festoons of ragged insulation, disappears down metal tubing on the wall, and reappears behind the switch above the lathe. When button's pressed to start machine the lights all fail: each time the fuses blow, plunging into darkness those who work beneath the cars, or in the pit below.

The cars of customers are in no better shape: the vet drives in with track-rod trailing on the ground; how he turned the corner none will ever know. Another has a car the wings of which are rusted through and through; corrosion runs like veins across the cellulose, a jig-saw held together by the tarnished paint. The welder weaves his molten metal like a thread to sew the tattered fabric into shape; next week the motor's back, another shunt has shattered all the welder's patient toil.

Too little work there is as yet, a nightmare at the end of every day to fill the time-sheet out, account for every minute spent there on repair when half the time there's not enough to do. Every hour must be attributed to job for which a customer must pay, some are shifted onto wrecks that lie neglected in the workshop's far recess, cars with con-rods poking through the shattered side above the sump: for those who fail to dip the oil the frightening sight a timely warning gives. A Rolls has joined this company of crocks, a valve has fallen from its perch above the piston's crown, see how the mighty fall!

At end of week when work is done and dirt and grime is washed from hands and hair, the motor-bike's bestrid to make a visit to a former friend, one Ferdinand, who lives in village not far off, on other side of hill; summertime it is again, the lanes are shaded by the leafy elms on either side whose branches meet above the road. The friend is met and way is made to meadow by the river's edge, there to swim and lie in sun and chat awhile, recalling times of youthful past.

Ferdinand a sister has, Phoebe is her name, she shyly stays at home until one day she's asked: "Why don't you come with us today, to sit and talk on river bank, or learn to swim in muddy water of this slowly flowing stream, its bed bestrewn with old tin cans and twisted cycle frames, and barbed-wire fencing where the cows come down to drink?"

Gladly Phoebe says she will. Thus many sunny days, and evenings too, are spent this way; and skiff is hired from wild-eyed elf who minds her father's boats on edge of marsh, to paddle through the rushes tall and tangle with the irate anglers' lines and floats.

Summer slowly drifts to autumn, shorter grow the days, and cooler too; the wind in fitful gusts it blows, bringing with it showers of rain. The wheels of motor-cycle slip on surface of the leaf-strewn lane and scatter conkers fallen from the overhanging trees. No longer is it fit to sit on river bank, or wade into the water, cutting feet on rusting wire half buried in the mud: the air's too cold and damp. Instead, when passing by on bike, a call is made to see if Phoebe's in or else if Ferdinand is there. A ride upon the pillion is proposed, as far as cafe at the crossroads, where the sad and lonely proprietor dispenses cakes and tea.

The homeward route runs through the winding lanes at first, beneath the trees now bleak and bare, the branches black against the evening sky, lit by an orange afterglow left by the setting sun. The days are short, soon darkness falls, and still some miles to go before the end of journey's reached. Black tarmac slips beneath the tyres, the bank each side is lighted by the headlamp's blaze, and speed's increased as is exhaust-pipe's steady roar.

Without warning all the lights (both head and tail) go out as once again the fuses fail. Sitting by the roadside in the dark, with fumbling fingers is the wire inserted in the box that's bolted to the frame, through which the coloured leads go in and out. Illumined by a little torch, the job is done, the engine springs to life. The road is for an instant flooded with the brilliant brightness of the beam - and now as suddenly it's gone, plunged in a deeper darkness than before.

What is there then that can be done? No chance that hidden fault can be discovered in the night, it will be hard enough to find by day. Too many miles remain to push this cumbersome machine, no other means there are to traverse road that leads to food and warmth and comfort sitting by the fire. A recklessness of spirit impinges on the mind, subverting it to course of action most inadvised, to wit, to ride on in the dark without the benefit of light, until some untoward mischance should halt the headlong foolish flight.

No darkness is complete, eyes grow accustomed to the faintest trace of light that radiates from stars or from some other source more near at hand: just discerned can be the line that's painted on the verge in brilliant white as, gathering way, the cycle races on along the road, audible to ears but invisible to sight. As the roundabout is reached, a car approaches from the right, but none's permitted to impede this daring reckless flight, a ghostly rider for an instant lighted by the headlamp's beam, until is reached home's welcome hearth.

Each day the time spent at the cold and dirty garage drags with not enough to occupy impatient mind, no future here exists, there must be more to life than this. A calling now is sought more satisfying to the soul, that better serves the people's needs. Everyone must always eat, surely agriculture is the answer, feeding every face, making up for wasted years of futile war. A new beginning now is made, a fresh departure on life's way that leads one knows not where.

Life's journey's often likened to a voyage in which a ship, bound for a certain port, is battered by the waves and rocked by fickle winds which drive it off its course; sometimes the haven after many years is reached, sometimes there's made an unintended landfall in a country strange and unforeseen, or disaster strikes and boat is wrecked upon the rocks, the crew escaping only with their lives, their hopes of fortune foundered with their ship.

Thus it is with he who would a farmer or a market gardener be, whose tale this is that now unfolds - how his dreams all come to naught, beaten back by adverse winds and sudden squalls: and yet at times does fortune smile, wiping frowns from off her face, and let him prosper for a while.

It seems so simple, sowing in the soil the seed from which soon springs the crop that yields a hundredfold and just as readily finds buyers at the market in the square. Unaware the youthful novice is, so full of hope is he, of the hazards lying in his path like landmines laid by hand of unseen enemies, the farmer's many foes. Pest and sickness, drought and flood, summer heat and winter frost, all combine to thwart the grower, force him into bankruptcy, drive him to despair until sometimes he takes his life, hanging from the beam in barn or shot through head by gun that stands in office by his desk. It is this contest to the death that gives its spice to mundane life of drudgery and endless toil: the prize of wealth is won by few.

Farming is the basic trade on which all else depends; other crafts cannot be followed till all bellies are well filled. The more the food each farmer grows, more are the workers freed to make the luxuries of life: and yet the grower gains no praise until a famine casts its shadow on the land; meagre is the recompense received by farmer for his never-ending work. It is the satisfaction of a worthwhile job well done (of benefit to men, unlike the service of the sword) which really is his real reward.

With these thoughts the question comes to mind, what is the force of life, what is it makes the plants to grow, what is it drives them on, each fighting to survive? Far easier to release the grip in letting go, slipping into slumber from which there never is awakening, held for ever in the cold embrace of death. Each flower and furry beast is filled it seems with power of will; does every bird and tree a spirit have, as does the labourer guiding plough? What is it makes them cling to life and procreate, before returning to the soil from whence they spring? Perchance some answers will be found in course of lifelong struggle to survive by cultivation of the ground. In old age, maybe, when fires of passion will have burnt away and dying embers shall alone remain, when head's no longer ruled by heart, the intellect will take the leading part and reason unobscured reveal the truth that now is sought.

A re-training scheme exists to aid those men who wish to till the soil who heretofore a rifle bore, with which to kill and maim. To different holdings are the students sent, to serve a year as pupils, on pay that's subsidised by generous government, to learn to live by plough and not by sword. Blind chance now takes a hand and opens door to horticultural scene, in preference to the acres broad where wheat is sown and cattle roam, and so commences course whose dedication is to vegetables and flowers, and fruits that in the glasshouse or the orchard grow. In wintertime when days are short and need for work is less, a day a week's devoted to a lecture or a tour; noted nurseries in the district are visited in turn, that all may see the varied crops and modern means by which they're raised. They are a motley crew who come to listen to the lectures of the local man from Min. of Ag., entrusted with the task of instilling into minds the elements of horticultural practice on commercial scale, his class composed of men and women, young and old, unconnected in the past with any rural craft: some elemental force has brought them here, a basic instinct buried in the brain of many folk which draws them to bucolic life until sad disillusionment sets in. The most unlikely one to be a nurseryman now stands at bar, his glass held in his hand; he takes his lunch in liquid form, no need for food has he. Outside the day is grey, no sunshine filters in to cheer the taproom bleakly furnished: wooden benches and a table freshly scrubbed stand on the floor's bare boards. He matches mood, this man, dressed drably in a crumpled raincoat and a trilby hat - one might suppose a bookie's clerk or rent collector's what he's been. A custom it becomes to meet him here on lecture days and talk of this and that, but never of his past or from whence he's lately come: why he's taking horticultural training is unclear. Misdirected he has been by those who have the job of finding niches for the men returning to an unaccustomed state of peace, their lives disrupted by the war. The course he will not last, from these meetings he will disappear, to transfer to a training for which he has more flair.

The die is cast by chance, fate alone decides, what sort of introduction to the horticultural scene a man may get: fruit or flowers, cabbages or spuds, if he wants the trade to learn he must go where he is sent. One young man is drafted to a holding where a pair no longer young, unversed in modern methods, live like poorest peasants in some forgotten past that hand of progress left untouched whilst all around, right to their gate, the modern world with haste moves on.

The ducks and goats he feeds with oats, he boils the swill to feed the swine; the tools are worn, the horse is lame, the fences tied with twine; the business slowly sinks beneath the weight of muck, but under midden is no money hidden.

The District Officer is told: the young man cannot learn a thing from this old couple who themselves do nothing know; with sympathy he hears him out, then moves him to another farm where he will learn the proper way to till and reap and sow.

On other days a trip's arranged to take the students on a bus through country lanes, the trees now bare of leaves as winter starts to lay its icy hand on field and hedge, the herbage dying down as shadows lengthen, weary sun not rising far, exhausted by the heat of summer days. They're taken to the glasshouse gardens hidden in the valleys or terraced on the side of hill, where proprietors are proud to demonstrate their expertise, display their knowledge and their skill.

An experiment in hydroponics first is seen. A concrete trough has been constructed under glass, in which it is intended to cultivate carnations, a crop that suffers much from wilt disease when grown in beds of soil. Diseases of the earth are intensive culture's greatest curse, needing drastic measures for control to be achieved: heavy work and time-consuming when whole beds must be replaced, so much simpler if the troughs could just be drained. Too easy this would be, these plants do not adapt to water, to grow like lilies in a pond: aerated earth that quickly dries is what they like. The trial is soon to be abandoned, nothing has been gained, no more is heard about the scheme; and yet, all problems can be solved, some day perhaps there will be found a way of growing in a liquid instead of in the ground.

Next visit's made to nursery where chrysanthemums are grown; it is November and they're all in bloom, a lovely sight. The holding is not large, yet a prosperous air it has. The owner greets the students; a man of modest stature and no longer very young, most business-like is he in suit of black and homburg hat, starched collar round his neck: if seen in town he'd be mistaken for the landlord of a street of houses, back to back. He shows them round, describing all they see and explaining how it's done. Not only does he cut the flowers to sell to florists in the town, but raises new varieties, which, when named, bring fame and a little bit of fortune to the village where they're grown when at international exhibitions they are shown. New colours come as 'sports', variations that by chance appear among a bed of long- and well-known sorts - remember now what Darwin said, "Varieties are many, but species very few".

Attempt is made to demonstrate the many facets of the trade, to let the students all the options see before deciding what it is they want to do. This is why next week the day is spent among the apple trees, in an orchard spread out on the Weald. The fruit is long since gathered in, and now reposes in the store in an atmosphere of ethylene; here it will in healthy state remain, crisp to bite and sweet to taste, until the market's short of stock and prices rise again. The foreman shows the way to plant and prune, to spray with winter-wash and fertilise the soil. In further field a youth is pruning tree that's very tall, barely can he reach the topmost bough with his long-handled tool: the branch repeatedly repulses every effort that he makes to cut it off. The visitors they gather round in ring, silently the students stare. Red-faced the boy persists, at last the twig falls to the ground. The watchers give a cheer.

Perennial problem for most crops, as already has been pointed out, and for tomatoes more than any other, are the rots that harm the root, reducing growth and yield of fruit. To kill the fungi in the soil, many are the drenches that are tried: cresylic acid, methyl bromide, Jeyes Fluid and formaldehyde. Unpleasant is their use, and feeble their effect.

At last a method has been found with effectiveness profound to exterminate this plague that with every passing year grows more and more severe. It is to sterilise with steam, to heat the greenhouse soil from end to end till all the weeds are killed and mud begins to boil. It is a mammoth task to bury grids beneath a foot of earth and screw together two-inch pipes that lead from mobile boiler standing fuming on the road outside. For weeks and months the labourers toil, no respite day or night, until the job is done and time has come to plant the next year's crop. Costly is the coal to fuel the fire maintaining stream of steam, and wages for the muscled men who never tire; it's money well invested as in summer can be seen, every plant is strong and healthy, standing stiffly in the mid-day heat, and not a weed in sight.

The visit of today displays the process now in progress at a glasshouse nursery quite nearby. Tomato plants will fill these crystal sheds in summer time, bare and empty are they now: devoid of life the houses are, apart from that from which the vapour rises through the vents and meets the cold clear air outside. The boiler stands without, resembling Rocket or some other loco from those early days when trains first ran on rails: it too has wheels of steel and smoke-stack tall to give good draught; through the fire-door open wide the smutted stoker shovels coke to feed voracious maw.

Into greenhouse file the students: there they see the sweat-stained pair who shift the soil, who heap the earth on buried grids from which the steam spurts forth until completed is the 'cook', passing through the pipes laid on the floor. A steady hiss the only sound that can be heard: the acrid odour of formaldehyde hangs on the air from washing of the rafters on the day before.

"There is a need for care" the chargehand says "you must not tread on sterile earth lest reinfection might be spread. The pipes are hot, the pressure high, make sure the joints are tight, the gauge is right, and stand well clear if hoses burst, emitting scalding steam from point where torn."

The men who dig have dug the next cook in, they pull the steaming sheet to cover earth, retaining heat, and stain their hands and clothes with liquid mud that from it drips. Endless repetition goes on day and night, every day and every week the winter through, until all houses, fresh and clean, stand waiting for returning spring.

Higher now the sun's trajectory, milder is the air. Long enough the Earth has rested, in its bosom life begins to stir. One last visit's made, to nursery built on slope of hill. Each house a little higher than the one below, no light's obscured by one in front, all plants receive an equal share.

This property is owned by army man who's now retired and runs his business with precision, like battalion or brigade. A record's kept of all that's done, how cold the night, and hours of sun. Already plants are planted out, not too early, never late: for everything its special date. Row by row tomatoes grow, held up by strings that hang from roof, their necks encircled in a noose; the scent of jute pervades the air.

When visits such as these are made, everything is tidied up and well displayed. Useful is the information thus obtained, the chance to study different systems that one hasn't seen before. What is never seen is the muddle and confusion, the carelessness and errors that are part of every day when the whole thing's not on show and the strangers are away.

A year is set aside in which must be acquired the skills that young apprentice will require to gain a place as worker in the horticultural field, and earn his living in that world where Nature rules. Allocated to a nursery garden long established, all seems rather strange at first, one might even say perhaps unreal, as if one strayed across the border to a foreign land where engineers are unfamiliar, rather rare. Machines begin to take the place of beasts to draw the plough, but labourer still is tied by habit to the old organic way of tools held in the hand.

Entry to the nursery's gained from lane that runs between the cottages that form this village in the Downs - too small to call a village, a hamlet's what it really is. A church of flint it has, and next to this a farm on thin and chalky soil which, when it rains, turns puddles white. On the left, behind the houses, runs a river through the meadows where the cattle quietly graze, its turgid water slowly flowing 'twixt the muddy banks by which the rushes thickly grow. On the right the nursery gate, guarded by two giant sequoias standing sentinel like soldiers, dressed not in tunics but red trunks. On beyond, the rising ground is clothed in apple trees and shrubs of every kind and flowering plants to meet demand: and further still the rounded hills, the Downs, where cowslips grow and bugloss blooms, and song of lark mounts up the boundless blue which stretches out of sight to distant cliffs and sparkling sea from which the breeze brings salty tang: or clouds of cumulus ascend on thermal airs, creating lofty castles high above wherein may live the Lords of lightning and the thunder storm. Round the valley's rim on either side are woods of elm and oak: in topmost branches roost the rooks, and here they build their nests, returning every night from gleaning in the farmer's fields, circling overhead and rising on the wind: with their cawing and their calling, what an awful noise they make.

Lower down on southern side old apple trees are sparsely spaced, remnants of an orchard long ago: hollow are their gnarled and twisted trunks, the wood has rotted from the centre yet they go on yielding year by year, fruit picked at every fall.

Between the redwood trees that piquet gate and steeply rising ground beyond, greenhouses have been built around the square of frame-yard and the booth from which are sold the fruit and flowers and shrubs and trees. This is the only level part, from here this little empire is controlled. Two brothers run the business which once their father owned; now they themselves are getting on in years, but have as yet no fortune made. They're more like Midas in reverse, everything they touch, it turns to dross.

The younger is an active man; slim and strong in spite of age: forbidding is his glance, fools he does not suffer gladly, he does not suffer them at all. His younger years he spent in Winnipeg out on the prairies where life is hard and climate harsh. Returning home to settle down he built himself a cabin in the wood; wild ways of youthful days now quite forgot, sequestered life he leads alone, loving best the flowers he cultivates, and faithful friend, his collie dog.

The elder brother is a man of manner more relaxed, now crippled by the pains that come with age. Dressed in ancient suit and fresh white shirt and cap on crown of head, his boots are black and polished bright, his hair is white and 'tache to match adorns his upper lip. His movements are restricted by the need of stick, with help of which he slowly makes his way each day from stucco mansion on the street, which is where he with his sister lives (she keeps a most sedate and proper bar established in the room beside the entrance door). He goes on past the mighty redwoods at the gate, to the greenhouse where he works. There he sits at potting bench in winter and in spring, pricking out the seedling plants in trays or putting them in pots: a labourer brings him soil to use and takes the trays away. At other times the customers he serves, sitting in the booth, taking orders for herbaceous plants and trees and shrubs to be delivered at a later date. He is a kindly man who treats his staff in manner mild, more heated is discussion with his brother when more money's needed to replenish stock or are required new tools of trade; but the worries of the business leave undisturbed his sleep in spite of fact that health of firm's no better than his own.

Broad horticultural spectrum here is seen, all the ornamentals and many sorts of flowers, and fruits that grow in field and others under glass. Grapevines grace this greenhouse where the old man works, last remnant of a common crop until the conquest of the southern lands allowed the culture of this fruit in climate more benign, blessed with sunshine most the time; and so it is with peaches too, already gone, giving way to the tomato crop: their name alone remains on glasshouse door where formerly they reigned, reminder of more prosperous days and wealthy patrons of Victorian age.

Now in winter, stripped of leaves, the vines are just bare bones, skeletons that lean against the glass in rows, their fleshless arms outstretched each side. The glasshouse walls have arches built beneath the ground, through which the roots protrude to gain the water from the rain. On the borders underneath are stood the trays of pots the old man's filled with slips, the latter rooting in the compost while awaiting coming of the spring.

On upper slopes long beds are dug and with herbaceous subjects filled: the soil is thin upon the chalk, infested with the roots of couch, a most pernicious grassy weed from which the ground cannot be freed: in spring and autumn are they sold, these plants, in summertime their flowers are cut and purchased by the florist trade.

A little lower are the lines of shrubs, following the contours of the slope. All sorts and shapes can here be found, with foliage red or green in every shade and blotched with cream, some cursed with barbs and spikes and cruel thorns to tear the flesh and pierce the skin. They must be dug when they are sold, loaded on a barrow till it weighs a ton, and down the hillside dragged to where the roots are wrapped in jute; this is how the winter's spent, when growth lies dormant and all nature seems to sleep.

The sapling trees, they too can now be moved, before the lengthening days shall make the sap to rise. Conifers and hardwoods, junipers and limes, apples pears and peaches and various sorts of nuts; also plums and cherries, some grown for fruit and others for their flowers. Down by the path, where the ground is nearly flat, they form a shady spinney or a copse, wherein the weary gardener hides a while, whilst having surreptitious drag on a fag he's rolled by hand. Early sets the sun, a disc of red like pool of blood that colours crimson cirrus clouds, a sight that gives delight to shepherds on the Downs; its light is filtered through the branches bare, silhouetted black against the lurid sky, and falls on gardener resting here. From smouldering heaps composed of couch grass slowly burning in the bonfires round about grey plumes of smoke arise and hang on windless air; the peace gives rest to troubled breast and respite from all care.

The foreman is a moody mulish man, not liked by everyone, but jealous in his job, resenting interference no matter whence it comes, from labourer or from boss. Every workplace has its air, its atmosphere, that's partly place and partly comes from those frequenting it for many years: thus these three, the brothers and the leading hand, have stamped their brand on mood of this their land, a curious mix of two strong wills and gentle moderation interposed.

Silent is the foreman at the dawning of the day, a grunt is all the greeting one will get: and yet as sun ascends the sky quite loquacious he becomes, melting like the early morning frost upon the grass. He alone may fuel the fires that burn all night, maintaining warmth around the tender plants that stand on shelves or grow in ground within the houses clad with glass; no overall he wears, no cap to cover hair, he's clothed in dust from toe to top of head.

Trained in gardens of the rich in days when servants worked from six to six, this clever craftsman has a name for all the plants he has to tend, some of which are hard to find, hidden as they are among the weeds or in tall grass that rampant grows for lack of labourers armed with hoes.

To the novice he is kind; when has lifted that dark cloud that in the morn for him hangs overhead and weighs his spirit down, then his sardonic humour shows its face and conversation freely flows, although the topic of his private life is strictly out of bounds.

Christmas sees the crosses made, and wreathes of holly and of every sort of evergreen that grows in nursery garden stocked with shrubs of strange exotic kinds, collected from the ends of Earth, from the Himalayan foothills, from China and Nepal: for floristry's another art that's practised by the elder brother now that he's confined by the weakness in his knees to sitting on his stool beneath the leafless vines. The decorative designs of these symbols of both sadness and regret will brighten up the cemetery and graveyard situated in the church's shade, reminders of the people who used to pass this way.

From time to time the old man rises from his stool to stretch his feeble legs grown stiff from sitting at his bench, and wanders round the smaller houses where as hobby he has foreign plants that formerly were only in the tropics found. Bougainvillea climbs against the glass at further end, a mass of red and mauve when summer comes, and open-mouthed cymbidium orchids gape with grin of sickly green. Ferns push up from floor, protruding through the staging's slats, on which stand many more whose Latin names escape the mind and baffle tongue.

Incomplete would be this inventory if were forgot the potted plants that flower in wintertime and in the early spring when outdoors the earth lies bare and leafless trees are unadorned. Newly built, the glazing bars are gleaming white, the bricks still rosy red: within, the benches down each side are corrugated tin, covered with clean ashes on which a little moss begins to grow, giving warm and humid atmosphere a fecund fertile scent. This greenhouse isn't large, there are not many pots of plants, and yet a good selection's here assembled, suiting every taste: the pink and white azalea, brought here in a box from Belgium where they're grown in special soil; cyclamen that bend their necks, producing blooms that hang their heads, but not in shame; funereal cinereas, dark blue and purple, sometimes splashed with white; calceolarias sporting brightly coloured pouches marked with spots; coleus grown for variegated foliage, for they're lacking fancy flowers; solanum capicastrum, cousin to potato and tomato, in the winter brightly berried; and the dainty malacoides and obconica, that with the buyer little favour find.

Preparations now are made to plant tomatoes where in yesteryear the peaches grew, endowed with velvet pastel-coloured skin, a luscious juicy fruit within: and withal the branches covered with a pinkish blossom 'ere the snow has melted from the frozen land outside. First the cultivated soil is watered with formaldehide from cans filled from a forty-gallon drum. No gloves or masks are ever used: the hands have wrinkly skin and eyes begin to smart, but chest is freed of phlegm and throat is purified withall. Worms lie bleached on surface of the soil, and stiffened toads, now lifeless, crouch beneath the heating pipes, escape denied by outer wall; bugs and beetles and the weevils, all are dead, but root-rot fungus, hibernating deep below and out of reach, is left untouched to reinfect.

The fumes are left to dissipate and soil dry out before the planting can begin. Attention's turned to smaller house that nestles in a corner of the yard, in which are cucumbers by custom grown. Fresh beds of finest horse manure are made in here, laid on boards lest roots should touch the unclean soil of greenhouse floor. Thus it is no rots can reach this crop from underground, swiftly spring the fibrous stems from strawy bed and climb the wires to which they're tied.

Amongst this galaxy of gorgeous flowering plants and shrubs one could suppose this simple salad might unnoticed pass - but no, imagination's seized by rapid growth of slender shoots from which depend long fruits of weight and size, contrasting with the papery leaves and twisting tendrils reaching out to find support. Great the prospect offered by this quick-maturing crop, commencing cutting while the winter's grip is still upon the land and prices scrape the sky. Flush follows flush, there isn't any week when no money's coming in, until, exhausted, in the fall the plants just shrivel up and die. For impecunious man this must the future be, not greenery to ornament the mansions of the rich, but quick return from good nutritious food for common folk, in fact for everyman.

The old man in the doorway stands, surveying scene pulsating with prolific life and rampant reproduction in this little house that's made of glass: now he speaks, the words drawn from the well of deep experience, years and years spent in this garden, every flower and tree familiar friend, "When God did plan to make a man, it was the cucumber caught His eye."

Spring has early come this year, not the normal dull and damp to which this kingdom is accustomed, girt around by sea from which the winds transport the rain: in April does the sun beat down with summer heat, constant use of watering can is needful to ensure the plants survive that in the greenhouse grow. Instead of standpipes and a lengthy hose each house a concrete cistern has, sunk deep below the soil and fed from greenhouse gutter by the rain: cans are filled from these to irrigate the crop, a parapet prevents the gardener falling in and getting wet.

In the centre of the yard the frames are full of plants of every sort, waiting to be purchased by the passing trade. Large and heavy are these lights, thick wooden sashes round the sides supporting glazing bars and glass; hard work it is to raise them every day to water pots, or when a sale is made.

The trees awake as leaves break out from buds and blossom bursts from branches of the apples and the pears, the apricot and crab. The haunting call of cuckoo in the wood that covers higher ground commences, intermittent through the day from dawn until the dusk, unearthly music of the satyrs' dance. It is as if this Saxon hamlet, hidden in the fold of Downs, is place where did originate this heartless bird that finds a foster for its chicks, a place with all pervading air of mystery and romance.

At first tomatoes prosper, twisted up the twine that from the roof depends, three trusses swelling fruit on each, green to start then turning red: now the blackbird spies them, luscious looking, tempting meal. At first he pecks those lower down, in easy reach, then those that higher hang by hopping on the pipes that distribute the heat. A single peck at each he gives, perhaps he does not like the flavour after all. The sight so angers younger brother, quick of temper, short of fuse, to see the loss occasioned by the mocking bird, he fetches gun from woodland cabin where it's kept and fires it from the greenhouse door, careless of the panes of glass and shot embedded in the crop.

With increasing summer heat the root-rot in the soil begins to take effect, tomato plants are not so lush and stems grow hard and thin; the flowers aren't setting well, the fruits are getting small, although the flavour's very fine: the lack of water in the sap increases sugar concentration, making taste more sweet.

That most pernicious grassy weed, the couch, infests the beds in which are bred perennial plants. Deep dug when vacant after sales, fragments of the roots persist, broken from the matted mass removed with fork, a whitish bundle like a ball of string that's come unwound. All through the summer days of drought the master and his men, having honed their hoes to razor's edge, attack the menace when it's weakest, famished by the lack of rain; but there's no way it can be conquered, the grass will always win, all this effort is in vain.

The trees of which the grove's composed, the ash and willow, beech and oak, as well as those that bear the fruit, their leaves now fully formed provide cool shade and hide the labourer taking break from noonday's torrid heat at hour when silence falls on all the land, and thrush and blackbird cease to sing till sun's no longer overhead. Little rain there's been, the level of the water in the cisterns is fallen very low, there may not be enough to see the season through until the summer's end.

The summer slips to autumn, the heat's not so intense. From the sea now comes the wind: angered by departure of the sun for regions equatorial, its anger whips it to a frenzy. All the night it roars through tops of trees, the ancient elms that crown the rise each side of vale, and rocks the rooks that snatch some snooze before grey dawn breaks in the east. It rushes down and rattles rafters, loosening glass in the greenhouses huddled near the path: when the brads fall from the rotting bars it sucks the panes up in the air and flings them on the grass. In the morning when the gale relents and wind is less, the heavy ladder's lent against the roofs and broken panes replaced.

Across the road, behind the cottages that line the lane, there is a plot of land the brothers rent, and here they raise chrysanthemums to cut at Christmas, filling glasshouse when tomatoes are torn out. Fertile soil it is, lying in alluvial plain and not on chalky hill; beyond, the sluggish stream meanders through the pastures on its way to open sea, passing under wooden bridges painted white, with rails preventing ramblers falling in among the rushes and the slimy mud.

In the spring the little slips are planted out in rows and left to grow, until there's need for canes to give support, to each of which they're tied with string. At the fall they've grown so tall, they've reached full size: they too they suffer in the gale. Blown about, some lying down, at once they must be quickly raised and straightened up before they bend their necks to see the light and tissue stiffens in the sun.

Tomato vines have now been cut from strings and pulled from ground, the latter littered with ripe fruit too small to eat, and some remaining green. Sad it is, this time of year, the crops all dead and haulm destroyed: a filthy job and boring too, to drag this rubbish from the soil and try to make it burn on bonfires smouldering day and night all autumn and the winter through. Chrysanthemums bring brightness to the shortening days made shorter still by frequent rain and lingering fog. Tomatoes gone, there's room for flowers, and none too soon, for frost and wind will damage plants if left outside. Fully grown, they're dug from ground with soil adhering to the root, and brought by barrow 'cross the lane to empty greenhouse, greeted by the gaping door. Into trenches are they placed, the excavated soil returned and heaped around their stems. Rough treatment this for plants in bud, but there's no sun to scorch the leaves before they've settled in and roots revived.

To slow the growth the vents are opened when it's not too cold, they must not flower a month too soon - they must wait for Christmas Day. At night the coals are smouldering on the boiler grate lest damp should penetrate and propagate grey mould.

Six stems are borne on each of plants, and each of these one bloom it bears, all other buds have been removed, pinched out between the thumbnail and first finger of the hand. Some flowers are incurved, petals tightly packed to form a ball, the reflexed ones turn down to form a skirt or farthingale. Many shades and tints there are: pinks and yellows, scarlet and pure white, deep crimson and a mauve; but best of all, the autumn bronze, deep chestnut with a gold reverse.

The time has come to cut this colour, rich and warm; the florist waits, the potted plants all sold, to fill his window on the morrow, Christmas Eve. Out come the sharpened knives, the hands move slowly through the rows, and in a single swathe the flowers are cut and bunched and sent away. Next day at dawn, more than before, there stands forlorn the empty greenhouse, stripped of beauty, nothing left but naked canes, necrotic leaves still clinging to the stumps of stems, like wreckage left by shipwreck on the shore when storm has passed and wind abates.

The winter's cold and dry, with frost by night and sun by day, and still the bonfires burn the roots of couch; added now are prunings from the trees and dried-up leaves, and these with suddenness flare up in leaping flame, igniting nearby fruit tree and running through the sere and yellowed grass: in spite of cold the lack of rain has left the herbage like to tinder, earth that's ready to be scorched. Will it spread, devouring all the trees that here have stood these many years, until are reached the cottages, of which the roofs are made of thatch?

Madly beating ground with back of spade the flames are held in check and village from disaster saved, which might have happened had the wind got up and driven flames with lightning speed across the field. The only loss is one old tree long past its prime.

Unstoppable is march of time as world rotates around the sun: longer days and warmer weather herald Life's return from bosom of the Earth wherein it slept as if 'twere dead. In one greenhouse bulbs in boxes stretch their necks and, like bunting broken at the head of mast, reveal the colours hidden in their buds. On the sunny slope that faces south are sown the seeds from which will spring the annual flowers, maintaining continuity of cutting for the cut-flower trade.

In spite of this return of spring and rise of sap in all the trees, a great surprise (and shock for some) it is, announcement of the younger brother's marriage to a lady with a mind to run the firm. For many years the foreman's had free rein, to him it seems as if the garden is his own; his surliness and moods have been ignored because he works more days than those for which he's paid. Now all this has changed, his predominance is under threat as another era ends. He surely will not stay, mastered by a matriarch - it's certain he will quit.

Almost idyllic has it been, to work here in this pocket of the Downs, among the scented shrubs collected from the highlands of Tibet, the galaxy of flowers and out-of-season blooms that colour most of year, the lions of stone that guard the steps that lead down to the lawn, coldly staring at the gardener going about his tasks: but it isn't near enough to satisfy a peasant's soul, quench ambition's fire whose leaping flames inspire the mind and render restless itching feet. To cultivate the crops that stand in rows beneath the glass, whole houses filled with single species, every plant the same, that is the heart's desire, to feed the populace with food for healthy life that's laced with vitamins and iron.

'For Life': the plants' pulsating life on every side, and yet Life's secrets still they hide, no hint is there of what it is or what it's like. These brothers here have lived their lives among the flowers, they know their names and what each wants, how much heat and type of feed: and yet they cannot tell how water rises from the root and reaches topmost tip of tallest tree. The stream of knowledge is a trickle here, there's need to journey far before the source is reached, the fount where all life's mysteries are made clear.

The younger brother's always led his labourers, shown the way, dragging barrow up the hill no matter what it's weight, regardless of advancing years. Now this toil it takes its toll, from time to time he's victim to a fainting fit, struck down unconscious on the path, or as he climbs the slope to reach his cabin in the trees. None there is to follow on, no kith to carry burden when these two are gone. It too will surely die, this nursery garden of the past still living in the present time, relic of another age. Reluctantly it must be left, to start a life that's dedicated to the culture of cucumber in a manner that is state of art, modern, up-to-date.

Although departed from that place where has been spent the previous year, on the grape-vine word is heard, it is said that he is dead, the newly-wed, that he has died.

The plain is crossed by railway track, raised up above the river on embankment lest in winter when it floods it should get wet. Leaning from the window of the train one can perceive a passing panorama spread out before the eyes. To the west the river, and on beyond across the fields the market town. Low line of hills lies on horizon to the east, but the foreground's filled with a thousand houses made of glass. From this point of vantage all the detail of the nurseries can be seen, vast blocks of buildings, each several acres in extent. Gazing down upon the serried ranks of timber houses, glazed windows gleaming in the light, what strikes the watcher most is absence of all sign of life: there is no man that moves between the houses, or on the roads that separate the blocks. Beneath the glass the leaves press up, green curtain covering all who work inside - a thousand men and women working there, yet not one there is that can be seen.

The train is met by man in rumpled suit of Lincoln green, to match the countryside in which he works and has his being: his head is covered by a cap. Is this the chauffeur, or the foreman then? No, it is the nurseryman himself, the wealthy man, his wealth revealed by Daimler limousine that stands in station yard outside.

An overview of horticulture has been had. No longer at the whim of chance, instead a conscious choice is made, to learn to cultivate the long green fruits that so profusely grow in rows of strawy beds beneath this sea of glass - the rise and fall of gables simulates the waves.

Unaccustomed is the sight of modern nursery maintained in manner regimental, regardless of the cost. The concrete yard's as wide as barrack square: the guardroom's at the gate, it's where the workers punch their cards at start of day, and when they leave at night. Like guardsmen on parade the stacks stand tall and straight in single file: at their feet the boiler pits sunk in the ground, each covered with a roof of corrugated iron. Close by the coal is neatly heaped, the wonder is it isn't painted white. An ornamental garden runs along one side, a blaze of colour in the summer, set to lighten hearts of hands exhausted by the heat, reduced to shadows of themselves by constant perspiration, toiling from the early dawn until the setting of the sun.

The dog is large and fierce that's chained to kennel at the foot of smoke-stack in the yard: at night he is released to roam about and keep intruders out, who otherwise would climb the fence and steal the hard-won fruit. Each new hand when starting work must have an introduction to the dog, who will then permit him entry in the morning when he comes to punch his card. An unwary rep will run the risk of being chased, taking refuge on the ironwork of the water-storage tank.

Two crops alone are cultivated in this nursery conurbation dedicated to their care, the rosy-red tomato twisted up its string of jute, and cool cucumbers tied to wires, raised in structures more recently constructed than those that formerly were used to house the vines. Ample height there is to stand beneath the gutters linking eaves, wide enough on which to walk when broken glass must be replaced. Folklore tells of one who cycled down the narrow defile, risking laceration should he fall upon the sheets of glass. Enter in the door, the atmosphere is sweet with smell of strawy dung spread as a mulch along the paths that separate the rows, and that distinctive scent of string that pervades all nurseries in the spring, until strong odour from tomato leaves and stems obliterates all else. The many cords attached to wires close under roof seem like a mist that hangs above the thickly planted vines that with great vigour grow; the plants are all of even height, the foliage curled and twisted as if in ecstasy they writhed, filled with youthful joie de vivre. Trusses push their yellow flowers from out the stems between the leaves, from these the pollen pours when shaken by the force of water from the hose directed by the nursery hand each day when strikes the hour of noon.

This is nature's workshop: no ring of steel on steel as anvil's hit, no panels beaten into shape by oft' repeated blows, no welder's arc or grinder's spark to light the gloom like fireworks on the Fifth: produce is produced without a sound, in silence do the living plants perform their never-ending task. It's only in the night the silence is disturbed, as lonely stoker drags his shovel on the concrete road, going round to extricate the clinker, then fill the furnaces with coke: but there is none to hear, the many acres are devoid of human life until the dawn lights up the eastern sky. Then, like the Tour de France, the cyclists fill the lane, racing to arrive before the clock the hour has struck at which commences daily grind.

The soil has all been steamed when houses empty stood in autumn time. A crew went on ahead and slashed and cut tomato haulm and cleared cucumber houses of the dead remains. Then followed the elite among the men, the six who moved the earth in every house to bury grids a spit in depth, screw on and off the lengths of two-inch pipe that carried steam from engine out of doors, dragging back the grids each time a 'cook' was done. One man the boiler minded, maintaining head of steam, repeatedly refuelling the fiercely burning fire. Once a day and once at night the clinker was removed, a solid mass of molten slag that blocked the flow of air; while this process was performed the pressure dropped and steaming ceased for half an hour, a respite for the men who excavated earth with shining shovels which reflected feeble light from lamps suspended from the wire; food and drink were then consumed to see them through the rest of night, or refresh them in the day, restore to them their might.

When at last they reached the door, when the lengths of pipe had been removed and laid on floor of house next door, and only rubber hose remained, attached close by the boiler belching smoke from stack like locomotive pulling up a steep incline, this was the hardest part, to turn the grids about and load them with a double depth of earth, to struggle with the heavy headers and never step upon the sterile soil which stretched to furthest end, vapour rising from the surface as it slowly cooled. Worst of all, at night the steam collecting under gable by the door reflected modest rays that emanated from the lamp that was hanging overhead. The labourers groped among the scalding hoses and the pipes, very little could they see: their shirts were soaked with sweat, clinging to their crouching forms. Outside the frost was white upon the grass.

Further down the lane two men between them work a holding on their own. They could not afford a man to fuel the fire, they buried grids and pulled the sheet, then one ran out, flung in some coal or coke through iron door, and hurried back inside again to start to dig once more.

Two shifts were worked, for months the steaming never stopped. No word was ever heard complaining of the toil: the men they never tired, but at the end of shift repaired to tavern, there to quench their thirst and quaff some ale.

Now it's April and the plants well grown, tomatoes twisted half way up the twine, suspended from the rafters overhead. All of equal height, in serried ranks they stand like some great army on parade, prepared to march in columns by the right when there is given the command. Impressive is their vigour and their health, and yet the foe is never far, lurking near at hand, creeping up with stealth. So it is that in the midst of all these sheds filled with sturdy plants enjoying freedom from disease, there is one in which has taken hold the dread botrytis mould. The hand whose task it was to train these plants and trim their leaves has hanged himself, driven to despair by the pressure of the work and the need of unrelenting speed to keep abreast of the growth of the many thousand plants entrusted to his care.

This grey mould disease, it prospers in the warm and humid atmosphere enjoyed by many hothouse plants, although tomatoes grown in unheated houses do not suffer this: they have instead the cladosporium for a scourge: is there no escape? On the other hand, the growers of the finest wines in France leave the berries on the vines until grey mould appears, and then they name it Noble Rot!

Nothing noble is there in the sight that greets the eyes on entering in amongst this decimated crop: great weals of rotting tissue, where the furry fungus takes its hold on stems, disfigure plants. These must be removed by slicing with a knife, another job to slow the speed of he who is already overworked. "All dead stems must be removed and in the boiler thrust, that all the fungus may be burnt." Thus speaks the boss, but surly stoker has a different thought: "This rubbish will not burn, you choke my fire. I insist that you desist, put no more through iron door, or else there'll be no heat when it's required, and it is I that will be fired."

The stoker's short and squat, broad shouldered to bear the burden of responsibility to which oblivious he seems to be. Least regarded of the staff, black with dust, the colour of his clothes is that of coal he shovels all day long, and in the winter all the night as well. The jobs of all rest in his horny hands: should heating fail in falling snow and bitter wind that freezes fields, the hedges and the trees, the tender plants that shelter under panes of glass they too would soon be dead. This stoker is of habitude a silent man unless provoked, a loner who the company of other men avoids, and is by them avoided too. A man most taciturn who works alone, in the mess he's never seen, where other workers eat their grub and play at darts in their brief breaks between hard slog: in fact few words does he exchange at any time with those with whom he works - what ever is he like at home with those with whom he lives? Why is it those on whom society depends for basic needs are those who by this same society are most despised?

Within the trade this nursery's fame is widely spread for quality of fruit and crop of heavy weight; because of this there is today a visit to be made by Netherlandish growers with intent to steal the secret of a more successful venture than their own. It is the name of firm that is at stake: if they should see inside the house where rampant fungus rules, if they should tell of what they'd seen, of how disease is uncontrolled, it would be shamed, its reputation lost. That is why, as they come by, they see a notice on the door embellished with a hideous skull and bones in form of cross, warning of a fumigation with a deadly poisonous gas.

These natural hazards, it would seem, are sent to try the growers' patience and their skill; so much time is taken up in mortal battle to survive, that time for better culture, bigger crops, is very much curtailed; but in truth, in fact, it works to their advantage, restricting output and preventing flooding of the markets, maintaining brisk demand and underpinning prices.

Scientific stations of research, officially established for the betterment of crops, impart advice impartially for which they do not charge: no individual grower gains an edge, all must adopt the new techniques, incurring extra costs for handling heavier harvests and buying new machines. The public profits from the cheaper food as prices fall in markets well supplied: this is only fair as public funds have financed the stations from the start. At this present time more modern methods are gestating yet and well established ways are still the norm, producing ample profits for the growers who've grown fat; a harsher regime looms ahead, when some will loose a lot of weight.

Unpropitious is this introduction to the world of monoculture keenly sought, fraught with more diseases than have previously been met at that nursery nestling in the Downs where are cultivated species of a spectrum broad and wide, an ecology in which the balance is just right.

At start of day the fruit is picked, cucumbers cut without delay. The twisting and the trimming follows on, the race against the speed of growth which by the grower's rarely won. Hot and bright the summer sun, inducing shoots to be produced at every joint where leaf is joined to stem. High overhead, across the wires supporting strings, there spreads this rampant growth: below, the hand climbs up his steps and slashes at the surplus shoots, retarded by his awkward stance.

The thinking man is struck by speed with which these shoots progress, and needs must take the ill-afforded time to measure increase in the length of plants by day and night. Well it might be thought that in bright light of day the plants would grow the most, resting when the light had gone. This indeed is not the case as now is found: an increase of an inch is shown when measured in the morn, much less when length is checked at eventide. Why this should be one cannot say, it's just a fact consigned to memory of the mind for future use, to help to find the answers to the questions which as yet have not been asked.

Business men are quite content with status quo, the ebb and flow of life they know, provided profits are maintained. Some there are who say advance has gone too far, that land is poisoned with inorganic salt, and nitrate fouls the watercourse. They would that we went back and farmed with dog and stick as did our fathers long ago, spreading dung upon the field and letting nettles grow. The younger men and idealistic youths discuss the pros and cons and give fair ear to those who preach conversion to a life more healthy, nearer to the way that Nature did intend: the older men indulgently just smile. Soon the noise subsides, the subject is forgot and nothing more of this is heard.

Cucurbits grow on built-up beds of fresh manure bought in at some expense. Constructed in the winter when there's little else for hands to do, they run in rows beneath the eaves from end to end of greenhouse blocks. In each house one hand now sits alone on box, tying in the shoots with bast that hangs in bundle from his waist; or else he stands and strips unwanted growth, then sweeps it from the floor. The smart exterior's mirrored by the plants inside, of even size and neatly tied.

The culture of cucurbits is a mystical affair, surrounded by the magic and the myths originating on the day when gardening began, when first old Adam plunged his shovel in the soil. Perplexing is the choice of dung: manure from milking parlour's cheap, but reputed to be cold and wet compared with equine waste, the straw that comes from stable floor. Most highly rated is the product of the well bred bloodstock trained for stamina and speed, qualities the grower would implant in plants of which his crops comprise.

Myths and legends, they declare that humid must the air be kept, an atmosphere both warm and wet within the glasshouse where are cultured these erotic fruits, their tendrils stretching out until they touch, then cling together in a tight embrace. In the middle of the morning, before he has his bit of bait, the hand will hose the floor and damp the plants, and play the water on the pipes and watch the steam rise up and fill the air in space above.

Modern man's misled by all this ancient lore he dare not disobey lest crop collapses like gourd that shaded Jonah from the mid-day heat, the rituals without reason regularly performed according to the edicts of horticulture's pundits and its priests. Perhaps it's true that in most things that people do there is an influence that's persuading them that they must act in manner without reason, guided by some superstition lacking sense.

There is a little café at the corner of the lane that serves the nurseries lying side by side for distance of a mile along this private road. Here forgather some of those who work nearby, buying lunch or cups of tea. They are the single men and girls who have spare cash, who can afford extravagance of eating out, even if it's only beans and chips, and not ambrosial food of bloated rich. Behind the counter near the till, there stands proprietor, a man who lacks all colour, grey of countenance and dress. He lives alone, no wife or kids to cheer the lonely hours when cafe's shut: by day with fortitude he bears the banter of the boys, giving little in exchange. Of his hopes and fears he gives no sign: can he really have no friends, is there none in whom he can confide? Racing is, it seems, the only thing that interests him, the list of runners on back page, the commentary each afternoon from BBC, broadcast on the raucous radio that livens up the kitchen with its never ending cacaphonic bawl.

Here may be found the student types who stay awhile to learn the art, then move on to managerial posts or buy a business of their own. Here again there may be met the social mix of those seduced by Nature's call to seek some idyll tilling soil: some for sure will find success but not that perfect peace of mind which here on Earth does not exist; the rest return to urban homes, and there find refuge from a life of hardship and financial risk.

The sailor man is one of these. At thirty years he still can't settle down. By trade a mason, service in the navy gave to him a taste for travel and the sea; now he's seized by sudden whim to work the land and leave the town where he has lived since he was born.

This café's where he's met a girl, a packer from some packing shed that's situated further up the street. They meet here every day, for this year he works ashore. He has a fancy a nurseryman to be, a fad that may not last for very long before again he hears the call, returning to the sea. Overboard she's gone, swept off her feet by wave of wild desire for roving seaman stranded on the sand. For her what hope is there, what future lies in store? When crops die off and winter's nigh this man will not contented be with washing glass and digging soil: whalers seeking crews will tempt him south to join Antarctic fleet to quench his burning thirst for new adventure, new dangers to be met: will he return, will he come back? As time moves on and carries all before it in its track, the answer will be most likely never known, except by girl still standing on the step.

Another is an architect, a third the son of household name, the name on every can, the great industrial man whose face is never seen: instead of occupying boardroom seat he too is drawn into the net, the web of fate that lures both men and women too from town to countryside to taste the pure delight of working, not in cities built of stone, but in the natural world of muddy fields and dripping leaves. A little nursery now he owns, he works it with his own bare hands.

The question often comes to mind, how different is a millionaire? When passing in the street does he stand out from other men, do people stop and stare? With regret it must be said, there is no way to tell a pauper from a prince: the latter does not sport a topper or a coat with tails, or leather boots with shiny spurs. The only sign is at his gate - the griffons perched on pillars made of stone supporting iron-work painted black and gold, giving way to sweep of drive and avenue of oaks and house half hidden in the trees. When he's out he mixes with the throng; he's lost to sight, quite undistinguished, just another mortal man like all the others in the crowd. Returning from the pub at night he stops to fire the boiler of the greenhouse that he's recently acquired.

A stoker here is often seen, very different is he to the one already met. Tall and thin and gaunt of face, but full of fun, loquacious too. Black greatcoat flapping round his legs, he cycles up the path and dismounts by the door. He never doffs his dusty cap, a white silk scarf adorns his neck. He takes a seat and puts the 'makings' on the table covered with a chequered cloth, and slowly rolls a fag between the coal-black fingers of his hand: it is no masterpiece, tobacco shreds hang out from end, and when it's lit the burning ash falls on his silken scarf, which in an instant catches fire. Quickly does he douse the flames by tipping up his cup of char.

Sitting at the table in the window one can feast one's eyes on all the passing sights, which in truth are very few; but every day about this time there comes in view a comely lass, sweet sixteen or thereabouts: no surprise is this, a girl going to her work along this street that leads to greenhouse nurseries, nothing else, were it not that in this land of welly boots it is the tric-trac of high heels one hears. No overall upon her back, a cute black dress she wears, and golden earrings jingle, dangling from her ears. Wherever does she toil, whatever can she do, does she pick tomatoes or pack them in the shed, does she make their tea, or merely tease the boys?

Few the women found here on this site, they mostly work in Rose Land as described on further page, but incomplete would be this listing of unusual men if a mention is not made of luckless Luke who just survived the shelling but is now severely shocked, suffering from a damaged brain. From time to time he senseless falls to ground in crumpled heap: then slowly he revives, and, lighting fag with shaking hand, he rises to his feet.

Such is his wound, some days he does not wake from sleep when morning dawns, until another circuit of the sun's complete - a whole day lost from life as if it never was: yesterday for him did not exist until he's told by mates at work "today tomorrow is".

A wooden cabin by the river is his home, on the bank by water's edge. Here his friends he entertains, how strange to eat a meal prepared with skill and care, not by a woman but a man: one would expect a mug of tea and can of spam.

On summer days when evening's warm and meal's devoured a skiff is hired from elf-like miss, a wild-eyed faun who haunts the marsh and shyly minds her father's boats: weary working men relaxing on the river, peacefully paddling undisturbed. As they loiter by the rushes rustling in the evening breeze the girl herself comes sculling past, blades flashing in the fading light of setting sun. Her skiff the surface skims with silent swiftness of a bird, then disappears around the river's bend.

When darkness falls the friends depart. Their host they leave to sleep, lulled by lap of water 'gainst the bank, the croak of frogs and lonely call of waterfowl who dare not rest for fear of fox. He shares his bed, so it is said, with a black-eyed girl of the Hebrew race.

These are the odd, eccentric fringe who come with suddenness and then are gone, ephemeral, a soon forgotten few. Apart from them the labour force consists of steady working men attired in worn-out suits or torn tweed jackets tied round the waist with piece of string, who strive their families to feed by hours of overtime, for they are poorly paid. Not only that, in each back yard some sort of hothouse stands, half buried in the soil: the evening too is passed in stoking fire and cutting 'cues' to sell next day to highstreet store.

Amongst these modern nurseries of great size, here and there small holdings have been interspersed, where some two-talent man with more ambition than he has of business skill, dazzled by the prospect of a fortune leaping from this rich alluvial soil, has built a span or two of glass. He begs some aid to plant tomatoes in the open on the slope, to snatch some cash from land that else would be unused.

Swiftly are they planted out; impressed with speed with which it's done, he offers job: "At last it starts to pay, this plot on which I sweat alone, the way ahead looks more secure, a partner's what I need. Will you to my wish accede, and come full time to work for me?"

In his greenhouse cucumbers stand in rows, planted in the beds that tradition and mystique decree, raised up above the floor: and yet they look unwell. The leaves are dark, they're almost black, and flaccid too. The half-grown fruit have ceased to swell, they've hung like that for all the week. Why is it that the weeds and wildflowers prosper on the edge of road and in the ditch, while those for which man cares with tenderness and love contract disease? His faith's misplaced, his future's dark as this limp foliage on these failing plants.

The café's fine for lunch or other meals, but when it's time for bed, a lodging is required where one may rest the head: a room at rent one can afford has now been hired.

The house is large, imposing, set on rising ground amid the meadows also owned by her who owns the house, fields fenced by unkempt hedges and here and there some fine old trees.

It is the garden that reveals, as one arrives, the lack of care occasioned by the years of war and absence of the master who now hither comes no more. The unswept paving and the steps of stone connecting levels up and down, the sundials and the dried up fountains covered now with lair of dust, with lichen and with moss, the weeds protruding through the joints, all seem as if deserted by the gardeners in some other age in distant past, halcyon days when summers sweltered, when all day the sun shone down from azure sky. The sound of balls being struck and cries of 'net' or 'forty love' came from the tennis court, and zephyr breeze disturbed the leaves and tossed the boughs of taller trees; the children camped in wigwams on the close cropped-lawn now left uncut and overgrown.

In fact it's not so long this idyll's gone, vanished in the smoke of war, the conflict that destroyed so many hopes as well as men. The artefacts that by the hand of man are made, they crumble all too soon, damaged by the frost and rain, and then are buried 'neath the herbage and the grass that spring relentlessly from fertile and from arid soil, while the treasured garden species struggle to survive in neglected dried-up beds where sparrows quarrel in the dust.

Two sons there are, not long left school, who share this mansion with their Mum. Little cash they have to help maintain the house and grounds, so that is why a room's to let where working man may get his rest.

A neighbouring farmer's rented an adjacent field and there has raised a crop of wheat. The grain has ripened in the ear, the weather's fine, it's time that corn is cut, but combine's much too wide to pass the five-barred gate.

"The bushes must be slashed, an opening must be made that will accommodate my combine, facilitate the entry of this broad machine." Thus the farmer speaks to son, the elder one. "It must be done by half-past one. Finished I must be before the evening dew shall damp the straw." He turns on heel, returns to farm.

The sons confer, daunted by this task to be completed ere the hour is out. "The aid of lodger is required, that man who clears the greenhouse in the fall, accustomed to the use of well-honed sickle and the bagging hook. Thus will be our hospitality repaid."

The farmer shows surprise to find on his return that he can drive with ease between the trees, complete his task an hour before the sun is set.

Within the house are spacious rooms where once was happiness and joy, but now the master's missing and the mistress is distressed by debt and inability to pay the bills the postman brings. On the table by the window of the lounge a bottle stands, the label says it's gin. Does this some solace bring, mitigate the hate that fills the breast? This hate, it haunts the house, it stalks the landing late at night, emanating from the hearts of those who in this house reside, deserted by the man they used to love.

Returning from a day of toil, tired by summer heat that on the glasshouse beat while cues were cut, tomatoes picked, it seems a guest has come to stay, a lady in her twenties one would say. When all have risen from the evening meal, she asks "Why don't we visit inn, just you and me, imbibe a little beer, and pass the time at darts?"

Uncertain is reply. Weary from the long day in the sun, rest upon the bed with a book one hasn't read might be preferable to walking down the lane and climbing up again.

The offer is accepted in the end, the suggestion is agreed, but, it must be admitted that it could, that it should be done with better grace.

The game of darts is a game of chance as much as skill, the outcome determined as often as not by the width of the wire. Some games are lost, and others are won; time is being called, it's all been good fun.

The light begins to fade as inn is left behind, strolling slowly up the slope of the narrow winding lane to the house that lies ahead. The banks are high that line the way, the field above is out of sight, and she turns and she says: "Ideal for an ambush, this spot, I bet you could wish for a sudden attack, the chance to display your courage and strength my life to protect." Alas, no such thought had entered the head nor had crossed the mind - non-committal the answer, in words that are mumbled: it just isn't her knight.

All too soon the summer's done, the crops begin to die, exhausted by the heat of sun, the foliage hard and yellow from subjection to the constant white oil spray.

Not all of autumn's sadness and decay. Even here, where cucumber is the king, and salads hold their sway, a space is found for chrysanthemum, the autumn queen, the Queen of Fall. They stand outside for most of year, not planted in the ground but in large whalehide pots. When one house is cleared of plant remains and dangling strings, and floor is swept of residue and bits of straw. In one single day the whole crop's moved and brought inside, stood in ordered rows, divided into ranks according to their height as if the sergeant had just marched them in and dressed them by the right. Planted in their individual pots the roots are undisturbed throughout their life, resulting in a crop of flowers of splendid size, much bigger than the ones so rudely wrenched from open ground.

Now a visit's made to Rose Land, 'cross the river, on the western side, secluded valley formed by rising hills. Here the growers raise their roses for the cut-flower trade, well established in this vale for many years in nurseries each of many acres in extent. Built in blocks, each house is very long: the man who stands at entrance can hardly see the one who exits at the other end. Undisturbed the bushes grow from year to year until so tall the stems are out of reach. Little tilling of the soil takes place, the hands just keep on cutting buds of flowers. Small wonder that the owners have grown rich, much money have these growers made, big business is the rose that signifies romance. No longer does the master toil or stain his hands with greenhouse soil, blue suit he wears, and homburg hat; at start of work his Humber Snipe sweeps through the gate, a chauffeur at the wheel. The men they stand aside to let him pass: he looks ahead, at them he does not deign to glance. Many men are here employed, and many women too. The latter move around enmasse, a horde that terrifies the men, and puts to flight with horrid oaths the drivers of the trucks that bring supplies.

All that can be has been learnt from working for these prosperous men who demonstrate that money can be made from cultivation of the glasshouse crops. The time has come to leave the nest, to see how high it is that one can fly unaided, all alone.

Like carrion crows or vultures on the Andean plains, these men who come to pick the brains of those for whom they work take off again when feast's complete and all that's left is bones. The parting of the friends does not take ceremonial form, they do not gather at the station and promise that they'll write, a promise that they know they'll never keep; they drift off one by one, one day they disappear without a word, never to be seen again, of them nothing more is ever heard. For weeks and months they live and work most proximate, it is as if they looked into each other's soul, then seized by whim or sudden thought and by obsession driven on, one by one they slip away, no trace remains, it is as if they never were.

Four Solo Flight

The search begins to find some land that's not too dear on which to build a greenhouse, or perhaps there'll be some there. Small plots are hard to find, the farmers buy and sell a hundred acres at a time, they will not split a field and sell a piece, except to builder building dwellings, paying thousands for each plot.

The metropolis is fed by market gardeners growing crops as close to shops as they can get, but as the city grows in size they're forced to relocate, and benefiting from the increased value of their land, build new premises in latest style and increased size. Other growers set less store on proximity to those to whom they sell, and value more a climate mild on southern shore, blessed with longer hours of sun and less of rain, but linked to London by a frequent train. Not forced to modernise, and strapped for cash, outmoded are their buildings now and not in good repair; like their owners, some display advanced decay and signs of age. This is where the bargains can be found.

True it is, it must be said, the seaside towns have grown to some extent, but not enough to dislodge growers who with status quo are quite content: rows of houses now surround the greenhouse nurseries just as rising tide creeps up the shore, leaving islands of dry sand; the glistening glass reflects the sunshine's rays, bright oases in drab desert of grey slates and asphalt streets, rus in urbe, the countryside in town. Faithful to the old traditions, the customs and routines that for fifty years have served so well, chrysanthemums still follow on the summer crop. The early flowers are cut while still they stand outside in field, swathes of vivid colour that enhance the beauty of the coastal borough.

Built to house the vines on which the grape is grown, the headroom in each greenhouse is extremely low, the gutters nearly on the ground. They mostly stand alone, not joined together in a block, set down it seems as if by chance, conforming not to any plan; some are built against the great flint walls that to the fig-trees gave support. Lacking paint and bleached by sun, warped by heat and soaked by rain, the feet of glazing bars begin to rot, and screws come loose that hold the hinges of the vents, which, when they're raised, slip off their pins and fall with clatter on the roof. Sheds there are, they too are scattered round, they're built of brick half underground.

There is a feeling in the air, an atmosphere of times long gone when Victoria sat on throne and men returned from Boer War, and sun shone on the heads of happy men in bowler hats who prospered on the proceeds of tomato crop which grew more strongly than it does today, before disease did ravage roots, the soil infested with the filaments of pathogenic fungi. Willing hands worked lengthy hours with pittance for their pay, keeping neat the land outside and painting white the greenhouse bars. Tonight as light departs and darkness falls, there can be sensed the presence of their ghosts, the spirits of the men who spent their lives among the plants in these glass barns now falling into ruin, in final stages of decline.

As ancient owners pass away, and sons and daughters wish to wash their hands of what was once their fathers' pride and joy, they themselves being settled in the City where they work in counting house or store, so the nurseries are for sale. It is a buyer's market, but derelict they are, who would so foolish be to try to earn a crust from buildings so outmoded, which have long since had their day?

The nursery stands back from the road, quite surrounded by the terraced dwellings of this little town which boasts a number of these holdings which were once enclosed by open fields and pastures where the cattle grazed.

November's day is dull and damp, the leaden sky weighs on the soul as each greenhouse is surveyed: vacant for a year at least the weeds reach up and touch the roof and cover all the floor, dead and dry and dusty now, dried up in summer's heat; the only water they received was that that filtered through the broken panes on rare occasions when it rained. Entering in and going inside, the air is still and filled with choking dust, the fungus spores disturbed by unexpected movement after months of solitary neglect, shaken from the shrivelled corpses of Nightshade and Fat Hen: all around upon the ground are strewn black berries fallen from the poisonous plants.

Huts of tin, old Nissen huts of corrugated iron, these stand on southern edge beneath the hedge of thorns, in which were mushrooms grown, and one was used for turning dung. They have not been here long, but are already rusted through - they have the air of army camp deserted by defeated troops who beat retreat, fleeing in the face of hostile force. Some metal sheets have broken loose and flap about and creak and groan when caught by intermittent breeze. Desolate the scene, depressing to the mind, reminiscent of the ghost towns seen in Western films, where once prospectors searched for gold until the seam had petered out.

A discerning eye redeeming features can espy, facilities that are not always found in premises much better kept: the houses of convenient width are in a block, without external walls each keeps the next one warm; the spacious yard is concrete covered end to end, with generous gully taking rain and excess water to the drain. Each house two standpipes has of two inch bore, and wind-pump feeds from well a cast-iron tank set on a brick-built tower.

Of course there is a shed half sunk below the ground as was the way in those far days when first were made these market gardens for the culture of the grape. Beneath the bench are wooden trays, a treasure-trove of metal junk accumulated over all these years: bolts and nuts and screws, spare hinges for the vents, strips of steel with which to fashion parts, objects made of iron in strange contorted shapes the use of which is quite unknown and can't be guessed. No need to purchase washers, wire, or nails, somewhere here there can be found the bits and pieces that daily are required.

The boiler pits are wide and deep and open to the sky; built of brick with concrete floor, they're really rather fine in spite of moss that grows in all the cracks, and weeds that spring from ashes used to insulate the brickwork of the boiler underneath.

Short and squat the smoke-stacks are, of insufficient height one thinks to create draught and draw the fire on winter's night when extra heat's required; yet have the boilers stood the test of time, providing heat on every night for fifty years. For fifty years this rusting iron's subjected been to flames of fires and constant coursing of the water through their tubes - how much longer will they last, before one splits on frosty night and water falls with steady drip on glowing coals and fills the pit?

In men's affairs decisions must be taken, with frequence does the need arise. Choices must be made at crossroads on the lane of life that twists and winds between the fields of circumstance on either side that look alike, all lacking landmarks or finger-post to indicate the way that's best to choose. No master now to say nor yea nor nay. Standing all alone, supreme, of destiny dictator, captain of the Fates (or so it is it's thought), and yet inexperienced, with insufficient knowledge of a past on which a future judgement may be based. No longer is there anyone to whom to turn for guidance or advice, recklessly must die be cast, and trust to luck it comes up six; procrastination does not lead to any place, it is a cul-de-sac, a dead-end street.

The die is cast, the deed is signed, it is as if a ship is leaving port and safety of the shore to cross an ocean deep and wide, a voyage fraught with violent storms and hidden submerged reefs that rip the hulls of careless captains' ships or unwary masters' barques.

A start is made to clear the weeds and mend the glass, it's not as hard as it appears, and spirit rises as the nursery's finer features from apparent dereliction now emerge; freed from weeds the soil is seen to be a deep and fertile loam well fed with fertiliser and spent manure from mushroom bed.

The old year's nearly done and soon will winter's hand stretch out and touch the land with ice and frost: at once must seed be sown while still there is some warmth left in the air, but heat is needed in the night, it's time the boiler's lit.

Diminutive the boiler is, sunk in a pit outside the door, reached by a flight of steps by which the stoker may descend to fill the firebox full of fuel. With water is the system filled, and sticks and paper laid on fire-bars ready to ignite the anthracite. Just when it seemed its life was over and the boiler'd breathed its last, the water starts to warm and flow again, like blood in vein of man on brink of death who's been revived and brought to life once more, restored to health and vigour of his youth.

All is well till airlock blocks the flow and boiler overheats, and jet of steam ejects from vent and scalding vapour fills the air. At this juncture does the clergyman appear, recruiting members for his church, prepared to talk in solemn tones of peace on earth and bliss above: instead he finds all hell let loose, the spouting steam and flaming coals synonymous with life below.

Prosperous is the nation now and commerce thrives, which is perhaps the reason why the reps are swarming like the bees that fly from neighbouring hive. The first arrives from Holland, sent to get the money which has not been paid, collect the debt that by the previous owner's owed; a wasted trip, he gets no cash, for previous owner's broke, and for fraud he now in goal resides.

The second is a pleasant chap who comes on bike, a cycle with a box fixed on the back. He's sent by Mr.Stench, for whom he sells manure, nothing but the best from the stables where the thoroughbreds are kept. An order he receives, for is it not essential that the beds should soon be made, in the manner that the pundits have decreed?

Now the tables they are turned: some irrigation harness he is sold, it was lying in the shed, and now it's on his bike; not only that, but Nissen huts as well, the old and rusty sheds that flap and grate whenever blows a gale, these too he's bought to take away some other day.

The third is of sadistic turn of mind. His spiel he first repeats, but no order does he get, and a tone of disappointment enters in his voice, and hardens as he utters a terrifying threat: "I've heard it said with certainty, the District Council has an order made, that by compulsion they shall buy this land of yours. You have not been here long, not much longer will you stay." Strange thing for him to say, there is no shred of truth in these the words he speaks.

By now one house is planted up. Swiftly have the seedlings grown, the roots have filled the pots and been transferred to beds of horse manure from which the stems reach up, their heads tied tightly to the lowest wire: the great adventure has begun.

Mild indeed the weather is when next a salesman calls. He assurance gives that on this favoured coast the snow it never falls. Hardly have these words of comfort and of hope been spoke, hardly have his footfalls died away, the wind backs to the north, the sky is overcast as threatening clouds blot out the brightness of the sun; gone the mildness of this climate maritime, its place is taken by the icy arctic air, and soon both sky and earth are turning white.

Next day the dawn breaks grey, it's hardly light, and over all a foot of snow. Each day is just the same, the sky is covered by the cloud, there is no sign of sun; at night Jack Frost takes hold, and bitter is the air.

The plants they cease to grow for lack of light and insufficient warmth in spite of fiercely burning boiler fire. No need is there for routine work, the world stands still within the nursery wall, the only job that must be done the frequent shovelling of coal. The leaves grow pale, oedema occurs where transpiration can't escape as vapour in the frosty air.

Huge the heap of anthracite that's stacked on concrete yard, a railway wagon-load straight from the pit, great blocks of coal, boulders blasted from the face of mine deep underground. These must be busted with a sledge before being barrowed to the boiler-pits and tipped, falling on the floor below. The weeks go by without a change, the plants stand still but stay alive: it is the stack of coal that dwindles day by day, the heating costing more and more. Right at the start of risky voyage has ship of venture met with shoals demanding navigational care.

Less short and dark the days become as winter passes; warmth returns as does the sun, and in the air there can be felt a hint of spring. The plants revive, they have survived, and now they quickly grow, and on the mainstem fruits appear as embryo. The old traditions of the past that can be traced to prehistoric time insist that fruits should not be grown upon the central stem but on the shoots at either side. These edicts of botanic priests are now ignored, too much time's been lost, too much coal gone up in flame. Was not this crop selected for its speed, its roots enriched by race-horse dung for stamina and pace? Severe the handicap of cold and frost imposed by Chance, the steward of this risky course: it is by reckless disregard of rules that has, against all odds, the selling-plate been won. The first fruit's cut on date predicted when the seed was sown, taken from the stem and not from shoots retarded by the snow.

A second heated house is planted up to follow on the first; quickly does it start to crop, now that the days are longer and the weather mild. The dangers of the winter are for the present past: each flush of fruit is followed by another in the warm and sunny days of the early part of summer.

Not for long may grower bask in pleasant sunshine of the spring, relaxing in a chair upon the lawn, watching through the glass the lengthening shoots and spreading leaves, for now the spider mite creeps from the crevice where in hibernation was the winter spent.

So small it's hardly seen by eye at all although it's coloured red, it breeds with shocking speed, devouring chlorophyll and spinning web. If this mite is unmolested, soon the leaves are turned to white and wrapped in silken thread; and then, these mites, they climb through vent, whence, caught by movement of the air, they're carried on the wind from house to house, tiny galleons on the air with wind-filled sails of gossamer that enter in some open light like pirates sailing up a creek: disembarked, they swarm across the new-found shore, they pillage and lay waste the foliage fresh and green, unless they're driven back by some acaricide or pesticidal smoke.

Control of pests and of disease that's caused by fungi in the earth or in the air most surely is a major part of grower's work. They do not wait upon his pleasure but like lightening strike and multiply in hours of darkness overnight, and that is why in spring and summer on most days there can be heard the throb of pump outside some glasshouse door.

With haste is made a spray machine, fashioned from the pieces found amongst the junk that here remained when previous owner went away, fleeing creditors he could not pay. Driven by the tiny tiller which is used to turn the greenhouse soil, it pumps white oil to furthest end through yards of hose that lie pulsating on the path. As well as underneath, the leaves are treated from above, to cover every side: the lance is thrust between the stems to try to reach the foliage pressed against the glass, and trap the insects in a film of oil, hold them in confinement till they starve. The process takes much time, time the hand would spend on trimming if he could, because the shoots they never cease to sprout, forming thickets on the upper wires in which the blackbird makes her nest.

Not only is there need for pest control, but whitewash must be spread upon the glass to mitigate the glare of sunshine when the summer's at its height; this entails the dragging of the hose along the narrow gutters, just another job to swallow up the hours.

As each summer day dawns still and hot, the hum is heard of early bees, slowly moving through the garden flowers. A little later, as the rising sun strikes fiercely through the glass at tender leaves, the greenhouse vents are opened up, admitting cooling breeze, a bee or two as well; impossible to keep them out with nets or take from every plant the flowers they pollinate - some fruit are fertilised, swelling at one seed-filled end until they seem like Indian clubs and cease to have much worth. Is there no end to obstacles that Nature places in the grower's way, lest he should lazy grow and richer too?

Some houses still have not been filled for want of time to make the beds and raise the plants. Instead they're planted with chrysanthemums in spring, the tiny slips set in the earthen floor to stand where they will flower. Undemanding are their needs, a little water now and then, occasional tying up with string.

There is a market in the town to which the traders come each day before the dawn to buy the fruit and veg they need to stock their shops.

The growers came the night before to stack the salesmen's stands with trays and crates while buyers slept and market was deserted and silent as the grave. A few dim lights cast feeble rays between the stands enclosed by fences made of wire; overhead the light was lost in lofty vault, roof's canopy that covers all. The watchman stood at gate, afraid to move, to walk down aisles in shadow shrouded, fearing that a miscreant might attack - some rascally tramp who hid here in the dark.

The fences that surround the stands, excluding all with bad intention seeking something they might steal, have been erected at the close of trade, they will be taken down next day. There is a gate, the growers have a key; but posts are bent, the wire is twisted out of shape, one can't get in without a fight. Inside, aroma rises from the boxes and the crates containing most exotic foods, flown from furthest ends of Earth; the lid removed from one on top reveals the luscious fruits that tempt the taste of those who bring their gear: they must not the salesman's trust betray, the evil thought they must repulse, the while they stack their boxes where they can, and check the stocks on other stands to see what hasn't sold and what there is in short supply.

On that night there came a man, a humble man who strove alone to grow some crops upon a plot of modest size, enough to feed and clothe himself and his long-suffering wife. He had not been before, he was a stranger in a place that he himself found strange, for no one else was there. The gate he could not find, the mesh looked all the same: no padlock on a chain, just twisted wire secured to frame.

With fists upraised he beat the fence, with frenzied cries he called the salesman's name. His shouts rose up to darkened roof and echoed round the market hall, and then were lost in foetid air.

Did he at last break in and leave his load, what did become of him? There's no way that one can tell, for there was no one there to see or hear.

The salesman acts as agent for the nurseryman, it is by him that he is paid. He is the vital link and sure defence between the seller and a public hard to please. That is why when he commands he is obeyed: he is the arbiter on quality and presentation's judge. Tonight an extra load he needs to meet increased demand when trade commences in the early hours, not at local mart of which the previous tale was told, but at the one that at the City's centre lies. Without delay the van is loaded and the driver takes the road - it's already late and darkness lies like mantle on the countryside.

The crates are safely laid inside the stand, the van is turned and heads for home and waiting bed. The City falls behind, the houses are more sparsely spaced, and here and there some fields appear, lighted by the streetlamps' amber glow. These lights, suspended from their spindly concrete pylons high above, illumine now two figures on the verge, one standing upright waving with his arms, the other prone upon the grass.

The van it comes to rest beside these persons in distress: the man who's lying there no movement makes, he may be drunk, he could be dead. No explanation does the other give, but bundles friend into the cab upon the seat, for he is very strong and lifts him like a babe, then seats himself beside his mate.

An infirmary is near at hand, it's only two miles back, it's surely where these two would wish to go, as indicated by a nod. Before the destination's reached, suddenly the stranger calls out: "Stop the van!" It comes to rest beside the curb. Through opened door he pulls the huddled heap that is his mate, who gives no sign to show if he is still alive or now is dead; he lays him on the ground again, stretched out as if he sleeps. No further word he speaks, but with a gesture waves the driver on, who, quite perplexed, continues on the homeward run.

What had happened to the pair, what befell them in the dark? Have they in safety reached their home, what secret did they wish to hide? Today in morning light it seems unreal, as if it never had occurred. The only proof that trip's been made to market late last night, substantial cheque for goods supplied.

The days grow shorter, darker too as rain sweeps in on wind from sea, the equinox long past. The summer crops are swept away, chrysanthemums are all that's left on which to pin the hope of further cash to see the winter through and some to spare to buy more coal and recommence to ride the cycle of the seasons as they pass.

The water-tower is low and square and built of brick, unlike the ones one usually sees, taller, with a tank atop of latticed steel. When standing in this reservoir the sea it can be seen: the sea is not far off, the nursery's near the shore. In the fall autumnal gales blow unimpeded from the ocean, from Atlantic's watery waste. The rising wind comes howling from the beach and roars between the gables of the flimsy houses made of glass and ageing sashes, wrenching at the rotting timbers, loosening bars and shaking glazing till a square flies free and shatters where it falls. The heart is filled with fear as, sitting by the smoking fire, the night shut out by heavy drapes, the unremitting sound of storm outside is interspersed with crash of breaking glass and rafters thrashing in the wind. What sort of fool is it, that every day is teased by Fate, afraid of every accident that might occur, bringing bankruptcy in place of life of ease, picking fruit in Nature's garden, like some Adam with his Eve?

Now that tempest's past the rain sets in and starts to fill the boiler-pits, grey ashes floating on the rising tide that threatens to extinguish flames if it should reach the fire-bar tubes and suffocate the fire. An acrid odour rises from this murky pool, the smell of coal-dust mixed with wet cast iron, enhanced by heat of red-hot ash that's quenched with hiss and spurt of steam. The rubber wellies wading through this flood are almost overwhelmed as large-bore hose is wrestled into place and water's slowly siphoned from the sump and channelled down the drain.

The constant fear that boilers fail from fractured tubes or flooding in the night before the dawn, or do not draw because the damper's incorrectly set, creates an image haunting mind, invading sleep; a dream occurs sometimes at night of iron towers deep underground, black with scale and red with flaking rust, and underneath the glow of smouldering coal throws shadows in the darkness on the walls of this cavern dark and dank.

What is it that inspires this parody of greenhouse heating in those hours when thought meanders uncontrolled while body rests, dredging memories from subconscious mind, distorted by the lapse of time? From these depths there are recalled scenes seen some years before, of broken ships beached on the mud below the tide. Proudly once they sailed the oceans of the world with care-free crew familiar with the ports of call from here to far Cathay; split in half by raging storm some time before, the sea swirled through the jagged gash and flooded floor of engine-room, vast chamber like the chancel of a church, illumined by a sombre greenish luminescence filtering in through open wound in side of ship. In the centre, rising like Poseidon from the waves, the triple towers that housed the pistons and their rods that drove the vessel through the seas as seamen stoked the fires beneath the boilers now submerged and partly covered by the silt brought by the waves of tide's recurring ebb and flow.

Stairs of steel led up to galleries on either side where once the engineer was wont to stand who listened to the engine's steady throb and watched the flywheel spinning as he checked the pressure gauge for head of steam.

Up on deck the sun shone bright, it hurt the eyes accustomed to the gloom below, but none was there except the sea-birds perching on the single stack. No lock was on the door to bridge, it was as if the master left his post the hour before, the charts spread out beside the wheel, untouched by intervening years: they were encaptioned 'China Sea', blank sheets marked only with the variation of magnetic North, maps waiting for the touch of trammel and the point of pencil clasped in the navigator's hand.

All that's left now are the flowers. At last the buds begin to break and petals stretch, revealing beauty that's been hid since early spring. As colour spreads along the beds the heart is lifted as there now appears this triumph at the end of year.

Not content to see them packed and then despatched on railway train, they're followed on the next, and city's reached some time before the dawn. The stones with which the streets are paved are cold and damp, reflecting feeble rays from gaslamps fixed to corners of the buildings that surround the square, and centre-stage the Opera House now sleeps, fronted by its classic pillars and its pediment in ancient Greco-Roman style, and at the side some crates of leeks.

Round the back the vegetables are sold, and at this hour it is as if it's Bedlam that one's at: buyers haggling over artichokes and bargaining for the spuds surround the brightly lighted stands, the porters push and shove their barrows through the throng, calling raucous warning that everyone should mind their back: and in the basement are the flowers. Arranged around the walls the contents of the open boxes are displayed that everyone their beauty may admire and, keenly bidding, raise the purchase price. In the office at the back the principals in black with homburgs on their heads and glasses rimmed with gold.

A winter's evening, clear and crisp, when all is held in ice-man's grip. Crouching in the brick-lined boiler pit with shovel grasped in hand, the anthracite is thrown upon the flames that fill the fire-box of the furnace till it holds no more, then into place the iron door is swung. Gently sizzling as it slowly cools, the clinker's glowing disc lies on the floor.

Straightening up, the head is raised and gaze is fixed on darkened dome that is the sky, Kelvin's Kingdom wither flows all warmth on winter night, and energy is lost in cruel cold among those glinting shards that are the stars, hard and sharp, a thousand knives. During day a feeble sun shines briefly to reduce deficiency of heat, but after dark the stars reclaim this energy that's rightly theirs: with endless toil a man must pay the price for his short life.

The greater part of year is subject to a climate temperate, mostly mild, cold enough at night for crop to need some artificial heat, too warm by day when sun beats down, except the vents are opened wide. All night the fuel is burnt at great expense, by day the heat is all released. In early days when first were grown tomatoes under glass, the cost of coal was very low and price of fruit was high. Now it's gone the other way, no longer does this happy state exist, and cost of fuel begins to matter very much. To a grower, in his daily fight to earn a crust, it seems absurd to spend each day in keeping cool, each night reintroducing heat.

In the glasshouse good control can be maintained of moisture in the air and in the soil, and temperature as well: for light reliance must be put on fickle sun which shines one day but not the next, rising high in summertime for far too long in northern clime, and quite inadequate is length of winter's day. If in eternal dark the plants could grow, freed from the bondage of climatic whim and inconstancies of each succeeding season, what benefits would then accrue.

The light of day falls on the leaf, it's trapped by chlorophyll, and there its strength is used to synthesise some sugar and some A.T.P. So simple now it seems, to substitute a spoon of glucose for the sunshine's beneficent rays. In darkened building, or in cave deep underground or buried in the side of hill, no one would ever know the time or what the day may be, if it's cold outside with north-east wind and showers of snow and sleet, or if it's hot with breeze that scorches leaves and so dries the pollen's dust that its robust virility is turned to impotence and infertility. No pest or mould need penetrate this fort protected from assault by filtered air and air-locks at the door, an aseptic area it could be, and free of weeds as well.

In the glasshouse every plant must see the light, unobstructed by its neighbour or some structural member that supports the roof. In everlasting darkness, where sugar substitutes for sun, the plants could fill the whole of space, stacked to ceiling from the floor. Free from toil of weeding soil and hoeing rows, from shading glass and endless pest control with spray machine and yards of hose, few labourers would in future be required.

The siting of the works would not depend on drainage or the quality of earth or a sunny aspect facing south, but close proximity to market in any part of world, and production artificially controlled to meet the variation in demand. Best of all, the freedom from reliance on those hungry boilers keeping cold at bay, the bitter winter winds and biting frost that if they can will kill the crops.

This is then the dream: not the normal nightly dream of chaotic thoughts and wild imaginings of mind released by sleep from consciousness' control, running freely through the fields of fantasy; no, this is the aspiration driving quest for answers to life's many mysteries, yet avoiding bog to which the ignorant are lured by decoys that seductive sophists put in place.

Research must now be put in hand to understand the chemistry of life, to see how sugar can be introduced and used instead of sunshine's vital rays. Plants that grow in gardens, in the woodlands and the fields, they make good specimens for culture in the lab: they can be had at any time, just by going outside. Simple lives they lead, they do not walk or run or move around, rooted as they are to the ground on which they stand; rarely is there any function they perform but grow from seed to adulthood and reproduce before they reach the compost heap. The system of controls maintaining such a spartan life has great simplicity itself, responding to the change from light to dark and hot to cold and very little else; for nourishment they soak up salts dissolved in moisture in the soil: not for them the hunt for prey composed of protein nor the daily grind at work. By constant observation and measurement of plants, their rate of growth, development, decline and ultimate demise in varying conditions of experimental tests, deductions may be made regarding metabolic process and chemical exchange.

Books are read when time allows between the bouts of nursery work and keeping of accounts and calculating V.A.T., books of biology and natural science and the chemistry of cells, for never does it flag, this new-found interest in the inner workings of the plants, that may one day lead on to fortune, and maybe even fame.

Close by there has been built in recent times an institute for crop research with aim of aiding growers increase yield until they self-destroy with glut of fruit and too much veg. Great blocks of labs in modern style house bio-chemists brewing potions for controlling growth or curing pathogenic ills. A glasshouse complex stands beside, the crystal panes embedded in the aluminium bars: in here are crossed the breeds producing seeds of plants resistant to the deadly wilt and virulence of virus brought by aphis, carried by the dry and arid wind originating in the deserts of the East.

Six steam boilers stand like stallions in their stalls, sheathed in shining steel as were the chargers of those knights in former times who jousted for a lady's hand. Their warmth is forced round all the site through four-inch pipes held up by stanchions made of iron; the hot breath hanging from their nostrils is the vapour seeping from a leaking gland.

Imposing portal leads to entrance hall flanked by reception lounge and licensed bar; on beyond lies spacious lecture hall where growers gather for their monthly meetings in the winter when the work by darkness is curtailed. The speaker stands on platform at the front, beneath a massive screen on which are beamed the diagrams and tables of statistics at which he points his laser while he spouts his abstruse theories to an audience held spellbound by his words - all except for one, who, brought against his will, falls into slumber most profound and loudly starts to snore.

Beyond the labs on upper floor where sit the Ph.D's in silent contemplation, wondering what it is that makes the sap to flow and why the leaves all face the sun, the library is found, its many windows facing south toward the distant town and shining sea: in between some market gardens and some pastures, emerald green, the edge of which is being encroached by waves of residential new estates, slowly moving inland like a concrete tide of bricks and tiles. This book-lined sanctum's where are sought solutions to the problems that surround the new technique of growing in the dark. The rays from autumn sun slant through the windows' sashes, warming alleys separating shelves stacked nearly to the ceiling with the horticultural literature, the scientific journals and reports of meetings of societies of learning, and the papers that polymaths have published, and periodicals in many foreign tongues. In this hallowed place does silence reign, broken only by the rustle of a turning page as, sitting at a table, a scientist in lab-coat studies his selected text to aid him in his work.

It is as if here at this Institute all knowledge that exists concerning glasshouse crops and plants that need protection from the worst of winter's weather has been gathered up together: somewhere inside these papers, books, and dry reports must lie the clues that lead to goal of searcher's quest, the means by which the plants may thrive whilst kept in darkness, without light.

From the abstracts an account is found of how, before, it had been tried, to feed with sugar in the dark: but abandoned was the work when no response was made by plants to scientist's demand that they should grow at night as in the day.

Thus it seems no rival's near to snatch success from under nose, and many days are spent perusing tomes purporting to contain all knowledge that is known to date of how they live, the lilies of the fields, the lowly moss and stately trees.

Professor Hastings is librarian here, a man behind whose name a string of letters follows on, for he has qualified in every branch of science that to horticultural expertise pertains. The rivalry between the learned men is very keen, for each success in science brings advance to some career. An ignorant gardener groping in the mist surrounding matters far beyond his ken cannot compete or offer threat, and so is treated with a condescending kindness, and assisted in his search for how this photo-synthesis it works.

"I've read these long accounts of how the light falls on the leaf, of how the glucose is produced, and A.T.P., but there's a need for something else, these two alone are not enough."

"What you see is energy" explains the guardian of the written word, "it powers the chemistry proceeding in the plant, but only if it's given guidance, so that it knows what it should do, else it will dissipate in gentle warmth, lost to cool surrounding air. Another factor must be found, controlling action of the cell, whether it should multiply, or merely slowly swell."

Now is remembered an exhibit seen a while ago of some new way of propagating tiny pieces taken from fresh tissue of some growing plant, which then are sealed in pots and cultured on a gel containing all the nourishment a plant could ever need. At that time so small and insignificant it seemed, no interest did it arouse: but now, it's not too late to see that somewhere in this mix there will be found the factor X that will unleash the potency of sugar's latent power.

Once more the pages of the tomes are turned, descriptions read of work performed by biochemists of renown, but no trace nor mention of this factor can therein be found.

The annual national horticultural exhibition's being staged this week here in the City Hall: an honour is it for the town, in recognition of the nurseries old and new that crowd around the urban fringe, enjoying southern sunshine since first the figs were planted 'gainst the tall flint walls that had been built expressly for this use.

Delegates have come from other parts to view the latest gadgets now on sale, the plastic pots that will replace those made of clay, the irrigation hose that's punched with holes and waters all the bed at turn of tap, cardboard boxes folded flat instead of those that growers used to use, bushels made of wooden slats; more deadly sprays that really do destroy the pests and fungus spores, and careless growers too who have not dressed to kill, donned their rubber gloves, their gas-masks and their plastic macs.

The show is over and the day is done: now commences the reception given by the Mayor, to which all growers are invited, those who from afar have come and those who to the town live very near. A chance it is to speak with those from other parts, comparing notes, exchanging fresh ideas, and meeting men one knew when working where the river and the railway run together side by side, and the nurseries fill the fields for mile on mile.

It is one of these who is accosted now, a man rejoicing in a not entirely inappropriate name - Tenacre is he called, in his locality a leading light who lectures growers' meetings when he's not chairing their committees.

"What news is there of those I used to know, what tidings do you bring from the nurseries on the plain, where heretofore the art was learnt, how to grow the long green fruit on beds of sweetly smelling dung and straw?"

"Alas, the news it is not good. Success had gone to rich man's head, complacency as well. He thought his world would never end, but go on turning profits every year, unaware that Progress never rests, seeking new techniques, reducing need for labour, and increasing weight of crop of fruit. More and more are boilers fired with oil, giving constant heat all through the night without the help of grimy stoker wielding shovel, blackened by the dust of coal. So now I have to tell you, all his money's gone, the nursery's up for sale. Thus it is it passes, the glory of this World."

A timely warning, this. So far the luck has held, the boiler tubes have failed to split, but still the rain it fills the pits, time is wasted pumping out through two-inch hose and shovelling sodden ashes fallen from the fire; and every night the winter through, on into early spring, removal of the red-hot clinker and the filling of the firebox with fuel enough to last until shall come the dawn.

Modernised the heating is, the ancient boilers left to sleep deep in their pits, resting undisturbed where they have lain these many years. Replaced they are by hot-air heaters gently blowing warmth that flows through plastic pipes that will not burst; their burners, softly humming to themselves a lullaby, are fired by diesel oil, controlled by photo-cell, the 'magic eye'.

Spring has come around once more, bringing with it sunshine and a milder air to blow away the frost and fog and wintry mists. Just planted the tomatoes are in double rows a foot apart; one by one first flowers of lowest truss appear, like yellow stars at eventide revealed by darkening sky. The strings in place, there is hiatus while one waits for plants to grow, while new roots make forays into freshly cultivated soil. This gap is filled by propagating plants for those who plant tomatoes late; easy money thus is made, for rapid is their growth this time of year, and little is the need for artificial heat.

Already plants have been supplied to some who have no time to grow their own, or lack the heated glasshouse space, and promptly do they usually pay although they're poor and not well britched. One has come today with cheque in hand, he stands here yet in house wherein the plants are raised, the propagating house, a cigarette between his lips.

Well known it is to all who grow tomato crop, racimes of ripe red fruit depending from the vines, that from tobacco leaf the virus comes that twists the leaves and sterilises truss. That is why this man of conscience taps the ash into his palm, and holding up the flap of jacket tips it in the open pocket of his coat, regardless of the risk he takes of setting self on fire.

On edge of life does live this man and wife. Beyond the town and cultivated land they dwell in shack that's not much more than shepherd's bothy built of brick, the mortar flaking from the joints, with roof of turves surmounted by a tangled mat of grass and weeds. Greyhounds do they breed and train to race on nearby track; undisturbed they live in isolation at this remote and lonely spot, and none disturb with whine and bark of restless dogs, who in a street would cause distress to those who in the night seek peaceful quiet in which to rest.

A cultivated patch they've cut from wild hillside, and here they plant each year tomatoes on the slope that faces to the north of east, catching rising summer sun at start of day, for it isn't warmth alone that makes them thrive, but energy contained in every solar ray. Their bothy stands at wilderness's edge: beyond, a grassy path still leads along the scarp above the steeply sloping side of vale gouged out by ice in bye-gone age, but few the feet that tread this way that leads but to a treeless waste, once browsed by sheep before the import of New Zealand meat. Now these hills serve only as retreat for those who seek a brief escape from cacophonic world, a chance to sit and think and dream a bit.

Inside this poor abode the furniture is sparse and far from new: two chairs, a sofa, and an outsize telly 'gainst one wall. The sideboard is the centre-piece, the polished wood reflecting still the candlestick that stands each end and cut-glass decanter on a tray; glasses too, and bottles now half full, and packs of fags piled at the back, for man and wife maintain their health with whisky and tobacco smoke, and scanty winnings from their racing dogs on lucky days.

It's not long after that the cheque returns from bank, and on its back is euphemistic message and request for re-presentation at a later date.

A new development's announced this year, effect of which will be profound for growers of the glasshouse flowers. Originating on Atlantic's western side, a herald's come to bring the news and tell the limeys what it is, this thing of which they've vaguely heard. A meeting's been convened in lecture hall which now is thronged with nurserymen all eager with expectancy to hear the words of prophet from the west who's just arrived.

This is no dry and dusty sermon spoke in slow and measured tones by academician going grey, his life spent poring over papers in some cloistered college on the banks of Cherwell or the Cam. This vibrant man with vivid style is full of phrases up-to-date, with frequent reference to the power of flowers: whatever can it mean, this 'Flower Power', battle cry of New-age Man? Instead of tables of statistics, hard to see from back of hall, psychedelic graphics he flashes on the screen, to match his flowery speech and histrionic skill. Well entertained his audience is, but as they file outside to find their cars, stumbling in the ill-lit night, they realise that they know no more than when they came two hours before. Little substance had the lecture, lacking flesh on which to chew, just the bones without the meat.

The substance then is this: whereas up to the present time chrysanthemum has been the autumn queen, brightening up the shortening days and beautifying the altar of the church at Christmastide, henceforth this flower will fill the florists' shops throughout the year; and not the classy mopheads in their many subtle shades bought only by the well-to-do, but sprays of daisy shape at price that common man can well afford to pay.

This flower blooms only in the autumn as the days grow shorter and the nights grow long; as daylight lengthens in the spring the stems grow tall and profusely are the leaves produced, but of buds there is no hint nor sign. The trick is now to cheat the plants: when days are long, in summer and in spring, black-out sheets are pulled across, restricting light to mimic fall, and buds begin to form. Conversely, as the days grow shorter, colder too as winter days approach, lamps are strung along the newly-planted beds: intensity of rays need not be great, enough to cause disturbance of their sleep, for broken nights prevent initiation of new flowers until the stems have reached sufficient height. Creating artificial seasons by this means, repeated plantings every week ensure continuous crops throughout the year. The system is precise, calling for complete control of heat and light, of harvest times and planting date.

There is success at once for this new type of flower, each plant a single stem with several heads kept compact by applying alar in a timely treatment, long lasting in a vase or purchased as a potted plant.

New techniques demand new premises to suit the methods coming into use. The old glasshouses interspersed between the dwellings and the shops will soon become beyond repair; the land on which they stand is highly prized by entrepreneurs for building blocks of flats or homes to house the old where they may end their days in climate mild beside the sea.

One by one the nurseries go, the gaps in town soon filled by showrooms where used cars change hands, or offices of auctioneers in which the sale of houses is arranged. The proceeds from these deals provides the cash the growers need to start again in open fields, their crops protected by new glass, modern structures of the best design, heated by steam boilers electronically controlled.

When a business old is closed and preparations made to clear the site, then an auction sale is held, at which good bargains may be had: timber glazing bars and wooden vents with which to make repairs when rot has gone too far and sashes are replaced; and stacks of glass can be acquired to fill the gaps left when the gale has passed, ripping panes from off the roof and smashing them upon the grass.

The gypsies here are always found, short swarthy men in trilby hats and well upholstered women, swarms of happy children hanging from the cabs of battered vans, for they must buy the scrap by which they live, the four-inch cast iron pipes which cost so much when they were new now smashed with sledge, and coal-fired boilers follow suit, redundant in this age of oil. Absurd the bids they make at first for stores unused and nearly new, greeted with the jeers of auctioneer and laughter from the crowd; then silent do they fall as more realistic prices start their meteoric rise. Some there are who loose their heads: desperate to obtain the lot on which they've set their hearts they bid a price above the cost when new.

There is a tide in the affairs of men, and foolish would it be if one were left behind, stranded on the sandy shore, when the waves have swept the others out to sea, carried on the current to where prosperity and fortune can be found. So it is with sad regret that all has gone, the ghosts of those first nurserymen who toiled here in another age no longer haunt this sacred site, now desecrated by the dwellings of the urban men who care not whence may come their bread: only faded photographs and memories remain. Soon forgotten are the early days when all the future was in doubt, success and failure in attendance, waiting at the gate without, to see which one would answer call. By strength of sinews have the obstacles been overcome, now briefly does good fortune smile as inadvisably endeavour recommences, the mind seized by same madness as it was before.

Five The Temple of the Sun

The scattered village lies betwixt the open fields and apple orchards on the slopes through which a shallow valley runs, ending at the disused mill; in wintertime the winding lane is flooded by the stream which wanders past the village hall. Once these ancient timbered cottages were home to labouring men who toiled all day, milking cows and making hay when all was done by hand or horse - each farm had many such. Now they're gone, replaced by tractor and all-terrain truck: one cowman comes by car each day from council house in town. Rich business folk reside in former cotters' homes, commuting to the City to gamble on the stock exchange or work in merchant bank.

Here it is that stands the glasshouse just acquired, great glass basilica, apt to house an airship or Graf Zeppelin, a hundred yards in length and lofty; its unsupported trusses stretch from side to side, high above the soil; great squares of glass rest on the spindly metal bars, when blows the wind with any strength these panes they ripple with the force in waves: or if one stands upon the floor within, high above the head the framework creaks and groans, but never yields. A total change it is, contrasting with the cramped and rotting structures so recently vacated, now gone for scrap and cleared from site. Ample space there is for climbing plants, twisted straight up strings instead of tied to sloping wires: no more training in neat patterns, forming tent of leaves, the plants now stand in ranks like soldiers on parade, between each rank a path down which the officer in charge can pace, inspecting every plant, adjusting its accoutrements and murmuring words of criticism or expressing praise.

The space above the crop is vast, it would appear to be a waste to heat this vacant air: in fact it is the other way, it acts as buffer 'tween the plants and icy blast that strikes the outer side of glass. Wide vents that run the length of roof emit the surplus heat on summer days when Phoebus shines in clear blue sky from early morning till the dusk.

It is a temple to the Sun, replete with worshippers who turn their leaves to face their god as he from orient to occident his traverse makes; see them at the fall of night, clasping tiny hands above their heads, praying for return of light.

The heat for cooler days and nights comes from a boiler making steam that's passed through pipes that lie on ground, but as yet this monster is residing on a neighbouring nursery, where no longer it's required. Relocation is a daunting task that must be tackled, there's no time for more delay. A crane is hired, and men skilled in its use, a welder too who'll join the pipes and fix the stack.

Overhead the power-lines pass, on which all day in summer sit the turtle doves, in contentment gently purring to themselves. For fear the jib of crane may foul these wires the power's turned off for several hours - most inconvenient for the folk who hereabouts reside. The stack's cut off with glowing torch and showers of sparks and hoisted clear. The boiler shell's in cables cradled: in its turn it's lifted up and swung around, now lowered onto flat-truck's bed, and once again securely tied with ropes of hemp.

The truck is trundled off with swaying load, and on the top a reckless man is standing, going for the ride. A concrete strip serves as a road, a dog-leg half way down, and falling land on left hand side. The trailer lurches at the bend, should one wheel slip off the narrow way - one dare not think the awful thought, what fate could wait the man on top.

All the gods who guard the garden, spirits dwelling 'neath the bark of mighty oak that dominates this part, give protection and their blessing to this project fraught; the boiler's lowered in and work commences, reconnecting multitude of wires that lead from switches to contactors to controls that measure heat and level of the water round the tubes.

Painted red, this monster of great girth glares down with menace on the men below who watch the burners as the pressure rises and the steam begins to hiss from newly fastened joints, its belly filled with fire, with anger too and ire it seems, judged by a rumbling from inside; at central point the brass-bound gauge a glowering Cyclops' eye gleams darkly in the fading light.

The new chrysanthemum that yields its crop of blooms throughout the year has occupied this great glass barn for some time past, but no profit has accrued: all monies have been swallowed by this great machine that warms the flowers in autumn, in the winter, and in spring.

So recommences culture of the salad crops instead of flowers in circumstances much improved: now larger yield can be achieved with greater ease from sterile soil, steamed with aid of fearsome monster just outside, singing, like a kettle on the hob, the same old song of which it never tires.

Ancient custom did demand a mould of horse manure in beds raised up above the floor to generate a warmth from decomposing straw. Now instantly comes heat at touch of switch, and nourishment in form of powder sealed in plastic bag.

The plants spring up from sandy soil, watered by that lay-flat hose so cheaply made it hardly costs at all, and climb straight up the strings till out of reach: the fruit hangs down on every side, hidden by the side-shoots' leaves.

No longer is there need to spray the whitewash on the glass to break the fierceness of sun's rays on summer days, so large are vents, so far the roof above the tips of tender plants.

The fight against Red Spider Mite goes on without respite, although defence is much improved by method new, insecticide dissolved not in water but in air; yet to treat the plants each night when sun has set and work is done except this chore, is wearisome to him who'd rather be stretched out on bed at home once more.

Plictran's an insecticide of manner mild and not too toxic if it's spilt, but there are those who say it marks their fruit and spoils the beauty of their 'cues': to see if this is true this is the site the makers choose at which to put it to the test. A row of plants is purchased for the purpose, and once a week a spray of Plictran is applied by lab technician sent from works, and with a glass he studies fruit; at last he finds a minute mark that naked eye finds hard to spy. "It is enough," he cries, "the case is proved, this brand must die, no more by growers to be used."

However, help is near at hand, nearer than one dare to hope, a little mite that eats the pest and not the leaf. This carnivore is very small and hard to see, but breeds with great rapidity and unexpected speed. This new friend has come to stay, working ceaselessly without requiring pay, more effective than the poisonous pesticides, freeing grower from the need to spray.

Life is easier now: outside the farmer struggles with climatic change, the rain and sun and frost and wind which floods the ground or dries it up, freezes it as hard as iron or flattens corn with summer gales, whilst under glass all is tranquillity and peace. The truckers come to take the trays of fruit stacked in the yard as breaks the storm right overhead. They shelter in their cab as fire-ball bursts with vivid flash and thunder roars and rain descends and gutters overflow: and all the while the grower stands serene, surrounded by his crops, unmoved by what goes on outside, protected from electric shock by massive metal frame which surely will conduct the lightning if it strikes this spot.

On other days the sun shines down with pleasant warmth, and driver, when he calls, comes ambling over, lightly treading on the well mown grass, to ask for aid in solving crossword in his paper, his puzzlement displayed by frowning face.

Storm strikes again although it's June, all night the rain comes pouring down, the road is more like river come the morning light. A neighbour has not kept his culvert clear, the rill that runs down from the hill is choked with twigs and mud and overflows across the well-kept sward: it forms a lake against the greenhouse wall. Through chinks and cracks it's seeping through, it runs down paths between the crops and soaks the soil. Is this the end of hopes for harvest in the coming months, the plants submerged and earth no more than boggy mire?

In his absence is the neighbour's culvert cleared, the sticks and stones removed that last winter gathered here, swept down by storm and winter rain, and by the occupant ignored. At once the stream resumes its normal course: slowly does the flood subside, no damage done to plants inside.

The long hot summers of the post-war years, which started in the spring at time of Easter's feast, maintaining heat until October's end, are now no more, just memories of golden years long gone that won't return until a thousand years are passed. In their place a shorter summer, more intense, no clouds at all, and higher temperatures than ever known before, not every year, just now and then. Such days suit well the sale of salads, briskly are they cleared, the salesmen's stands.

In such strong light the leaves do not expand, but stay no larger than the palm of hand; in June the nights are very short, the side-shoots have no time to grow (the cells they multiply by day, in hours of darkness do they swell), the leaves are closely spaced, yet on these stubs there hang great fruits - they alone increase in size. Cut they are each day, the cutting never stops, the piled up pallets whisked away each afternoon to market by the man who drives the transport van; the stacks begin to grow again before the darkness falls. There is no time to trim the plants or twist them up the strings; the foliage hangs about them like the flounces of a skirt and hides the heavy crop. Soaked in sweat as fruit is cut and packed in trays, perspiration fills the eyes, peering through the shades that filter out the scorching rays of burning sun. Blindly are the paths between the rows traversed, the harvest slashed with flashing knife until approach of night calls halt to work that will resume with reappearing morning sun.

It is the most successful season ever, one that will not be surpassed, but no great fortune's won, so hard a master is the soil; from here, be sure, the tide will turn, and economic factors will ensure a slow decline, the cyclic boom and bust that for business is a must.

All is not plain sailing though, for Nature takes a hand. There must be sent a scourge with which to whip the nurseryman, to keep him in his place, lest over confident he may become. An infestation is the form it takes, a plague of outsize aphids, fit to frighten Pharaoh when he wouldn't let the Hebrews go. A common pest of cabbages and corn, of garden roses and the greenhouse flowers, till now it's scorned cucurbits and the like, victims of Red Spider Mite. Because of this no readiness there is to greet this unexpected guest, it is not faced with fusillade of smokes and sprays; the threat is great, what should be done, how shall this dread invader be repelled? Imperative it is to act, and that without delay.

There is a jar on greenhouse shelf in easy reach, a potent poison that on lettuce was employed. It is decreed that seven days should pass before the crop is fit to eat, after treatment with this useful tool - too long this is, the crop will spoil in summer heat: but regulations they require that this includes some extra days beyond the date on which all dangers dissipate.

A chance to take, a risk to run, to cut too soon before it's safe; a foolish act indeed, but by a desperate fool it's done: the leaves aren't drenched, just lightly doused. With great relief no word is heard, no report of death of diner in circumstances untoward is printed in the daily press, just one more undetected crime burnt like a brand on mind to in the future haunt the soul.

No surprise it surely is that after so much summer heat the winter weather sharply contrasts, bringing snow that covers all the fields and makes it difficult to drive. Now fuel is running low, the level in the tank that feeds the boiler with its diesel oil has dropped and stands in danger zone. In previous years this product was delivered by next day, but now one knows not when it is that it will come; the stock is dwindling fast, for not much longer will it last.

Finally it comes in sight, the tanker's backing round the bend, but now it stops, and driver leaves his cab. He kicks the snow to see how deep it is, and shakes his head. "I fear this heavy load will cause my truck to slide, and slip down slope the other side. The prospect fills my heart with dread."

"It must be filled, this tank of mine, it must be done today, for if you go I do not know if you'll return before it's dry. Life and death it is to me."

"Death indeed, for me, not you, if tanker overturns with me inside. The bank's not high but it is steep, and path's not wide."

Toe to toe, each adamant to win the day, a deadlock has been reached, and all around a white expanse of virgin snow, crisply glistening in the sunshine's horizontal rays.

It is the driver in the end who yields at last, compelled by force of will to do what he considers most unwise. He mounts his cab with resignation and resolve to back up if he can to point from which his hose will reach.

All goes without a hitch, they do not slip, so great the weight the tyres must grip the concrete surface underneath: the big black tank is slowly filled. The ladder's climbed to walkway on the tanker's top to check the dips that slide through slits to show that all is drained and none remains of precious oil - "Take care," the driver cries, "take care you do not fall." He takes his leave, the truck now lightened of its load departs with ease.

It is required by law that vessels under pressure, filled with steam, shall be insured lest anyone gets hurt, should any accidently split along a welded seam. This means that every year upon a certain date an inspection must be made, to certify the safety of the shell.

Before this can be done the monster must be cleaned until the metal's brightly shining, just like new. The man-hole covers must be moved, and doors that hide the tubes. The querns, unbolted from the fire-box face, are lowered down and rolled away with care, for fear they get away and break a leg or crush a foot. There are one hundred tubes to clean, a tedious job and tiring too, to clear them all till free of soot.

Entry to the space inside is made through man-holes adequate for agile cat, to see that all is well where normally the water heats: lithe and slim must be the boiler man when he inspection makes. Should a man fall sick when he's alone inside, loosing consciousness when no one knows his whereabouts or what he's at, he may be undiscovered many days, till naught remains but bones left by the rats.

The heart is filled with fear lest cracks are found or unsafe tubes, repairs that cost a thousand pounds or maybe more, but reassuring the inspector is, a man with pleasant manner, not sarcastic or unkind as are one's rivals, even those one thinks one's friends.

Formerly he went to sea as engineer on those great ships that sailed out East before men went by air to India and Hong Kong and countries further on. Smartly dressed he is in suit, befitting to a man meticulous at work; overalls he takes from leather case, freshly laundered, newly pressed - this is why the boiler's inside must be free of dirt and speck of grime.

Surprising is the ease with which he slips through opening at the boiler's base and disappears from view.

The final act is raising steam. The doors replaced and shell refilled till gauge shows full, the burners spring to life at touch of switch and through the peep-hole can the flames be seen. The water takes its time to heat, like kettle when it's watched: at last the needle starts to creep around the rim of pressure gauge, the light reflected from its glass. A sizzling sound at first from safety valve high up behind the stack, and now with high pitched hiss a gush of steam from vent-pipe to the open air. A feeling of relief is felt, there is another year before returns the nagging fear, the dread that tubes may next time fail the test, or cracks appear.

The need the mouth to feed and pay the bills leaves little time for else but work, the fight to solvency maintain; but this battle brings to mind the benefits that would be seen if plants could grow in total dark, if no longer pests did penetrate on silent wing, nor mould invade from provenance unknown.

Thus thoughts are turned once more to finding ways to fill with sugar veins of plants, supplanting sunlight as the source of force supporting life. To this end a test is planned, cucumbers planted in the fall, a single row maintained in comfort by hot air, blown through a plastic tube.

The plants are thriving in the sunshine of the early autumn days, although the nights grow longer, lighted now by Hunter's Moon. Fruit begins to sprout, a little longer than the fingers of the hand, protruding through the lower leaves as if they too would wish to see the sun.

November comes and gloom increases, growth of plants slows down, and now it ceases as the shortest day draws near. The foliage keeps its colour, freshly green, stiffly standing, but when measured there's no increase in plants' height, nor in the length of fruitlets poking out, searching for the daylight which they crave.

Every means is sought by which to introduce some glucose into xylem and the phloem: the leaves are slashed and soaked in sweet solution, grains of granules introduced through stem incision, sticky mix poured round the root, but no movement do they make: obstinate, they give no sign of growth, they show no interest in life.

Negative are all the answers that from this trial are gleaned; they neither nod nor shake their heads, these plants, they only stand in silence, making no attempt to speak.

However, now it's known no easy answer can there be, no smooth road to fortune leads, success a mirage yet. Nonetheless, parameters are fixed, a fence inside of which solutions must be found. The sugars will not enter roots, their molecules too large and hung about with barbs like anchor's flukes that foul each other and the walls of passage where they wish to pass; nor at any other point can introduction into tissues be achieved, somehow it's into flow of sap it must be mixed.

Other information comes to light from out of gloom for which so well November's known: the sudden stop, the halt to growth indicative of pulling of some switch held in great Nature's grasp, effected by reaction that by hormone is controlled; but costly exercise is this, no other gain there is from burning so much oil, that can be snatched from Nature`s fist.

The status quo which has existed since long years before the war has now come to its end; nothing ever stays the same for long, it does not do to slumber nor to sleep lest wakening comes too late. The past has gone, the future takes its place instead.

First warning of impending change comes when the Arabs seize the wells from which is pumped the life-blood of the West, the fuel that powers the factories and the tractors in the fields. The steam for glasshouse heating and the sterilising of the soil, both depend entirely on the Middle-Eastern oil. Like the dawn of day at sunrise that lights upon the lattice of the derricks in the desert, it also dawns on minds of Arab kings to cut the flow of crude and double up the cost.

It can be borne, this extra charge, but market prices start to slip, as more and more is produce sourced from overseas, flown in at night from Israel in a Jumbo Jet, or rushed by road from Spain, where there's no need for artificial heat.

Spring slowly turns to summer and the weather's warm this year, but no glimmer of the sun breaks through the heavy layer of cloud that covers sky. Day follows day, but overcast persists, strato-nimbus higher up, and near the ground continual mist. Cucumbers freely grow, their leaves much larger spread to catch the lower light, and internodes are longer as the branches wander far, for lusher foliage needs more space to fill. The fruit swells as it did before when more clement was the weather and more kind, all of the size the buyer most desires and quality superb: on every side the plants abound. Alas, the salesmen cannot move their stock, insufficient buyers can be found; consumers cannot stomach salads on these sunless days, seeking more substantial fare with which to feed the man inside.

When first the nursery started up amid the snow, uncertain if it could be made to pay, insufficient was the crop to satisfy the salesman's needs; telegrams he used to send demanding more than could by grower be supplied: today this great glass barn's replete with fruit, there's hardly room to place the feet, and none that can be sold. The fear that crop would fail is now replaced by dread that sales will cease for ever more, the fruitful earth lie hid beneath the rotting mass that covers all the floor.

So it is that factors economic combine with factors meteorologic, together they conspire to undermine the food-producers' fortunes and drive them from the land, force them back to city and to town, to where industrial giants rule over slaves, bondmen bound to workbench, obedient to the foreman's fierce command.

In summertime each year a sacrifice is made to satisfy the god who rules the Wind: one glasshouse man is chosen his business to be killed, slaughtered to appease Aeolus goaded on by summer's torrid heat till he can stand no more, loosing patience with the Zephyr breeze, releasing twister over victim's head: his crops are spoilt and houses utterly destroyed, sometimes by hailstones large as eggs, at other times tornadoes tear the stanchions from the ground and twist the flimsy metal frame till nothing's left but heap of scrap. Blind fate strikes randomly at growers large and small, it cares not if they're rich or poor, the humble and the proud are treated just the same - a whirlwind will descend, it can't be seen but only heard: then it shatters all the glass and twists the flimsy aluminium bars, leaving wreckage in a heap on top of all the flowers: defenceless is the victim chosen by blind chance. How long before is drawn the straw that's short, and all is lost in tempest's wrath? Perhaps it's better now to quit when business goes less well than wait for fortune's wheel to turn, for fear of being crushed instead of lifted up. Growers who once proudly showed their premises on open day to lesser men who came to marvel at their crops and wonder at their palaces of glass now slouch around with downcast eyes and faltering steps, waiting for the summons from receiver to relinquish the little that is left, and sometimes life itself.

Instead of looking for another niche in some other facet of this horticultural trade, why not look to leap in one great stride to furthest point that can be dreamed, where plants will grow without the need for sunlight or the never-ending rhythm of sequential day and night? It can't be done in one great jump, not enough is known to cross the deserts of the mind, where knowledge does not bloom as yet; required is more research to reach Utopia, promised land. To this end a lab is built of concrete blocks, windowless it is, for utter darkness is the aim, unbesmirched by slightest light or single gleam. In here the alchemist can sit before his clean-air cabinet, where dust, disease, bacteria and yeast are filtered out, and potent potions can be mixed, their purity and strength remaining unimpaired.

The missing factor now is found, it is a hormone splitting cells, promoting growth; a second, too, that swells the cell that's thus produced. It would appear that one serves in the hours of day, the other after dark. Obtained from factory where these things are synthesised, they are in turn applied to plant kept where the light can't penetrate, to mimic day and dark of night.

Glucose is prime member of the mix, providing energy to power the metabolic process, since excluded now is sun, the normal source of fuel for growth. This sugar cannot enter slender roots, fine as hair to filter out unwanted bodies in the soil: these only swallow simple salts composed of atoms ionised in water fallen from the clouds, the rain that quenches thirst of Earth. This is why the stem is cut across and root removed, exposing ends of phloem and xylem tubes through which the chemicals the plant is fed may freely pass.

The shoots begin to grow from internodes of stems, the glucose does its job now that it enters flow of sap, pumped by peristaltic process through the plants. They grow in size, but then they stop, new growth they cannot make, they only swell the tissue that's already there; it is as if the sun it doesn't rise.

This hormone, then, that's long been sought, ephemeral it is, born of light and dying each night when once bereft of rays from sun; but what of its remains, what happens to its residue? The daily study of the structures of these molecules of life reveals at last the fact that, lacking power, the atoms rearrange to form a shape that needs less effort to maintain - two hormones for the price of one! Do all such hormones act like this, is this the case with love and hate, with anger and with fear? Many trials are made, and strangest thing of all, when absent for some days the growth is greater than when treated every day: and yet, it never goes beyond the tip, no new tissue forms, the cells they swell but do not split. In eternal dark it is not day or night, all sense of time is lost, the only measure is the metabolic rate, the period of the plant's response to chemicals with which it's fed.

The flow of cash is getting low, some other work must now be sought while seeking secret of the growth control, how the hormone may itself be overcome, made to stay in daylight mode long after sun has set and day is done.

Looking north across the coastal plain the distant downlands can be seen, blue ridge behind the haze on sunny day, dark shadow when it's going to rain. Nearer to, the castle and cathedral dominate the scene, watching over winding river and lush pastures where ruminate the kine. This is the view that now is seen whilst tending beds of year-round flowers, serving master once again as was done in times long past, new freedom now acquired, freedom from the servitude to soil, the hardest master of them all: with cash in hand an independent man, with time to talk to plants and wrest from them the secrets hid within their stems.

Every tradesman has his pride, his amour propre, concerning craft in which he's trained. This causes rift between the growers of the flowers that feed the soul and those who specialise in salads beneficial to the nation`s health: a cultural divide that's very rarely crossed. With reluctance then tomato man's accepted into band of those who raise chrysanthemum in this new-fangled way in which the planting and the harvest never cease, but go on hand in hand in each and every week.

A rigid routine must be kept, a protocol proceeding from advisors at the Institute for Crop Research who guide the grower through the whole procedure till the bunches of the white and yellow daisies lie in the cardboard trunks encased in sleeves of cellophane, awaiting transport to the market on the lorry or the early morning train.

It is the women and the girls who cut the stems and bunch the blooms and lay them on the wires, a quiet contented crowd (unlike the noisy mob that terrified the men in the valley where the roses used to grow) lighting up a fag and chatting while they work, exchanging confidences which are sometimes overheard by hand who squats in silence on the edge of other side of floral hedge - new knowledge thus acquired, not of how the plants do grow, but of what they think and talk about, the other sex.

The men who here do toil are mostly young, employed to do the work that needs brute force and little skill - to till the beds while crouched beneath the coloured nets used as supports for growing crop, and dragging chains across the floor to hold the hems of steaming-sheets, tarpaulins smeared on underside with boiling mud that fouls the clothes and scorches hands. The blistering sun beats down through panes of glass, the sweat runs down the back of man who forces tiller through the earth and fills his eyes and soaks his shirt; as his weary footsteps start to flag the foreman's voice is heard to speak: “Faster, faster, do not slacken pace! the beds must all be planted ere the ending of the week.”

The men and girls remain the same who work on glasshouse crops: same hopes and fears and loves and hates as ever were, ‘tis technology that presses on apace, introducing into greenhouse more and more machines to do the work that formerly was done by hand. Electric motors timed by clocks pull thermal screens, retaining heat that would escape through joints in glass: their wires and ropes proliferate beside the path, traps to trip the unsuspecting passer-by. From overhead the irrigation taps poke down with hoses unattached and scalp the worker underneath; jagged edges rip the shirt, and gadgets fill the space where flowers should be. Just think what bliss awaits the man who, growing in the dark, dispenses with the need to till the soil, to heat and ventilate.

Professing expertise in every aspect of the glasshouse trade, it’s essential too in this purlieu that skill shall be displayed. The unaccustomed work routine must surreptitiously be mastered without ineptitude being seen; at end of day exhaustion fills the frame, until the rhythm is achieved and tasks performed with practised ease.

Hitherto the need to spray was much reduced when cucumbers were the crop, the work being done by minute friend, the Phytoseulius Bug; but now another tale it is, these flowers are heir to every pest and dire disease. Ever present are the aphis, revelling in the heat, as does red spider mite, and white fly covers all with sticky mould; leaf miner tunnels through the leaves, and caterpillars chew the buds. The weevils and the beetles and other smaller fry would also join the feast, were it not for the frequent lethal drench that flows from sprayer’s hose as it weaves its way between the rows, snaking like a serpent round the beds, black belly slowly sliding as at the further end the figure in protective clothing and a mask upon his face drags it on along the endless paths whilst soaking all the leaves in this deadly poisonous mist. Like snake the liquid hisses gently as it leaves the lance, a low continuous sound that induces drowsiness and sleep in him who pulls the hose, so that at times he nearly falls, and falling wakes with sudden jerk, resumes his slow progression, spraying under every leaf lest any mite is missed.

White rust is worst and feared the most. Infrequently it comes, its visits widely spaced, but when it does great havoc can it wreak and drastic are the measures that the grower’s forced to take: whole beds removed, the plants all burnt, remaining crop well sprayed. New techniques require it seems new threats to health, new ills devised by Nature’s self lest men should sleep at night with mind at ease. When in the past this flower was grown by other means, its life was mostly spent in open field or greenhouse with a hint of heat; all now has changed, it's forced along at breakneck speed regardless of the time of year or length of day. To match unnatural ambience of this artificial atmosphere, so the fungi in this unaccustomed warm and humid climate do themselves new form acquire, assuming monstrous shapes not seen before, more vicious than the ones well known in times of yore, to haunt like ghosts the growers' dreams and restless sleep.

Unfamiliar are the signs of this new spore, unrecognised except by vague reports by those who live their lives among the fruits and not the flowers. When by chance when working all alone a mark is found, a small white ring on underside of foliage lush and green, it is not known if this is it, footprint of a foul disease, or just some dust caught up in web where spider lived.

Fearful lest an ignorant fool one should appear, loosing face and infallible repute, no mention's made of what is found, for surely others soon will see the foe now come to wreak revenge on those who try to bend the rules of Nature's laws, if such it really is? Oncemore within the breast a guilty secret's hid, to add to burden weighing on the sinful soul.

It really is indeed the fungus' spoor. It's recognised at once by those who've lived in half-expectant fear of infiltration by this dread disease into their highly valued crops, incurring serious loss. Some beds of flowers are ripped from soil by men in paper suits, and flowers and suits are all destroyed, and now is sprayed the whole of house with fungicide that's formulated for this special job.

Most circumspect must be the choice of fungicidal spray or pesticide for use on crops required for food, but on these ornamentals the deadliest of chemicals may be applied. When the rooted cuttings first are planted in the soil, there's Vidate pellets spread across the bed by man in mask and boots and gloves, from which arises smell of decomposing flesh, recalling 'membrance of the forest where the fighting once took place; the armies had moved on, the trees remained with battered branches stripped of leaves, and single stacks of chimneys stood where once the cottages had been, now nothing more than rubble and some lonely heaps of shattered stone; and over all the stench of death did hang, the terror that had passed that way the day before and left its shadow over all to awe the hearts of those who followed on - this is the odour that's imparted by the pills of

Vidate scattered on the ground by hand who slowly moves along the paths between the rows.

Gone is the moist and mossy scent of the greenhouse of the past with its algae-covered glass, its glazing bars of slowly rotting wood and ashy covered paths. Here instead organo-phosphate fills the air, insidiously it infiltrates the body and the mind and is made manifest in sleep by means of dream, a cavern underground, its massive chamber cut from rocks by fetid stream which feeds a pool, round like a well sunk in the stone, whose greenish-yellow waters lead on down to subterranean gate of hell.

The nose detects no smell in dreams, no odours permeate unconscious state, it is the eye of mind that sees the monsters and grotesqueries that fill the stage that's steeped in sleep, it is emotion that is moved by strange sensations emanating from these scenes, the fear and terror or disgust inspired by threats which always threaten but are always foiled by timely waking in a sweat; and in this dream the lifeless stones that tortured lie, held in eternal death beneath the surface of the earth, call to the living mind that O.P.'s bit by bit corrode. This nightmare is repeated many times, not every night but recurring without warning, preventing peaceful sleep.

Sometimes when awake a different dream occurs; although not sleeping, voices can be clearly heard, reciting prosy pieces with distinctly spoken word; would that they could be remembered too, but like all other dreams they quickly fade, gone beyond recall.

At last does patience win its prize, at last the plants, caught unawares, yield up the secret so long hid from searching eyes. It is on this wise then that Nature's trick's revealed, in circumstance that's costing nursery owner a substantial loss in crop, and yes, in revenue as well.

Amongst machines of every sort to cut the cost and increase yield are propane burners, pendant from the ridge of roof, producing gas called C O Two. This it is that plants breath in, the source of carbon for construction of the compounds of which all living creatures are composed. Early in the morning when the daylight starts to filter through the glass above the plants, insufficient is the warmth to warrant opening of the vents, admitting extra air: photo-synthesis is thus restricted due to lack of this essential atmospheric gas, unless are used producers of this vital C O Two.

Another type of burner's also used, that heats the house as well. Emitting flames it loudly roars, gas expelled by powerful fan to circulate throughout the space above the plants, an engine that by kerosene is fuelled. It is here, beneath the flames of this machine, that buds have ceased to form and shoots spring up instead, a leafy mat, a lawn where blooms should be. A strange effect, its track is traced, beneath the path that blast must take to circulate around the roof: by strength of growth and height of shoots is shown its route, it peters out behind the burner's base.

Now it is recalled that long ago in class the chemist told of how the atoms live, how they affiliate, then part and seek another mate, how some are strong and others weak, just like the people that they seem to replicate.

In this the answer lies, how it is that at the break of day the plants feast on the rays of rising sun and, energised, spring forth their shoots and make new growth; herein is found the way life works, how the catalysts are formed that weave new fabric from the liquid substrate in the cells; how the varying natures of the atoms is employed to make them break the unions that between themselves they make in manner of the men and women that they emulate, to operate the hormones that control the growth of plants by day and night.

Purine rings the basis form of growth hormone, nitrogen and carbon loosely linked to hold in place the catalytic sites. In course of day, when light probes all the corners of the natural world, much energy's absorbed by atoms roused from their habitual sloth and bonds are strengthened as electrons' orbits are extended, holding partners in their arms, tightening their embrace. When darkness falls and photons cease to flow from sun to earth across the space that intervenes, the bonds that bound the atoms during day are not so strong: with valency of three, nitrogen shows instability akin to that of stool that has three legs instead of four, and in the darkness of the night one atom's ousted by one stronger, a four-legged carbon one which in its wake brings friends to form new catalyst to swell the cells that rays of light did instigate the day before. Now is seen how hormones change their shape and altered functions are performed when spurt of energy subsides as sun sinks out of sight. Next day the residues they soon decay, to be replaced as cycle recommences when pale dawn lights up the eastern sky. The action may be likened to that of spring that functions in man-made machine to shut and open valves: electrons' orbits stretched by energy of light by day relapse to resting state at night, a ceaseless repetition in life's unending race.

However, when these burners turning kerosene to C O two are not maintained with care, the gaseous output is impure, contaminated with a stream of ethylene, a gas consisting of two radicals, each a carbon atom with a hydrogen in tow. One nitrogen ensconced in purine ring is ousted by this ethylene, and by one carbon atom is replaced: all further action is prevented by the hydrogen attached, acting, as it often does, as plug to seal a point where access might otherwise be gained.

Here then a tool for him who would control the growth of plant imbibing sugar in the dark, holding hormone in initial state until the cells have split. When hormone is applied alone to plants condemned to everlasting night it will at once convert to state in which there'll be no further growth: but if it's mixed with ethylene as well, the hormone will remain in virgin state, protected by the hydrogen that guards the gate. However, bit by bit the energy will loose its grip as drip by drip it leaks away as it must always do, until the hormone's quite decayed and cells no longer swell.

This effect it is that inadvertently has caused regrowth of shoots and leaves where disappointed grower looked for crop of coloured flowers and lovely blooms. With clarity the cause of trouble can be seen and understood with ease, maladjusted is machine, instead of C O Two it spews out Ethylene!

On the floor no word is heard, no comment's made for labourer's ear, the manager and master they confer in private if at all, for no attempt is made to cure the fault and purify the gaseous stream; but now the secret's out, it's ethylene that can control the hormone cytokinin, lock it in the mode that by researcher is required. Now at last in lab the shoots begin to sprout, new growth unleashed whilst still in dark, reward for endless hours crouched over bench in fruitless search for fuel to fire the cells' desire for reproduction and extended life.

At the Institute the scientist is sitting in his room, surrounded by the diagrams upon the office walls that show the synthesis of ethylene in heads of gilly-flowers as seeds begin to form. He has traced it from the start, but now the process is complete he wonders what it's for and where it goes, this gas that in copious quantities pervades the tissues of the plant. An attempt is made by visitor to understand the charts and follow all the pathways of the compounds as their various roads converge, uniting in their purpose, but it fails: many hours of careful study would it need for an uninitiated man to comprehend the chemical reactions and unravel all the trails. Unwilling to admit to this, a hint is given that it may be known, the destiny of ethylene and the use to which it's put.

At this the doctor rises from his seat, "Tell me all you know" he cries, excitement in his voice, but refusal does he meet: has not half of life and quite a bit of cash been spent to wrest the secret of their being from the stubborn silent crops? The scientist he begs and pleads, but the secret that he needs it cannot be revealed: the face of doctor reddens as anger rises in his breast and his voice acquires an edge. Time to take the better part of valour and to hastily depart.

The horticultural college is hidden in the trees; it stands upon a bank above the road that skirts the river, crossed by old brick bridge whose many arches span the waters swollen by the winter floods. Approached by winding drive and gravelled court, a manor house it must have been in former times; and further over, on beyond, a whited science block in which is being held this three day course concerning micro-prop., the art of growing plants in honey-pots from tiny buds or minute cells - at last there comes the one brief chance to be a student at this college of renown.

The youthful students, boys and girls, are absent yet, have not returned from Christmas hol's; this week twelve more maturer men attend, and a prickly rose. These men have mostly come from urban gardens and the parks, sent by city fathers to learn the state of modern horticultural art, as has the miss who, on her own, adorns the class.

The pace is brisk, from nine to nine the lectures run, and practise in the preparation of propagation mediums, made (by adding agar) into gel; acidity's adjusted with the aid of meter, then all is sterilised in autoclave. Placed on surface thus obtained is living tip of plant it's wished to propagate, from which a multitude of shoots will be obtained, produced by power of hormone that's included in the brew.

A cleanliness complete must be maintained; this potion is so potent that every sort of fungus, bacterium and yeast will come to feast upon this fare so rich in glucose, fructose, and the fertilisers spread by farmers on their fields. All pots and tools are purified with heat, and hands and arms with alcohol are cleaned.

Thus prepared, the pots are thrust upon the shelves in culture room: above each shelf fluorescent lights in banks with brilliance shine for sixteen hours in twenty-four. These lamps that cost so much to buy and run, producing heat that goes to waste, why can't they be replaced by chemical to keep these shoots alive and force their growth without the use of electricity or energy of sun?

A visit's been arranged: a neighbouring nursery will be seen, to demonstrate this modern way to propagate at faster speed and greater rate: the crop is roses, miniatures in pots, raised in their thousands in this new scientific way, more economic than the methods used in father's day. The glasshouse block is fronted by the lab. As if it is a synagogue or mosque all shoes must be removed, lest the hallowed floor inside might be defiled, and dread disease spread through the sterile site; the student group stands barefoot in the snow.

Inspected are the cabinets in which the work is carried out in atmosphere of filtered air, the autoclaves that treat with heat the gel, the room that's filled with roses in the honey-pots illumined by five hundred neon tubes.

Through the door that stands ajar the office can be seen - a ragged mat upon the boards, dusty cinders in the grate left over from the day before; coffee mugs adorn the desk, and on a worn old easy chair a mangy mongrel's heard to snore.

Some time has now elapsed since ownership of 'glass' was given up, fearing gales and tempest bringing ruin in their train; a time of clement weather and a gentle zephyr, warming sun, refreshing rain. Was then abandonment of business all in vain? Oh no, far-sighted view it was, undertaken in good time, well in advance; had not statistics, gathered from the past, foretold the future as an actuary would? Certainly they had. The storm that strikes tonight comes by surprise when all are resting in their beds, no warning does it give, a sudden sortie from the skies, ripping tiles and felling trees. From ridge of roof and end of wall large lumps of brick and mortared stone fall to the earth below with muffled thud that's hardly heard above the wind's unending roar. Recently the equinoctial gales have lost their sting, but briefly do they blow: tonight for this they compensate. No individual's singled out to pay the price for all as happened hitherto, no whirlwind strikes one man alone and leaves adjacent fields untouched: tonight the squall cuts in a swathe across the land from farthest west to eastern shore.

No more the need for watchfulness by day and night throughout the year, fearful lest the boilers fail or wind blows out the panes of glass, the plants exposed to winter's blast - undisturbed is sleep by raging storm, until on waking at first light of dawn the damage is revealed, the debris on the ground, the tilted trees, their roots indecently exposed; and now it must be said, relief is felt, like sailor thrown up on the shore by very waves that might have drowned him out at sea, almost an exultation at evading hand of fate: unworthy this emotion is when others suffer loss of livelihood and all for which they've strived.

A sorry sight is nursery where but yesterday chrysanthemums in coloured rows stood silently in beds beneath the lofty vitreous roof; now gaping holes admit the salty air that blackens petals of the blooms and scorches tender leaves, the vents are wrenched from off their hinges and some gable ends are shattered, quite destroyed.

The glass is scattered all around, between the plants and on the ground. The shards must be removed with care from where they've come to rest between the rows, half hidden by the growth, their razor edges pointing up in readiness to slice a hand or cut a wrist thrust carelessly among the flowers. Great heaps of glass are gathered in the paths and barrowed out and buried in a pit dug deeply in the ground.

Those protected by their premiums yearly paid will soon be back in business as before; for those who're not insured at all it may be end of road, total loss and nothing more.

A last return to library is made. Retirement homes now fill the field across the road, the concrete tide now laps the labs of Glasshouse Crops Research, threatening their demise as former fertile food-producing land now gives shelter to the old.

A search is made among the abstracts of the papers newly filed, to see what's fresh in biochemical research, to see if someone else intends to gain control of growth of plants by subtle use of natural compounds reproduced by hand of man. Inorganics, lifeless, hard and cold, will not submit with readiness to elements' exchange. Carbon compounds, on the other hand, compounded of constituents of water and of air, have like these a fluid flexibility and freely interchange, forging fleshy fabrics, which can by division of their cells be re-created by themselves. If Nature can create, unaided, living tissue, why not then a man? It is of this the authors of a paper write, scientists of BioMech, a firm that's recently been formed, this purpose in its boss's mind, but no progress have they made as yet, still baffled by the barriers that bar their way to knowledge of the natural world. Here then a hint that an even more ambitious project in this field has been conceived by these.

The staff of this establishment begin to drift away, there is no future for the growers of tomato crop, the fruit and veg now come from Spain or from the U.S.A. by aeroplane. The glass and aluminium blocks that glisten in the sunshine of the spring, sheltering newly planted rows of cross-bred hybrids, will soon, like those who work within, redundant be; the lecture hall will silent fall, as will the offices and bar. Where will they go, these rows of books that represent a lifetime's work for countless able brains, vast reservoir of knowledge not readily acquired? it must be hoped a springboard they provide from which may leap an industry revived, employing some technique that as of now exists but in the mind.

At commencement of this journey through the glasshouse crops, between tall rows from which the ripe red fruits hang down in chain, or cucurbits of great length lie lodged on wires above the head like zeppelins coloured green, tethered by their tendrils twisted round the crop supports, at the start the question asked was will the answers to the problems posed by life be found in comprehension of the force that makes them want to grow, these plants that spring from every side, leaving no uncovered earth?

Half an answer has been got: the method can be clearly seen by which ingredients from the air and earth are sorted into order, put in their proper place by catalysts that act as templates for assembly of component parts that move along production line until the final product is complete. No manipulation by the hand of man's required, automatically they clip together when they meet their mates, and simple salts are moulded in formation of most intricate organic structures of a complex kind. The mystery that remains, it is: whence comes the grand design, the master plan encapsulated in the nuclear code?

Four thousand acres once there were of cash crops growing under glass, tomatoes, cue's, and gorgeous flowers. Few now remain, food comes from overseas, grown by workers poorly paid, on salty soil in climate of excessive heat; the taste's impaired and flavour lost that was imparted by the British climate soft and mild and rich rain-soaked mould of English fields. Who knows what sprays they use, these men in foreign lands who've scant regard for E U rules?

As fades the light from evening sky when sun has set, its flames extinguished 'neath a sea of molten gold, so fades the former glory of the copious crops of red and green and beds of brilliant blooms that filled the houses made of glass, spread out along the coastal plain between the sea and rolling Downs or clustered on the rich alluvial fields through which the slowly rolling river runs, assuaging thirst of irrigation pumps. Glazing bars, by restless wind and long neglect denuded of their vitreous squares that heretofore admitted light, retained the heat, stand silhouetted 'gainst the darkening sky, last rays reflected from the broken panes that still in desperation cling to corner of the ridge, points of fire that blind the eye of those who come to mourn the loss of yester-year, skeletal remains that turn to dust and in the darkness of the coming days will disappear.

And in this darkness does atomic garden start to grow, pale green the cells that gleam like jewels when lighted by inspection lamp or caught by camera's flash; more sturdy are the plants, freed now from need of sun or risk of pest or debilitation by disease. Away from light life can't survive except it's guided by alchemic compounds newly come from lab in garden shed, proverbial place of birth of children of the brain.

Man cannot live unless he eats, and these new plants aren't ready yet for farmers' use, supplanting those grown in the usual way. The need to feed, to earn some bread, impels the search for work, at BioMech perhaps. Why not?

BOOK TWO

THE ATOM KING

look unto the rock whence ye are hewn, and to the hole of the pit whence ye are digged

Six BioMech

Sam alone remains at home. Untimely death has carried off the parents both, taken whilst still in their prime. A few years older and piously disposed, to all he's known as 'Sankey', short for Sanctimonious Sam. He toils by day in legal office sifting writs and writing affidavits to be signed by parties to disputes protracted over endless months; when work is done the elderly he visits in their homes, those retired who cannot cope with all the forms to claim entitlements and benefits which are their due, freely giving of his knowledge of the law. He would that he could be a lawyer, not a lowly clerk, that he had gone to university, and there had gained a law degree. When his master's out, visiting a client or attending meeting of the local Lodge, then it is that Samuel sits before the old man's desk on high-backed horsehair chair, and riffles through the papers neatly piled in little stacks, dreaming of what might have been if his father could have kept him till he qualified; but poor Dad had died, and poor Mother too. Instead of being at beck and call, of doing all the chores each day, he could then have been the boss, occupying this chair by right, telling others what to do.

So it comes to pass that making do with what little power he can acquire, he chairs the church committees and runs the clubs for youths and Cubs. Attracted to the Church he was at early age, taken by his parents, who have sadly left the scene, to the monastery to worship with the monks. The Abbey's built beside the river broad and wide that flows through meadows moist and green in winter time but parched by sun in summer during drought, when kine must come to water's edge, and, standing in the shallows, drink. The walls of ancient edifice rise up from water's depth, and are connected with the other bank by long low sloping weir; over this the water slides and falls on stony bed the other side with constant unremitting roar, except when level's low it does not flow at all, and one may cross dry shod; at other times the monks are seen with wellies, wading to the little chapel in the woods.

At once was his imagination seized by solemnity and gravitas of ecclesiastic liturgy, the majesty of moving words and phrase and uplifting music of the mighty organ, rising from deep diapasons to the giddy heights of single soaring notes that seemed to penetrate the clouds and pierce the very sky, then fall back to earth in crashing chords, these were the things that gripped his mind and stayed with him when manhood was attained. The ceremonial pomp charged with the magic of the spirit world, the invocations to the saints of old whose mythic stories he's been so often told by his dear Mother, lady most devout who never questioned old tradition handed down from father unto son, the rituals with slow and measured dignity performed before the kneeling crowd who hold their heads in hands with covered eyes as if they dare not look upon the sacred rites, all these things combine to hold in thrall the mind of lawyer's clerk.

And so this layman serves the Abbey church and those who come from roundabout to pray and join in monkish chant and hear the Abbot preach. The Abbot is an influential man whose words play on credulity of ignorant peasant mind, and of their masters' minds as well; most men accept their tutors' teaching without question, too tired to think or contemplate their human state. Led on they are by distant star, a beacon faintly shining through the brume, but mostly masked by mist or lost in fog. This light impinges on the heart and not the eye: it hints at great Nature's power, endowed with purpose and a plan. By his oratory is carried off the heart of Sankey Sam, who unquestionly accepts the Abbot's every word, confident they lead on upward to the beacon's source.

The houses line the village street, the cottages and timbered inn on corner where it bends and lane descends from sloping pastures whence the goats are brought at milking time by farmer's wife. At further end on little knoll there stands the ancient parish church: nor tower nor spire it boasts, a single bell hangs under arch to toll the passing of another life; insignificant it is compared with monastery's magnificence that dominates the meadows lower down and the trees that line the river's bank.

The parish priest's a man committed to his cloth, he too a single man, untroubled by domestic strife. Of medium height and aged some sixty years, with eagle eyes and nose of outline acquiline, he leans on ledge of pulpit clad in black soutane, like some raptor seeking what it may devour. This is the Reverend Ed Mathias, a Doctor of Divinity. He preaches naught but what he finds in gospels' text, speaking in a manner most austere. Those who come each Sabbath Day to hear what it is he has to say like not this attitude severe; where is compassion, and sympathy for troubled hearts? Were not the ancient books inscribed for people of another time and place? How can they have relevance for, us here gathered now, two thousand years apart? No motor-cars nor aeroplanes they had, but rode on asses' back, and crossed the Alps with elephants: what a different life they led. No anaesthetics when they had to amputate, a runner, fleet of foot, instead of telephone. So different are these cultures, the same laws can't apply, the rule-book must rewritten be.

The Reverend Edward thumps the pulpit's ledge, "What poppycock I hear," he says, "men and women always are the same, they eat and sleep and work and play as centuries go by; they constantly contend with foe and friend on battlefield or courts of law, they never learn to live in peace."

The people mutter in the pews, in lowered tones they speak in groups of three or four, gathered underneath the ancient yews that guard the graves, between the leaning stones from which the weather has long since erased the names of villeins living in this parish long ago and in the days of yore - "His head is always in his books, his mind is in the past, it is as if he has not heard of scientific changes that have altered all the economic laws and liberated folk from the moral code that heretofore did hold them in its thrall."

Each Prophet brings the Truth, the Prophet thinks, and thus each faith should coincide; but Truth is twisted ere the Prophet's dead, and sects are formed by those who misinterpret Prophet's words. Myths and legends soon abound, springing from this fertile ground, and form the basis of false Faith that leads to actions ill-considered and opposed to Nature's logic. Abbot and the parish priest, they both profess the same belief, in fact they're not of one accord.

Very different brothers often are, and this is here the case. It is not shared, this love of legal life, the dry old books of precedent, the litigious clients seeking recompense for some imagined wrong, the lengthy letters written in a dingy office in the fading light of dismal autumn day. Committee work has no appeal, the evenings spent deciding who will bake the cakes, and who will cook the sausage roll.

Having gone this far in search for knowledge of the truth, for understanding of this universe and how it works, imperative it is to continue to the end and find life's spirit, know the soul itself if the possibility exists that it might, it could, be manifest to men.

No training has been had in bio-chem, just wanderings through this most mysterious land that is by atoms colonised, exploring avenues beyond the usual bounds, unrestricted by conventions instilled in well-schooled minds, explorations on which the academics certainly would frown. Being thus self-taught, what job is it that should be took, how best to be exposed to scientific thought?

Application's made to BioMech, a company that's new, very secret is the work they do. The Lab is like the others on the landscaped site, low and white, not like the buildings of the previous age, the multi-storied mills of brick or stone with many windows letting in the light that fell on rows of looms that clattered without cease the whole day through, forcing hands to talk by semaphore, gesticulating in the air; no more the chimney-stacks erect against the cloudless sky they stained with sooty smoke the century before, the power is brought by cables underground.

The buildings line the terraced slope that slides down to the edge of stream half hidden in the rushes or by the weeping willows sweeping surface with the tips of tapered leaves. Green spires of Cypress and the twisted pillars of the Juniper form screen to hide the service road that runs behind the factories on this industrial estate, this ornamented business park. Behind, a ridge of rocky outcrop rises, scrubby gorse grows in the gaps between the stones. In the distance, far away, horizon's lined with mountain peaks, the tops of which are capped with snow the whole year through. The fronts of factories face the smiling sun, their glass reflects the clear bright light as if on fire; inside the blinds are drawn across to stop the glare, cool and silent are the labs and offices where figures in white coats bend over bench and desk, the only sound the hum of fans that blow clean air.

An interview is granted, first with the foreman who explains the nature of the job; he demonstrates the plant that must be serviced, the pipes and wires to which additions will be made when they're required, to operate the new devices in the labs. After that the Boss appears, quite unexpected. "A new recruit?" he asks in kindly tone. A man of forty years, dressed in jeans and anorak, he has a dreamy look, as if he isn't here, his mind is in the clouds, his eyes still peering down the microscope through which he seeks the clues to solve the old enigmas which have baffled brains since world began. Perched on the edge of bench, he starts to reminisce, speaking to a stranger that he doesn't know as if his mind he must unburden, and all his thoughts reveal.

"After years of study, poring over books for night on night in artificial light, attending lectures during day on subjects most obscure, and graduating at the last with good degree, my mind was quite exhausted, weary of the figures and the formulae. At night my sleep was broken by wild dreams of atoms dancing in fantastic scenes that could not be imagined by anyone awake, linking up in monstrous molecules, endless chains that moved to Conga's rhythm and its beat, snatching at electrons from everything they meet.

"A life idyllic I did seek; a peasant's life did pleasant seem, to toil at tilling soil in sunshine and the rain, my hair caressed by zephyr breeze. To hoe the dusty earth and watch the copious crops leap from its womb as summer followed spring would surely solace bring to brain tired out by strain of constant study and the need to pass exams.

"One year a visit had been made on foot, alone, to lonely village set in centre of a broad plateau, surrounded on all sides by fields of wheat that stretched beyond horizon's edge, and interspersed with blocks of maize so tall a man could stand unseen behind broad leaves, and from each stem a cob stuck out, the golden seed wrapped tightly in its tasselled sheath. Few the houses clustered round the crossroads, behind them barnyards and great barns replete with bales; the only traffic on the narrow lanes the tractors and their trailers, and majestic combine moving slowly to another field, the driver high up in his howdah like an Indian emperor on an elephant, aloof, above the common herd.

"On one side of street the café stood, a restaurant at one end, and by the door the bar on which the locals leaned, silent men, their faces tanned and lined by constant wind that blows across the bare plateau with searing heat in summer and with icy chill when fields lie bare, waiting for the thaw of spring. No greeting did they have for stranger in their midst, only dark forbidding looks to warn against intrusion on their privacy, their closely guarded way of life, in which the only interference comes from the gatherers of taxes and officials of the state.

"The church across the street with noble spire that I could spy from many miles when crossing endless fields of wheat, caressed today by warming wind, it seems it's shut: the door is locked, the paint is peeling on the rotting wood, the dust obscures the window glass; is there no priest, does no-one enter there to pray?'

"He fixed me with his steady stare, he held me with his eye: all he said, was 'God is dead'.

"Between the backs of barns and edge of field there toiled a man and wife and their young son. A market garden they had made on wasteland, shielded by some twisted trees and guarded by a rusty wreck, a truck just left when engine spluttered to a halt. Various vegetables were growing there in neatly planted rows, brightly coloured dahlias, tall gladiolas and a patch of maize. Other plots they had, scattered round the hamlet, to which they took their tools and fertiliser bags in trailer towed by two-wheeled tractor, but all-in-all it seemed too small, the land they had, to yield a living for the three.

"Excluded all outsiders are from familial circle of these introspective clans who guard dark secrets from the world at large. Is it not remembered well, the trial of village headman, accused of killing one who wandered where he shouldn't late at night, how he stood at trial, short and swarthy, dressed in suit of black as by tradition is required, stood defiant in the court, remaining silent as he had when questioned by police investigating crime? Scanty proof there was that he had shot the man, yet his stubborn silence went against him, guilty was he found, and Madame Guillotine had final word.

"A life lived thus romantic seemed, hid away from bustle of the urban life, the dull routine of nine-to-five, the constant stress to meet new targets set for sales, the anonymity of those around, commuting in their cars at end of day to bijou dwelling on a new estate.

"One was inspired with great desire to do the same, to find a peace of mind among the men who wrest a living from the soil, from their private plots, and answer not to boardroom boss: but here at home in native land, where one would more welcome be.

"A plot of land I purchased on the edge of upland overlooking Weald spread out below. A forest is it called, but heath and bracken and the whortleberry grow where the trees were felled some centuries ago: in the distance where the sky meets line of hills, blue in the haze, the Southern Downs.

"The winter, wet and mild, was suited to the turning of the sod, the preparation of the soil; the spring was douce, the gentle rains alternate with the sunshine's warmth as planted in the fertile earth were bushes of black currants and lengthy rows of raspberry canes. Idyllic was the scene, but little time there was in which to stand and gaze.

"Came the summer, hot and dry. First the fruit trees and the bushes newly planted thrived, throwing out their shoots and fresh young leaves. Then they suffered in the drought, and struggled to survive. Fires took hold of strips of heath and blackened bracken, ignited by the flash of lightning in the sudden summer storm that swept the bare plateau. The sudden shower ran off the surface, rushing down the hill, enough to germinate the seeds of weeds but gone before it reached the roots of crops in need of rain.

"Up sprang the grasses and fat hen, the cleavers and the clover; now commenced a fight with these unwanted wild-flowers that would choke the fruit-trees if they could. Now no time there was to spare, no time to stop and stare, the stunning view remained unseen; the fruit had ripened, picking went on every day, and hoeing in between.

"No close-knit commune did exist, no village hid from public eye in which might live close to the earth poor peasants wresting wealth from stubborn soil. Instead, at night the Pub was filled with City men who farmed until their losses equalled tax demand, their talk was all of horses and their last divorce.

"A year or two of constant toil, fresh air and poor returns from market well supplied, did clear the head and disillusion dreams of simple life close to the soil.

"A new ambition took their place. Fascinated by the growth of plants that I had watched each day with trepidation, lest disease or pest should rob me of a profit well deserved, admiring how they grow, the silent ease with which they stretch and swell - the beauty of their shiny skins, the colours shaded, blending in, it fired imagination, inspired a great ambition, to synthesise myself some creatures like to these, in texture smooth or horny, with furry hairs profusely furnished, or spiky thorns that will protection give. I sought to learn much more of how they lived, the structure of their cells, and what went on inside. Once this knowledge was acquired, and metabolic secrets were revealed, a notion I did have, far-fetched it seemed to some, that I myself would make a living thing from elements alone. Is this not the natural way, the way that Nature made the biosphere, whilst things of steel and stone contrived by man are make-shift tools that do not stand the test of time?

"The animals, the birds and fish, they aren't like you and me, they do not think and speak, they are Nature's playthings, robots made of flesh to people field and forest, no more conscious of their state than are the grass and trees of countryside they populate.

"I know a man who lives alone except for dog. All day for many years the dog and man each other's company they keep. Along the lanes and through the wood they wander, the man he talks to dog from time to time: the dog he does not deign to make reply. So many years together, such close companionship, so many pleasures shared, no one would show surprise if at the last the dog had gruffly spoke - but he never gives a sign, he never ever speaks a word. An animal's without a soul, it can't compose a sentence of two words, it cannot even think; its brain responds to stimuli, the chemistry of instinct guides it through the day.

"Goods and chattels do men make from wood and iron and precious metals, is there really reason why animated artefacts should not be moulded from the carbon in the air? I too, a sapient man, can copy Nature and construct organic creatures from the carbon atoms that abound on Earth and in the atmosphere."

He rises from his perch on end of bench like some great bird disturbed by sudden thought, and wanders off through corridors that link the labs, to check the progress in the search for products new, produced by process unimagined hitherto. Secret is the work, one department knows not what another does, but all is integrated by the Boss, this man obsessed with one idea, to build, not as in the past with wood or steel, but with the elements of water and of air.

The break for lunch a respite gives from concentration on complexities of complicated systems, cables, pipes, and ducts through which may pass the fluids that, like blood, bring life to new synthetic cells. Repast consumed, there's time in hand to stand and chat in foyer at the front of building long and low, to gaze through window-pane that gives a view of grassy bank that sweeps down to the sluggish stream below, the placid waters where the halcyon plunges after fish, and gaudy dragonfly is flitting through the rushes tall.

"Who is that that stands down on the edge, head bowed as if she's lost in thought? Her face is hidden by her hair, her lovely hair so fair, spun from purist platinum."

"Ah that, dear sir, is daughter of Professor Yorke, Arachne is her name. She works in 'Personnel', last month she turned eighteen."

Each day when lunch is done, return is made to front of foyer, there to gaze down to the river, hope to glimpse her through the leaves of trees that line the bank, hope that she will turn her head that may be seen the features of her face as yet unknown.

Driven on by strong desire to hear the words that she will utter first to swain as yet too shy to come too near lest vision vanish, or prove to be not what it seems, a tentative approach is made. And when she turns her head to speak, will glance be cold and voice be harsh, will visage be ill-formed or downright plain? Does she exist in mind alone, of perfect form and character to match, a creature of a man's imagination?

The path across the grass leads not directly down to river-bank where now she sits, her skirt spread out around her feet; it winds and turns between the bushes and the shrubs bedecked with blossoms mauve and white that break from bud as summer takes the place of spring. With hesitance descent is made, moving twixt the sun and shade cast by these trees: and suddenly she turns, revealing lovely face framed in her hair so blonde.

Seized with shyness at this sight of blinding beauty, backward step is taken, behind a bush to hide confusion, speechless does the tongue become. What use to nearer go, robbed of coherence by this vision, by this stunning sight?

"Who is this man?" Arachne thinks, "this man who peeks at me, then blushing disappears. Strange indeed these men, between themselves they brag and bluster, while when they're met by gaze of those they would impress the most, their legs grow weak, they only stutter."

Seven The Meeting

The varied task, maintaining systems in each lab, and in each office too, makes possible the study of the system as a whole, enabling understanding of the work as it proceeds. Unheeded, toiling silently, without a word, up in a corner or under bench, festooned in coloured wires that must be fastened to their proper place on circuit board or jointing box, every word is heard as project is discussed by senior staff. Thus it is that full report can here be made of all that happens and is said in this laboratory wherein research the secrets probes of all that lives and walks this Earth.

Perambulating through these corridors and wandering round the office floor, flaunting length of cable, pair of pliers and a stillson wrench (thus avoiding challenge when invading boardroom meeting or slipping into Boss's sanctum), an encounter in the course of duty with the fair Arachne is engineered with ease; examination of a keyboard fault is excuse for introduction, and exchange of empty phrases as is the custom in these cases.

Official guests are meeting in the boardroom, bankers come to hear the Boss's explanation of the project and the progress made to date. The Boss is on his feet, the air is filled with smoke, and financiers, leaning forward, turn towards him with attentive ear:

"Hitherto all tools that men may utilise have fashioned been from inert lifeless iron and steel or composed of crystals grown from silicon. These implements that men have made to aid them in their daily grind and ease the burden of their toil must be maintained, or soon they'll cease to work; their wounds they cannot heal themselves, old age does take its toll, they do not have the power to replicate; and when they're dead their corpses litter all the land, for slow indeed is their decay, before once more their rust is turned to dust.

"Computers sometimes seem as if endowed with life, they seem to think and make decisions when their owners can't decide; it is not they who muse and cogitate, it is the architect who planned machine's design, who planted in its ROM inside the labour of his brain, the product of his intellect.

"Plastic products are organic, air and water woven into networks closely knit in chains securely tied, molecules of massive size bound with bonds that do not break. If the property of life such products are to have they must be formed of cells, or little sacs, each containing all the works they need to self-sufficient be. Given gift of life they'll have the power to heal and duplicate, and when they die to disappear without delay, solving ever present problem of disposal of the waste.

"Everything upon the Earth organic is, composed of living cells; there's nothing Nature's made that is inanimate, except the rocks that form the base on which all else may live. In space the astral bodies swirl about, but bleak and bare it would appear are surfaces of moon and stars; small in size the world may be, where else is there that can compare with Earth for fecund life and scenery? When first the world came into being, except the infrastructure made of rock, all things were fashioned from the carbon in the air; all inert objects are constructed by the creatures who are with breath of life imbued. It cannot be so very hard to do, to fashion animated artefacts, to imitate the way it was by Nature done. Why should not the process be repeated now? What can prevent me, with my mind well trained by years of study midst the dreaming spires, inspired by dreams and fired by wild desire, to go where no-one's been before, the intellectual wilderness in which the unknown can be found?

"At level of the ground a man may ride a horse and thus get round without the need for mechanical machine, moving swiftly over rough terrain; but in the air he cannot fly, he cannot share with birds the freedom of the sky. Oh! What prospect then unfolds for one who masters manufacture of organic matter - ability to breed a beast with wings and big enough to carry up a pilot into air above the clouds."

At further end of board a banker rises to his feet, who long has been acquainted with the Boss:

"A far-fetched scheme, fantastic dream, for one who once supposed the simple life of peasant, toiling on the land in manner of the days gone by, would ambition's limit be, fulfilling all of heart's desires.

"You've changed your stance, gone other way, beyond the fence of common sense, to realm of fantasies and make-believe. Can you your claims substantiate, what guarantee are we to see that profit can accrue; what is there yet to show for what we have already lent?"

The men of money get together, forming huddle at the further end. They wave their arms and nod their heads, and all the while the Boss his own he holds clasped in his hands as he awaits their verdict like a felon at the county court.

A decision they have reached. Hang Seng now speaks, he speaks for all, for all agree. "Very secret is your work, great care you take lest word escape of what you do and what you make. We too we give no hint of what to us in confidence you've told and yet, and yet the rumours circulate and they persist, that strange unusual creatures do exist in these your labs, of which as yet you do not wish that we should know. No smoke without a fire, it's said, and that is why we're all agreed to take the risk, to make advance, to pay a tranch. We wouldn't wish that we should miss some future day a golden chance."

Outside the house where dwells Professor Yorke, under window of the room in which it's thought Arachne sleeps, a nightly vigil's kept, in hope that glimpse is caught of maiden looking out before she goes to sleep. She never does appear, it is a waste of time, and cold it is as frost takes hold and whitens grass beneath the feet; overhead, the cloudless sky.

The sky so clear, studded with a hundred thousand stars, it's scanned each night until the names are known of those that brightest shine. Familiar sight it has become, leading eye beyond Andromeda and other galaxies too numerous each to name until it seems that edge of universe has been attained.

It is a sight which has induced so many men to ponder on that that's almost out of reach, the mysteries of this life and what its purpose is; but is it sensible to seek the answers in this lifeless space, this space filled only with the cosmic dust, with dust and ice and great clouds of noxious gas? Would it not much better be to look at things most minuscule, to study ways and habits of the individual atoms from which all great objects are constructed: are not the atoms' actions reflected in those of the creatures they compose? Are not their shapes displayed by crystals' cleavage, their properties revealed by compounds' colour and their smell?

Outer space, strange, unknown, but far from void, in its vastness terrifies with mind-boggling power of unleashed forces which propel huge heavenly bodies round the sky: unleashed, yes, lacking guidance nothing is achieved, these forces merely moving shapeless lumps of rock in solid, liquid, or gaseous phase around the universe's boundless space. The atoms of organic biosphere with these same forces are endowed, chained in a linkage which directs and guides their energy through winding pathways to a useful end.

Space is too great in size for detail to be seen by naked eye of common man; the world of atoms far too small. Attempted it must be to visualise these tiny pieces in mind's eye, to know them by their works and what they do, in imagination let them live, ever restless whirling round, changing partners in their dance, joining teams called molecules.

The sense of sight is much restricted, the limits of its range are red and violet and the wavelengths in between. Some other things are sensed by other means, by touch or taste or sound. Those which are not sensed at all, it is as if they don't exist; how can a man believe in that of which he can't conceive? And yet by constant study and research new concepts are unearthed, that which was hidden is revealed.

More rewarding is the study of the stars than staring at exterior of this house wherein there dwells the heart's desire; more remote she seems, further from the grasp of hand, than the constant planets which await the watcher every night. What is it makes a man pursue the chase of woman's love? It is the chemistry, the actions of the atoms by which he is controlled; it must be understood, the way these forces work. Thus it is conjunction's reached with Boss's mind, two heads with but a single thought, to understand the chemistry of life.

There is a meeting of the scientific folk tonight, the clever men from all the factories on the site and more besides. An invitation's been extended and accepted, perhaps a big mistake; one may well be out of place, not know what to say; and yet, there is a yearning to become a member of the upper class, to be accepted in the scientific world, in spite of lack of letters designating Ph.D or similar degree.

A serious disadvantage is it to be poor and always short of cash: to take a train when fellow men arrive in limousine or Porsche is in itself a social gaffe. Already is the room well filled, a haze of smoke hangs overhead. Incredible the babble of a hundred strident voices striving to be heard, rising in intensity of sound, without a pause to sip from glass that's gripped in every hand.

Cliques of three or four or more have formed, groups of friends and colleagues from the labs of factories on this site, this bio-technic park. Senior men, they're more concerned with money and administrative worry than with technology itself. How then to penetrate masonic ring, what could be said to interest these men engrossed in office politics in which they are involved? A haughty air they have, these scientific princes, far above most mortal men, versed in matters others cannot hope to comprehend, advising politicians, ministers and kings.

Standing tentatively on edge of one such group, waiting for the mention of some common ground, at last is heard a word on which some comment can be made. With voice that's hesitant and hoarse from heat and dryness of the arid air, opinion is expressed, interjected in the ceaseless talk, but it is ignored; its mark is missed like that of arrow which the wind deflects. A little later someone turns and speaks, at last a chance to integrate, but, unprepared, a mumbled answer from a humble man outside the upper circle's not what he expects: disdainfully he turns away, resumes his chatter to his confreres, tittle-tattle that concerns the ones with whom he works.

The noise grows louder, beats on brain and deafens ears as if one stood on saw-mill's floor; the heat's intense, the fumes of smoke swirl round the shades of lights that shine from ceiling on the crowd below, the sound of voices interspersed with sudden laughter bursting out like firework, lit by catty joke at friend's expense.

Pushing past these knots of raucous louts, cawing like the crows that gather round a carcass in the road, escape is made to foyer, where cloakroom girl is leaning on her counter reading book.

"You're leaving early, Sir," she says.

"A train there is that must be caught, the last tonight that takes me home."

Outside it's dark and quiet, and slightly damp; great relief is felt to leave behind the heat and noise, the brilliance of the lights that shone through blue tobacco smoke. The cool of early winter's night refreshes mind but not the soul, ashamed at having been ignored, of inability to make a mark among this upper crust of technocrats.

With no desire to meet another man and have to speak, to greet him with some inane phrase as courtesy demands, a path close under bushes is pursued, where shadows shield from beam of passing car that floods the road with light, lest seen by some scientist who's homeward bound, seated in his Jag-uar. Further on a narrow track leads off to left, and cuts a corner on the way to station where the passengers may meet the train. It steeply slopes to pass beneath the railway line, and as it does it bends to right before it rises on the other side. At lowest point there can be seen a luminescence faintly shining from a light around the bend and out of sight, and sound of muffled thuds are heard. Silently approaching in the shadows, there can at last be seen the back of labouring man, repairing rising track with shovel where the mud and stones were washed to lower level by incessant rain.

It is not wished to pass this man, to stop and speak and search for words that stick in throat: return is made to road and thence to station, where the train is caught. It is deserted on this damp and dismal night; dim lights that light the corridor enhance the bleakness of this carriage second class and all its empty seats. It is not very far, the journey's very short, no need to sit, but stand and stare at blackness of the night and sudden flashes of the shower of sparks thrown from electric rail.

From further down the corridor the sound of sliding door, and now two men appear. The elder is a man well built, tall and broad to boot, and bearded is his face. The other is much younger, slight of figure, like a girl it could be said. He too a beard he has, but whispy like a plant that's languished in the shade, that would be better shaved.

Some words the two exchange, slowly shuffling forward, leering with a sickly grin that accentuates the menace in their mien.

The wheels of carriage click as over joints in rails they pass, the corridor it creaks and sways, and faintly are the lights reflected from embankment in the night outside. Few they are who travel on this country line at night, scattered through the length of coach, and empty are compartments in this part: there is none to see what may befall. It's not so much a fear that fills the stomach as assailants slowly slide this way, it is a feeling of revulsion and disgust at sight of this repulsive pair.

The train now rattles over points as station is approached, and as it does for one brief moment are the dim and yellow lights that gloomily illumine corridor extinguished by the lack of current from the rail; and in this moment do the queer and ugly pair just vanish, disappear to who-knows-where, swallowed by the shadows as if just a dream they'd been, a nightmare seen whilst wide awake by mind in disturbed state; the train pulls into station and the passengers alight.

Sleep is sought as refuge from a troubled day: it quickly comes but little respite does it give the restless soul - no sooner have the eyelids closed than there appear in eye of mind a regiment of ghouls that gather round and taunt and jeer as did those boys on bonfire night, reminder of a time that had better been forgot. Familiar faces now are seen, of those who in the past connected were to incidents remembered since with sense of shame; and in this crowd of jeering demons reappears the pair who threatened on the train, ready to avenge all those unthinkingly abused by one they thought their friend.

No dream conclusion reaches, no nightmare in disaster ends, lest we all be dead, destroyed by monstrous beasties or misfortunes dreaded in the day that come to pass at night inside the head. Suddenly the sleeper wakes. The grinning face that's shining in - it is the moon!

Eight The Handbook

The Boss's mind is fixed upon this new obsession, day and night he dreams of what he's going to do, how he will manufacture products of quotidian use, that of themselves will grow without the need of artisan or some mechanical device.

Some there'll be that grow like plants and trees that grace the gardens and the fields, not with flowers and leaves adorned, but analogues of woolly garments, woven in a mesh of living cells, tissue of unusual hue and texture soft and very fine. This achieved the aim will be to build machines that move about, performing tasks like men or beasts, that heal themselves when sick or hurt, and replicate before demise.

The Boss, he has conferred with learned men, the sages he employs to ponder the perplexities of project of which his mind's possessed: a decision has been reached, at first they'll synthesise a plant, progressing to a creature more ambitious when creation's deepest secrets have been fathomed out.

A simple form of life, a plant, but large enough to see without the need for microscope or other optic aid, living on a liquid feed of basic compounds, oxides and metallic salts. On this the team have set their sights, to synthesise a little weed, before proceeding to a trickier task.

So common are the plants, the grass that's trodden underfoot, the trees who's branches sway in wind and shelter other forms of life, and yet how little is there known about the chemistry inside, and how electrons are exchanged. How is it that so many men, in course of many thousand years, have failed to understand the wondrous workings of a Nature all admire, which surrounds on every side? It is because so much remains unseen, the limitations of men's sight precluding view of much that they would like to see, and other things of which they hardly dream.

All things upon the surface of the Earth are thus composed, constructed from the cells that are too small to see, and yet abound in countless numbers, greater than the number of the pebbles on the beach thrown up by restless ocean's waves; centuries go by, people come and go, the scientists they poke and probe, and still a stubborn Nature will not all its secrets yield.

A cabinet is set in place, in which a study may be made of living tissue exiled from the world outside, kept in isolation like a prisoner held in solitary confinement, tortured till it all its secrets tells. A piece of plant the inmate is, that yearns to be outside, bathing in the sunshine, freshened by the rain. Food and water are supplied, and glucose in solution the driving force provides: a pleasant temperature's maintained lest it suffer from the cold; but no movement does it make, nor any sign of growth. No action does it take, no sign it gives that it still lives - evident it is it has no will, that the 'Spirit of the Trees' does not exist except in myth: in natural habitat it is the sun it must obey, that flaming tyrant in the sky.

It stands as once there must have stood the world, every sort of atom in profusion, all the elements of which the Earth's possessed in disordered chaos and confusion, but quite incapable of life. If this plant in this condition stays, will it tire of standing still, and suddenly break out and start to sprout? No, it won't, it will slowly oxidise until it dies. Was then the world clothed in spontaneous growth that sprang by chance? There is some doubt.

A signal is required that plant can understand, given from the world outside: the man in charge, who has the brain to think and will to plan, must give commands not with the spoken word but in molecular manner, mimicking the sun.

The master of the Cabinet of Growth Control, Arthur Fogwatt is the name by which he's known. A quiet and unassuming man, he lacks the bombast and the arrogance of those who fill the senior ranks and upper echelons of staff. Devoted to the little woman and the kids with whom he lives in cottage on the street, at work he shows the same devotion to the chemistry of life, seeking answers to the mysteries that it hides.

Some jealousy does Mary Fogwatt feel toward that Mrs. Yorke, professor's wife who seems to have it all: slender figure, rather tall, her blondish hair done in the latest style and faultless manicure, peerless daughter and for husband wealthy man.

However, Mrs.Yorke is rather bored: her husband's older, getting staid, and cares for golf in preference to the fashion store. She seeks diversion stalking Arthur, not because she likes his type, but because his faithfulness is like a citadel that seems impregnable unless perchance it can by stealth be made to fall.

Fogwatt now takes charge, he starts by feeding sucrose and some glucose, which will energy provide in absence of the sun, and also hormones that will guide the metabolic path. He has to learn to mix the chemicals that will desired result achieve, and fathom out from subtle signs their sequence which is paramount if they're to be successfully applied.

Many captives die in dungeon dark before is mastered the method of control, but they're only weeds, no good for other use: if pain they feel they don't complain, no league exists protecting rights of flowers and trees. Thus swiftly are the secrets squeezed by torture from the stubborn silent plants, patterns for the processes that the higher creatures use. Plotted are the movements of the atoms, tracing steps they take in their perpetual dance, changing partners held in orbiting electrons' grasp.

At this point there comes a tap on door, the dainty knock of one unsure if she will welcome be: Samantha Yorke now stands inside, she's dared to enter Arthur's den, intent on laying siege to stronghold that is Arthur's heart. Arthur's bending over bench, his pipette in his hand, as he adjusts acidity to six point zero three.

"Arthur dear," she starts, for well she knows the doctors all who under guidance of her husband toil. "I come to see what work it is absorbs you so, and keeps you from the social life that centres round the lab. Little do we see you since my husband gave you charge of this research." The path to heart of scientist, she does suppose, lies through his work: it seems there's little else that fills his mind, until it's time to hurry home, return to humble cottage on the street.

He gazes at this unexpected caller, peering through the pebble lenses perched on end of his proboscis. "Aha!" thinks he, "Professor Yorke has told her of the progress I have made, how the atoms dance to tune that I have played, and now she wants herself to see the marvels of this new technique." Aloud he says: "You want to see the hidden wonders of my work, the secrets of this life laid bare where light can't penetrate and eye of man can nothing see'?"

Samantha Yorke now sidles nearer to this artless man she would seduce: her heavy cloying scent (a perfume specially made here at the works from finest artificial esters, and a hint of pheromone) must surely fill the nostrils of his nose and some emotion wake in him that's unconnected to the contents of this cabinet that he's about to her display.

Arthur opens up his cabinet, and there for her to see are rows of growing plants at different stages, standing in a trough through which a liquid slowly flows.

"This living water's come from distant source, a stream that courses through the caverns deep beneath that further mountain range that's capped with snow for most of year; and as it tumbles over rocks and swirls above the silt that gathers on the bends, the chemicals of which the stones are made are worn away, and, decomposed, dissolve in flow and then are carried here to feed these plants for which I care.

"This one that you can see (he points with pencil taken from behind the ear), ever taller is its growth, its stem extending without cease, with embryonic leaves in pairs produced at every node, but never is there sign of flower or fruit. Maturity is never reached, everlasting is its youth so long as I deny the reproductive catalyst, and keep abscissic acid out of reach. This is how it is achieved, this is how eternal life can come to pass. If energy can be supplied, and food enough to build new youthful cells, and in addition an unchanging guidance given, as older cells mature and die a steady state of growth this will perpetuate.

"If nothing changes, what of time? Is it not that time it measures rate of change? If there's no change the time it would not be."

His mind is with the tray of plants, his thoughts are tied to inner workings of their cells: the heavy odour of this lady's scent is not discerned from other smells emitted from the rows of jars that stand around the walls on shelves.

"How could it be, a state in which the hours did cease, and time stand still?" the lady asks, her mind confused by these the words that Fogwatt speaks.

"We judge the time by Phoebus' movement 'cross the sky, or observation of the other stars, for each must follow path that Nature's preordained, indicating time of night or month of year; but these poor plants that see no light by day or night, they're only conscious of the rhythm of their growth. They cannot count the days, of the seasons they are unaware."

Samantha Yorke must now give up, admit defeat. Impregnable indeed integrity of this the Master of Eternal Night; his mind with biochemistry is filled, his heart is bound to those who sit around his homely hearth. If she was bored before she came, doubly now is she: not comprehending what he means, Arthur's lecture on the lives of his herbaceous friends has left her shipwrecked on a sea of ennui - in disgust she turns toward the door, and straightly does she leave.

The darkness yields its treasures, hidden hitherto in secret place. The mystery now unfolds, how it is that life exists, how the hormones change their shape when darkness falls on garden, forest, and on field; loss of energy of light transforms these catalysts, so that a different task they may perform.

Now that the plants that live in darkness are controlled, roots are produced and shoots induced at time that's chosen by the scientist in charge - no nonsense of a biologic clock here in the darkness, unillumined, free at last from dominance of light and dark, the tyranny of day and night, life controlled by rising of the sun and setting of the same, this fiery tyrant burning down on dried up fields or hiding face when warmth's required. First step has been achieved, control is understood.

By this means are found the different parts of plants and what their functions are: but how they're made and how they work are questions most obscure, to which the answers must be found before there can constructed be one tiny artificial cell. As each mystery is solved, so another blocks the path that leads to goal - ability to animate an artefact.

To make a cell is not an easy thing. Parts may be taken ready made from any source that comes to hand, but working drawing must be planned and bits by nucleotides identified.

Each cell its place must find in which to fit in final scheme. How is it done, what is the code that does assign the cell its place in line and special duties to perform? This problem must be solved before more progress can be made; a very distant prospect does a plastic Pegasus appear.

Early morning in the spring. The rising sun sends shafts of light to pierce the window in the east, it lights the chancel of the abbey church where monks commence the day with prayer; then filing out through door at side and passing down a passage the refectory's reached, where, seated on the wooden bench, they break their fast with simple fare.

The Abbot's in his office, early does he start, none can say he shirks his work. A roll and glass of wine stand on his desk within his reach, the only nourishment that he will take until mid-day.

Better times the room has seen, distemper's faded on the walls, the furniture is old and worn. Cardboard boxes litter chairs, filled with papal bulls and unpaid bills. In one corner is a wicker chair, in which is curled a feline loudly snoring; fine his form and long his fur - Magnificat his name.

There is a knock on outer door, and a stranger's ushered in. Short of stature, dark of hair, with features saturnine, he enters with a swagger and himself announces with an overbearing air:

"Good day, good Abbot Sir, my name is Death, I am the Atom King."

"You cannot be" the Abbot cries, "the atoms have no human form: unless combined in complex compounds they cannot live, no individuality they have, each element is all the same."

"I am a man, the same as you, born of woman, but no father do I have. Sired I was by Uracil, the acid that of mortality possesses key. You have the wish for ever-lasting life, because your spirit needs a frame in which to live. You seek the higher things that hold in thrall the energy that would be free, hold it in a prison of organic systems from which it slowly leaks, requiring constant prayer that fresh energy is sent, lest entropy should gain the upper hand. But I, my soul is made of unchained atoms, I am at one with them, seeking peaceful rest in everlasting death; I will drag you down with me to Hell, and those who follow you, for like everything there is, you are made of atoms too, when I call they will with gladness follow me. More of me you're going to see. In coming months I'll try your strength and test your faith."

With these words the stranger turns and passes through the door. The Abbot's spirit is perturbed, his will is weakened by the thought of easy route to everlasting rest.

The Abbot passes out to antechamber where his aide, a brother monk, sits at reception desk, processing letters and conversing on the internet.

"Who was that that you admitted, who has this instant left again, what sort of man would you suppose?"

"Sir Abbot, Sir, that man I hardly saw, he thrust his way through this my room, he hardly begged my leave; for at the cabinet I stood, before the drawer from which I lately drew a card. Almost it seemed as if an apparition passed me by, as if he wasn't really here: and yet a potent presence did he have, I felt uneasy in my mind."

"Clearly did I see him as he stood before my desk," the Abbot says, "his every word I heard, and yet there was about him something very weird. His presence filled me with foreboding: I'll now go and pray awhile before the altar, kneeling on the chancel steps."

An informal meeting is being held, the doctors gathered in old Angstrom's den. They here discuss the way an organism should be made. The Managing Director's in the chair: it's his affair to oversee and supervise the many minions who provide the services required to keep the factory smoothly humming. Rising from his seat he introduces topic for today:

"All projects must commence from single point, from which the structure bit by bit ascends, elaboration added on as each new floor provides support. They rise like lofty towers, the higher that they climb the further they will fall should anything go wrong, for are not atoms ever ready to relax their grip, return to earth from whence like slaves they're upward forced against their will?

"Before one brick is laid or foundation stone is set in place, the drawings have been made, and every detail's been defined, for else there'd nothing be but heap of rubble with a random form. So now more information must I seek before construction can proceed. The shape of finished product must be pictured in the mind and then by lines drawn in the sand 'ere can be mapped the route by which it's reached and pathway can be planned.

"Rational all must be, for Nature's laws are logic, not the whims of king who rules by arbitrary decree, pronouncing from the throne the idle thoughts that enter in his head. Nature does not by diktat rule, but just by common sense.

"Is it there's a single system that will work, homologue of living creatures that on the Earth abound, composed of channels spreading out throughout both plants and beasts, conveying food, abstracting waste? Or are there other ways by which these ends can be achieved?"

Turning to the Engineer, he asks "As regards mechanical design, what comment do you wish to make, what observation comes to mind?"

The Engineer has fitted out the factory with machines of every sort, performing functions day and night without the need for human hand or the overseer's eye, united by a web of wires and linked by copper pipe, and now this network he maintains: no one else knows how it works or how to trace the labyrinthine lines. Now this knowledge can be used to make the artefact on which the Boss has set his heart, to plan the route that fluids take, and calculate the stresses and the loads.

The Engineer replies: "Every engine must energy ingest in form that it can use, and by combustion burn the fuel, extracting heat that power supplies. The residue will be exhausted from the rear, that may be met the natural law that some must go to warm the air. There is no other way of which I know, but first have scientists to make materials I can mould to shape to make the ducts and tubes that for this purpose are required."

A plasmologist is Doctor Chalmers Slack, now called upon to speak.

"Two types there are of tissue, that containing chlorophyll that clasps magnesium to its heart, and that through which the haemoglobin flows, coursing through the veins as blood. There may be more that can be made" he says, peering through the lenses thick that hide his eyes, for he is very short of sight. "Suppose we change the atom at the core, the core of chlorophyll and haem. These two are not the same, why not devise another flesh, with qualities that we decide? Many permutations there must be to carbon compounds we can make, we are not tied to Nature's way. There are other means by which life can exist, variations we are able to devise that viability possess.

"Nature's laws aren't laws at all, just statements of the status quo when equilibrium is maintained and all the forces balance out. In fact by logic are they fixed, the consequence of how the universe was structured when it was created at the start.

"Each part was set to spin like gyroscope to hold it in its place, to give stability to constellations lest they wander off their course, giving cause for them to crash, fragments forming nebulae. So it is that systems large and small rotate, electrons orbiting the atom's core, the planets spinning as around the sun they circulate, and galaxies that slowly move across the sky, across eternal empty space. If all these things move round, there must surely be a central point, a hub of universe, from which all may be said to radiate. Where is this place from which to measure absolutely time and space? If universe is endless in extent, too far away it is for ever to be found, an endless distance from this spot at which we now are gathered to discuss these matters so profound.

"We must work within these Laws, circumscribed by what is possible and what is not: and yet there's much that can be done, that puny man with powerful brain can for himself invent."

"My friend" the Chairman says, "You seem to have this matter in your grasp. To you I give the task to see what new materials you can make from earth and air and water too, from which a living tissue can be made, with properties specific to our need."

Professor Yorke now speaks, rising from his seat, a man of medium height, clean shaven, his hairline in retreat. Leaning with his hands spread on the table-top, this is what he has to say: "When first were atoms made, free to wander where they would, they coalesced and formed the stones, and air and water too, finding satisfaction in a state of rest. To wrench them from their sleep and rearrange their lives, the plants were introduced, possessing power to trap the rays of sun and utilise the A.T.P. to synthesise new cells from salts drawn from the soil by roots.

"The cells are by Nature structured many ways, according to intended use. Many other variations there must be, for other uses which we ourselves devise; but the structure of the artefact entire will not wander from convention very far, it will not work without arterial ways and structural frame that form the basis of the animals and birds.

“ No magic means there is by which it could be made to work, the animated artefact, without the use of systems that are by catalysts controlled. The catalysts, they are the keys to door that leads to life. The inorganic chemicals are dredged from soil by hungry roots that search for nourishment that plant demands, and then conveyed to cells in which they’re processed into tissue new, not forged by hammer blows when hot as is the case when metal’s moulded into shape, but with a subtlety sublime by which they’re trapped and tricked into an unexpected union as they lie upon the catalytic bed. Passed along production line they’re modified again, step by step like pulley-block or train of gears, prised upward inch by inch toward the goal, a new organic molecule.”

Lunch has been taken once again, after which the progress of the work’s discussed, as usual standing in the foyer, staring through the plate glass windows at the lawns that stretch down to the willows and the stream: but there’s no sun today, grey and sad the sky, and frequent fitful showers make moist the mournful scene.

Redfire holds the floor; short of stature and of hair, he’s younger than he looks, so that he’s heard with more respect than he deserves.

“As I struggle in my lab, wrestling with the atoms, trying to force them into ordered line or into molecules of my design, the thought that comes to mind repeatedly and will not go away, it is that evolutionary chance could never shape the creatures of this Earth, moulding such recalcitrant material into such sophisticated shape.

“Ever does some energy escape, fleeing from its captive state, seeking freedom to return to space from whence it came, borne upon a beam of light. Surely logic does explain, that heat must flow to lowest level till a balance is achieved. If all the world and universe were held at zero on the Kelvin scale, then Carnot’s engine ought to work, because no energy would then get free: the only snag is that the orbits of electrons in their lowest state could not accommodate another mate, the fuel it would not burn and Carnot’s car, it would not go.

“Without the guidance of my hand they will not slot into appointed place, these idle atoms with a single wish, to oxidise till all is turned to stone and sand. How could life arise on lonely planet on its own, though air and water were in abundance found, and a climate mild and temperate did exist?”

“You say that other life in space there cannot be, one world there only is on which organic beings live and die in endless chain? If everything degrades and turns to ashes and to dust, caught up in cosmic wind and blown about the universe till changed to stars that shine in constellations, mythic gods much featured in the classic tales, how is it then that life goes on as if, it seems, it cannot cease?"

Resuming, Redfire makes reply: "All depends on catalysts, compelling elemental atoms to combine in patterns preordained. It is the origin of these that's shrouded in the mists that cloud the ignorant mind of man, a mystery unresolved as yet. Thus it is the aged are replaced before they die, and continuity's assured. When all appears in terminal decline, and savagery destroys the social scene, yet new life emerges from the ashes, and the rule of order reigns again. New cells are fit and full of strength (unless by chance deformed). With speed does every creature grow until construction is complete; thereafter slow decay sets in, and health and vigour are impaired.

"No automatic reproduction am I able to achieve except I first construct a cell containing all components needed for maintaining life; I see no other way by which organic creature may be made to live.

"Very complex are the creatures from the smallest to the tallest: could they not have been more simpler made? It would seem not. So complicated are our lives and everything we do, so many are the movements that we make, and each must be controlled by mechanism smoothly sliding into gear, that essential is this multiplicity of parts. No other means could be devised whereby the goal could be achieved - creation of a symbiotic biosphere that recreates itself for ever, year by year."

"Well it is, that which you've said, but you've not answered all I've asked. In your conception of the universe is there no place for other worlds that may exist, other peoples occupying planets somewhere else in outer space?"

"Just as Earth, an orb of rugged rock, was planted like a garden and watered from the air, sown by Nature with the seeds containing all the catalysts required, and by Evolution cultured down the intervening years, so endless other orbs may in existence be, bearing similarity to this, the world of ours. What it is I've tried to say, it's that it cannot be by chance, for chance itself is part of scheme, put in place that a purpose it may serve."

The Boss a worried look assumes, his head is bent as aimlessly he walks about, absorbed in thought, seeking answers to the puzzles which beset him, rob him of his appetite and interfere with sleep.

He has a friend to whom he turns when overwhelmed he is with all the troubles of this life, a learned man who spends his time in study of old texts in Latin and in Greek, and in Hebrew too: it is the cleric at the church, the Reverend Ed Mathias.

The cottage where the old priest dwells is next the church, where bends the road as it descends to village strung along the highway's verge; the garden rises up behind, it's full of brightly coloured flowers. The old man takes the Boss inside. Sparsely furnished is the cleric's modest house, so few his earthly needs. Shelves fill one wall, on which are stacked the tomes that hold the wisdom of the world; in one corner stands computer, connected to the internet.

"What trouble brings you here today to my abode? You have a distant look, your brow is lined, it seems you slept not well last night, some problem ever turning in your mind."

"Padre, friend and mentor of my soul, tell me, I have set myself a task, to build machines endowed with life, I know not where to start. A factory I have hired, and scientific staff who stare all day through microscope, yet still I cannot find the code that guides the cells and lines them up, each in the place where it should fit."

Each side they sit of table bare except for book that's lying there, bound in leather and embellished with gold leaf.

"What you need," the old man says, "is to consult the Maker's Handbook here," and speaking thus he pushes well-worn volume to the other, leaning forward in his chair.

"It's popularly supposed that of allegories it is composed. Much there is within its covers that's incomprehensible and does appear to have no meaning, muddled words that make no reference to what's gone before or follows on.

"The prophets wrote what they were told. I cannot think they knew or understood, what it was that they wrote down as best they could, inscribing phrases that they heard, describing scenes from visions that appeared before their eyes as if they dreamed whilst full awake; and in this ignorance tenses changed, the future stated as if past, and muddled pronouns make unclear to whom the reference does refer.

"Add to this the fact that ancient book was writ in times long past, in country far away, in language long forgot by all except the scholars, monks in monastery translating texts in many tongues. Taken by the captive tribes to foreign lands in which they were enslaved, distorted did the words become and some were altogether lost. It's like a ruined building, fallen into disrepair, ravaged by the passage of the passing years: some walls still stand, as does a damaged tower, but pediment and frieze lie broken in the dust; much stone's been taken and reused to reconstruct in modern style; that part of origin more recent, it remains as builders left it, unaffected by the time between.

"The older texts unaltered were when first translated into tongue that all can understand, revealing rubble where it fell; in modern times rebuilding has been tried, inserting words where vacant spaces have been found, or adding others in attempt to make more sense: and thus the meaning has been changed, and contemporaneous reader led astray.

"It does contain, this Book, the answers that men seek regarding life, why it is and what it's for. It is the list of questions that it lacks, and this it is that baffles wise men's brains. It is as if examination were being sat, wherein the students find the answers on their sheets, and must the questions write that seem to them most apposite.

"When first these words were spoken and a record made in writing, written down, the modern scientific names were not invented then, nor were they known to medieval monks transcribing Greek and Aramaic texts into their mother tongue. Thus a problem did appear, how to translate words for which they had no corresponding term.

"The archaeologists who search among the rocks beneath the cliff find shards of pots they put together piece by piece, and fossils of the bones of creatures long forgot which when assembled show to all their former shape. This technique must be employed to find true meaning of these texts that seem to lack all sense.

"Now the mists begin to clear. Open book, turn to page where story starts. Very soon you'll see a phrase that's very strange, a fable fanciful as ever you did read. But now for 'rib' read 'chromosome', the double X, and start to comprehend."

The Boss leaps to his feet. "Now I see what I must do, how this mystery must unfolded be by close study of these prophecies from distant past." With that he rushes to the door and disappears along the lane, hurries back to factory floor, there to start a new research.

The study of the Book in this new light is undertook, looking for a scientific statement instead of vague and incoherent ramblings unconnected so it seems to what precedes and that that follows on, producing insights into matters that caused puzzlement before. Slowly slip in place the pieces to produce a picture of the underlying truth, that all by chemistry can be described, that all is positive or negative, no shades of grey lie in between.

Much remains in mystery shrouded; broken pieces lie around, masonry that's fallen from the battlements above, and, falling, breaks and scatters on the ground. The work goes on and on, and as fresh information is obtained and bit by bit creation is explained, new knowledge is transferred to lab where into practice it is put.

The work is split between the doctors here employed, each has the task to make a part, component piece of those of which a cell's composed. Thus it is that secrecy's maintained, each knows not what the others do; Professor Yorke and Boss himself the only two to oversee the final phase, the organs' integration as they're synchronased.

It is the break for lunch, all are assembled here in works canteen; crowded are the tables, great the noise of many voices and of knives and forks. Few the seats that still remain unclaimed, and that is why as she comes by Arachne shyly asks if she may sit here too: oh happy day on which fate smiles, for now there's no more space, all empty seats are filled.

A habit has it now become, to share a table every day, and when repast is done, to wander down beside the water, shaded by the willows from the heat of sun. Long the weekends they appear: once Monday was a bleak depressing day, now too soon it cannot come.

Back in the office cool and white the study of the Book's resumed, seeking out the secrets hid in phrases that repeat as if to emphasise, and yet no context have with verse before, no relevance to that which comes behind.

Repeatedly the texts are read, each time regarded from a different point of view; eventually some meaning's made of phrases that had baffled brains before. If by chemistry can creation be described, then words of Sacred Text can by atoms' symbols be replaced whose meaning is discrete, and thus ambiguity avoid, lest words be twisted into sense to suit some other cause.

The work is long and hard, so many words are missing or misplaced. Much remains as rubble, such as lies at foot of cliff, its meaning hidden yet from human eyes, but sufficient facts emerge like bats from caves, exposed to light at last, blinking in the sunshine's rays, to clarify a little how the Universe is made.

The Boss takes stock, he sums it up, the point of progress reached to date:

"It can now be seen that all from energy is made, that every action represents a gain or loss of this unseen force of which we all are well aware: by work is energy implanted in that it's wished to build, idleness lets energy escape.

"Anything that lives, it dies, its corpse decaying bit by bit: the complex molecules they fall apart as energy is lost to jackal or the worm, the fungus and bacterium, reduced to silicates and oxides, dust composed of simple salts. It is of these the stones are made, the stones and sand death's final stage. Dragged down by gravitational pull they form the rocky pit, the underworld whose name is Hell.

"The atoms of one clan are all the same, so long as all electrons are in place, and none knocked off the cycle track on which they circle round. Unlike those things that are alive, no variation do they show, no personal trait can they display, no way there is to tell which one is which. In the hour of resurrection atoms can be had from anywhere, for they are all alike. The plan to which a creature's made can be retrieved from hidden source, a microfiche of sorts, and used for creature's reconstruction, rebuilt from stones that inert lie on surface of the Earth."

The veil is lifted more and more, and gradually the essence is distilled. The precious distillate is passed to lab, where men in white translate the words into amino acids with which to build an entity that is entirely new. The lysosome and ribosome, the mitochondrion and chromosome, each component of a cell is made by separate team that works in laboratory their own, until the pieces are complete, and then they're passed to final stage, the room in which the plasmalemma's wrapped around, and there it is, the finished cell!

"Why do they have such arcane names that twist my tongue and still I can't pronounce, these biotechnic bits, and cans of chemicals that I must fetch from store and carry to the room where they're required?" It is the janitor who asks, young man who learning lacks, who didn't shine at school. "Why is it they can't have more normal names like mine, or else be given godess's names like stars and constellations and yonder young Arachne there?"

So in the end the cell's been made, though crude it is and primitive without a doubt. It doesn't do so very much, except to live and breathe. Uncertainty remains, it's not apparent yet, will it split and be two cells, or will it nothing do but vegetate?

The Boss he is triumphant, quite ecstatic one would say. Few there are who're in the know, the chosen few entrusted with the final task - to make the cells metabolise. They're sworn to secrecy, to total silence on the subject of their work, no word of this must reach the ears of world outside; and yet, a rumour passes in the village street that in the labs of BioMech there's something going on, improper interference with the things of Nature that Nature never meant. The tale improves with telling, embellished every time it's told, until it is supposed some monster does exist that stalks the Business Park at night.

The tale comes to the Abbot's ears, there's little that he misses of the local scandal and the talk. He turns it in his mind, unsure what line to take: to welcome it as great advance, or condemn it as improper interference with Nature's natural plan.

It is as if the scientists a rival order of religion are, cursed as are the churches by that same uncertainty, the doubt if they have got it right. It's not as if they have this status sought, it's forced on them by popular acclaim. They are men apart, who study things obscure, performing wizardry with waves of light and sound, and telling wondrous tales of how it all began, stories of Black Holes that can't be seen, starting with Big Bang.

The question turning in the Abbot's mind, and those of many others too: how to reconcile religion and the scientific view?

He is decided when he hears that congregation of the parish church are most opposed to tampering with the chemistry of life, a thing they do not wish to comprehend. The way of life, now that they understand: the habits and the customs are abstractions which each man chooses for himself to suit his individual taste. The Abbot must maintain his independent stance, a champion for the Truth, he must not loose his hold on those he would control. He is decided now, he will embrace new scientific thought, although he knows no more of how it works than those he's chosen to oppose, and integrate it with the liturgy of old, the rituals, the splendour of the furnishings of brass, the hypnosis of solemn oft repeated chants that master men's emotions and capture simple hearts. This is how he hopes to satisfy them all, seem to have a modern outlook and an open mind, whilst keeping to tradition and the glories of the past.

The Abbot's met whilst walking 'cross the grass toward the abbey church. Stern and forbidding mostly does he seem, but in the peace of evening, as the light begins to fade, his manner softens like the shadows stretched across the sward, and friendly greeting does he make, and indicates a wish to confidentially talk.

"I see you often with that gentle lass Arachne, sitting on the river bank or crossing barefoot over weir."

"We'd been to see the grotto on the further bank. On our return we called at inn now kept by bachelor man who's lately come from town, whose ambition is to earn a Michelin star, or maybe two or even more. His cuisine is very fine, and as he stood by table, napkin over arm, he asked: 'This grotto that you visited today of which I often hear you speak, please tell me where it is and how to go; I'd like to see it for myself.'

"We told him then: 'It's no big thing, a natural cleft in face of cliff, but if of interest it is, tomorrow morning cross the weir, as do the monks who seek the solitude in chapel in the wood, but turn to left and not as they, to right.

'That side the land is high, and that is why the abbey's built on this, and not beneath the cave where first there dwelt the saints who brought the Holy Word to people of this part when they were pagans still. There isn't much to see: an opening in the rock that's by bushes flanked, and overhung with greenery beneath the taller trees that cover rising ground as far as top of hill; within, a man may stand if he's not over-tall, and space enough to eat and sleep and little else. In recent times there have been set two statues up against one wall, figures representing characters from Holy Book, but out of place they seem to be, here in this lonely spot, frequented only by wild beasts by day and owls and bats by night, where bringers of the Faith in olden times in poverty and hardship lived. More comfort they would find today in this old timbered inn, but first the monastry they had to build.'"

"So that is where you went. I saw you from my window high above the weir, walking hand in hand."

"Arachne is my girl of dreams, so perfect does she seem to me. Her image fills my thoughts by day, at night it sweetens sleep."

"Ah ha," the Abbot cries as he replies "I hope you never wake, this dream must never fade, it must always stay alive, for if it dies reality may bring disenchantment in its train.

"But I, I have renounced desire for wife, my family is formed of monks here in this monastery for whom I care; unfulfilled were youth's romantic dreams, and yet they haunt me still, most strongly felt at start of year, the season when all nature springs to life, released from winter's icy grip: some nights with torment are they filled, but still I tightly hold to monkish vow and dedication to the search for Truth and revelation of creation's purpose and its use. Is it well in doing so to Nature thwart, defying Nature's plan for man that, single minded, one may better aid the others, the Brothers in my charge?

"In spite of all this sacrifice, success escapes me yet. Divergent views divide the sects and dialogue of peace dissolves in acrimonious dissent that leads to conflict and to war." The Abbot turns, goes on his way, entering abbey church through little door set in its northern wall.

Evening's nearly turned to night, little light is left. In this gloom the Abbot kneels in prayer before the pew, his forehead resting on the rail. All is quiet outside, the birds have gone to rest at last, their tiny talons tightly clenching branch on which they roost; the rush of water over weir has ceased, the flow impeded at the distant dam by engineer.

The Abbot ever wrestles in his mind to solve the mysteries of this life that baffle brains among his flock, which is his duty to explain, but he cannot find a way: he only fobs them off with platitudes, with empty phrases and 'Hosanna' for a battle-cry.

Within the church the darkness is complete; he cannot see but only sense the presence of another who has in silence sat himself beside the priest.

As befits the peace that fills this edifice at evening hour when Nature's creatures fall asleep and man alone remains awake, watching lest the evil one should take him by surprise, in lowered voice and subdued tone Death speaks, for it is he, the Atom King:

"Of life and death you make no sense, the Book is sealed, to few its meaning is revealed. You have the power to comprehend, and yet you do not understand, for I your mind distract with petty cares, and your heart seduce with pleasures of the flesh. Good intentions you do have, but by the Second Law I rob you of your driving force, your energy, so that you sink back into slothful ways, relieving atoms of the strain of reaching higher orbits to maintain the search for great eternal Truth."

Having spoken thus, he rises from the pew and slips with stealthy footsteps through the outer door.

The cell lies on the plate of microscope, it lies there like a little eye, it stares unwinking at anyone who stares at it. For many days it's kept, fed with food to keep it fit, to see if it will grow, and finally will split.

Weeks go by and nothing does it do. In the end it withers, as does the hope that filled the hearts of those who tended it each day. The mood of scientists who in this department work, so high the week before, has fallen

like a stone, all are in mourning for this little cell whose life was very short; Arachne wipes her eyes, she cannot help but cry.
Disappointments are the daily bread of scientific searchers probing into matters that they do not understand; a few feet more are all that's gained in unknown territory that heretofore was unexplored. A second sortie must be planned; hope revives at prospect of another small advance.

Accompanied by village priest, the Reverend Ed Mathias, side by side with matching stride the river bank is paced, a place to which he often comes to ponder and to meditate, whilst watching eddies swirl around half-sunken stumps of rotting trees.

"Restless the people have become, that attend my little church beyond the bend, where road extends through pastures lush, leaving houses and the inn behind. They murmur at outdated moral code that encroaches on the liberty of each: they would turn the world the wrong-side-up, defying natural order, and instead impose the will of man. They seek eternal life on Earth, what benefit is that to those already gone? I tire of trying to teach the lore of logic to these stubborn awkward minds."

"Tell me, Padre, Father of my Soul, how can one tell what's right from wrong? Oft times it's hard to know, this ambiguity is cause of lack of faith in Nature's natural law."

"My Son (in spirit, not in fact), it is lack of knowledge of the scientific truths that fills men's minds with doubt. All can be explained in scientific terms, written down as mathematical equations, or shown by the symbols that in chemistry are used. No shades of grey there are, no abstractions that cannot be defined.

"The atoms have this great desire, to live in state of rest and free of stress, lying on the ground in form of stones, slipping down a crevice when they can, to reduce a little more the energy that they contain. This is their nature, this is how they're made: it's right and proper that they should.

"The spirit is a different thing, not composed of earthy matter, which is why it can't be touched or seen. In the Handbook it's described, but once again the scientific terms should substituted be for flowery phrases used by those who little knew of physics or the chemist's art.

"Impotent is disembodied spirit, lacking limbs with which to move and mind with which to think, until it's linked with brain in human frame - and then it seeks an increase in sophistication, searching for a life sublime and everything in perfect shape. Randomness it does abhor, this it must reduce, bringing order into all within its reach: a garden shaped from wilderness.

"Good and evil may now be defined, a yardstick does one have, a means to measure actions, to see if they are benefitting man, or if instead they're bad. Is life more organised, or does anarchy increase? This is the crux, a simple test - to see if entropy is more, or if it's less. For things that appertain to earth it's right to seek decay: the spirit, to endure, must go the other way, bind the atoms in a complex of organic life." Arachne now is met, she too is strolling by the stream, although the air is cool and sky is overcast with cloud.

The brook is left behind, all feet are turned toward the fields that lie close by, more quickly walking 'cross the close-cropped turf. Soon is reached a wood of slender birches; on their stems has lichen grown, the air so moist that quickly has it formed large clumps resembling nests of birds, some exotic species of a greenish hue that had adapted to this cooler climate some little time ago. The path leads to an open space surrounded by some larger trees, but lush and green it does remain, watered by the frequent showers from lowering clouds that hang above the mountains further on. In the centre of this clearing here there stands a man, a man who in a crowd would anonymous remain, a man who would not be remarked when standing in the street: and here now in this lonely place he would not attention claim but for the fact he stares intently at the tree before him, and does not a muscle move or in any way acknowledge the intrusion of three strangers on his solitude in this enchanted spot.

On what does lie the watcher's gaze with such intensity, what is it that so fascinates the man? Approaching near, the object of his interest now is seen: it is the Arboreal Animal, Tree Teddy as it's sometimes called. About four feet in height, it does seem like a teddy bear, except its rounded ears stick out each side of head. This habit strange it has, of standing stiffly with its back against the trunk of tree some two feet from the ground, as if it's held by strong magnetic force that stops it slipping to the earth below: unseeing eyes stare straight ahead, gazing into vacant space. From whence does come this beast both weird and strange that's rarely seen, that suddenly appears against a tree in this bewitchéd wood? Unaware it seems of being observed, it slowly slips until its feet are on the ground, although no movement of its body does it make. Its feet now firmly planted on the sward, it walks with wooden steps across the grass, ignoring those who watch it go with fascination and with fear, and then it stops and stands, as stiffly as it did when first observed against the tree. No more motion does it make, it simply stands, still gazing to the fore.

This is no place to linger, it is not good to stay where beasts as strange as this are found; a dark foreboding fear now fills the sweet Arachne's heart. With haste are steps retraced, the wood is left behind; the undistinguished man has disappeared, unremembered is his face.

The cells they have not ears to hear, no use to them to speak with words when it is wished to guidance give: to tell them what it is that they should do, some other method has by Nature been employed, a secret cypher that's encoded in the compounds that the nucleus surround.

"I cannot find their numbers," Redfire cries, exasperation in his voice, impatience in the gesture that he makes, waving arms in air.

"Is it not a fact that numbers rule all facets of this life, commencing with the date of birth? The days are counted as they go, as are the months and years, for fear that they should unidentified pass by and be forgot.

"The pages of a book, each has its number at the bottom or the top: if not, the place would soon be lost and in confusion would the reader then be cast, for are not all the pages just the same in shape and size?

"The cells of which a being's built, they must keep count, each must its number bear that it may know its place in life, what it should do and where. For see, the leaves of plants are with precision spaced, and shoots projecting either side repeat the pattern on each branch. The flower and fruit, it too it has its place, the same on every plant, for every plant within its species is alike. The cell a serial number has by which it's known how many've grown; there must be another number too, indicative of group to which it should adhere. Somewhere inside each cell there is a number encrypted in a code, a number huge and vast, written in a logarithmic style: but not in numerals Arabic or Romanesque, but in the way amino-acids are arranged."

He fails as yet to find this code, but this is not allowed to cause delay to progress of the project, for professor now invents his own; he does not wait upon completion of the work on artificial cell, proceeding at the rate of snail, so difficult to do. Instead he uses callus cells that unnumbered are, that just divide and multiply provided that they're fed - otherwise they die.

At last, the early problems solved, the cells they split, they increase every day: but always has the culturist control, adjusting feed and heat and thus increasing or restricting growing speed. Across the face of petri-dish they spread, all uniform like spawn of frog that floats on surface of a pond in early spring, before the snow and ice of winter's hardly gone.

As the weeks go by, the cells they multiply in one amorphous mass; now they must be taught to take a shape, to form a central core and epidermis on the outer side, by insertion of Professor's secret code. Complex are the programs in ribo-nucleic acid writ, strung in strands that nestle in the nucleus of the cell, inserted by the wily man who'll not admit defeat. Each cell now knows its place and what it is that it should do.

Since the day when he announced that he now knows the secrets of the cells, how it is they keep a count and each its number does display, the young Professor's kept his room, his lab in which for endless hours he works, the key turned in the lock. It seems by passion he is seized, without delay to put in practice what he's newly learnt, putting numbers on the cells that lie in petri-dish that stands on polished wooden bench.

Passing room wherein there works this fana-tic with feverish haste and single mind, to see if cells will now react and change their shape when number's called, and cease to grow when count's complete - passing by, a desperate cry for help is heard, akin to that that gives a drowning man who's twice gone down, and now awaits the final plunge.

The door is forced (it's locked inside), and terrifying is the sight that meets the eyes on entering in this den that's dedicated to discovery of the secret of the cells.

A layer of foam now covers bench and starts to rise as do the thunder clouds on summer's day, forced up by heat below. It's formed of cells that Redfire thought he could control now gone berserk. Driven on by heat they generate, they multiply themselves and geometrically progress. Lurid is the colour of this foaming mass, and putrid is the stench.

Redfire stands the other side, his face contorted by the fear he feels in pit of stomach, terror of this force unleashed by thoughtless act in instant when he concentration lacked. His limbs he cannot move, no motion can he make, except for hideous cry wrenched from his burning throat.

The fire-extinguisher is seized, the knob struck on the floor, and jet directed at the bench from which the ever-growing mound has almost reached the roof. At once a greenish gas appears, carried upwards by the heated air until the ceiling's covered end to end. Redfire falls to floor, overwhelmed by poisonous fumes, and now he's dragged from room, pulled by his ginger hair.

"Redfire's ill!" The receptionist it is that all the gossip gives. Seated at her desk in the foyer near the door, her duty is to note with care identity of all who enter here, informing Boss on secret line of those suspected of improper or nefarious design. It is to her that those too ill to work or otherwise detained must telephone, explaining what it is that keeps them from their daily task at BioMech, why it is they stay at home. So it is that all soon know young doctor's far from well, but what his ailment is remains a matter of surmise.

"Much learning's made him mad" the Boss announces to the few who in his office stand, his closest friends and confidants. "His accident has tipped him over edge, his confidence he lost when all went wrong, and turned to cancerous growth."

"Visit him I will" the Reverend Edward says, "is it good when mind's deranged to give the patient drugs, to ease the brain but harm some other parts? My duty is to strengthen soul that he may his will regain, and dredging strength from deep inside, return to health."

"As his colleague and his friend, this is something you must do. Only you, man of cloth, know what to say, how new hope can be instilled in spirit that's been crushed by too much work and little sleep; in the wake of disappointment and disaster came dismay."

The priest is ushered into room both cool and dim: the blinds half drawn foil ingress of the bright sun's rays. In one corner Redfire sits, slumped in an easy chair. He gives no sign of recognition, nor does he raise his head to see who it may be that comes to ease his deep distress. The usher leaves and silently he closes door. The two are left alone.

"I bring greetings from your friends who one and all wish that you soon be well. Arachne sends you flowers."

Redfire slowly raises eyes, and on Reverend Edward fixes stare. "Of sympathy I have no need, my life is finished now. Success lay in my grasp, but fickle fate, it snatched it from my grip, and now both day and night I feel the atoms round me, threatening death as their revenge, for did I not attempt to chain them, submit them to my will and make them do that which their master, Nature, did not intend they should?"

"Subservient to your will they are, if only you the strength can find to bend them by the power of mind."

"When I shut my eyes I see them yet, how they swarmed across the table-top. Nothing I could do could stop the festering mass, and still I hear them in pursuit. Your holy words, your saintly prayers, they are but emptiness, religious cant. No Spirit does exist, all is of matter made: that which you cannot see or feel cannot be real. Such things are fantasy, the fabric of your dreams. Soon will come the Atom King to claim my corpse, reduce my flesh and bones to inert stones, setting free the atoms that I thought I could control. Then when you gaze down through water of the swiftly flowing stream, translucent in the autumn sun, you'll find me lying on the bed through all eternity, imprisoned in the sand and mud, without the power to expiate my sin."

"What talk is this, why speak you thus, of inevitability of death, and you a young man yet with years to live, and much unfinished work, a project incomplete? The drugs that medics into you inject, they only mitigate your symptoms for a while, and in the meantime poison intestine. You must cure yourself, fight the demons in your head with weapon that one cannot see, the energy that drives man's will."

"Already battle's lost, I no more have the will: it is at best a natural force that emanates from human cells, emotion like the rest, product of the endocrine. I've studied all the scientific facts for years and years, and nothing supernatural have I found in all this time: the stars are naught but flaming gas, they are not gods as those like you proclaim, whose influence decides the fate of all mankind, astrologically foretold by stars' conjunction with the Sun."

In his chair now Redfire slumps, his head upon his chest again, downcast eyes fixed on his feet. No further word the priest extracts, in vain he tries to reach the mind become confused by over use, ignite a spark to light the dark of deep despair. He raises eyes as if in prayer to One above, and with long sigh he lifts his hands and tears his hair.

The Reverend Edward has returned to BioMech. He enters door, gives nod to girl behind reception desk, and strides on down the corridor to inner sanctum, where he finds the Boss, who, leaning on the table set against the wall, pores over charts that trace the route reagents take.

The Boss looks up expectantly at his old friend returned from visit to the sick: "How did you fare?" he asks, "Did you revive the spirit shattered by the sight of monstrous mass of cells unleashed from his control, that bid to overpower the man who would their master be, and suffocate the chemist underneath their stinking heap? Did you go some way to mending mind unhinged by disappointment on success's brink, for which he's worked so hard these many years gone past?"

"Alas, dear friend, I tried my best. In him I could no spark ignite, I could not kindle in his heart a flame anew. His spirit plumbs profoundest depths, forsaken by his former faith. Now he will not hear a word of hope: he's sure he's doomed to follow Death, and downward go to Kingdom of the Stones where reigns the Atom King, and Oxides lie in peace."

"Much hope I had your words would lead him back from state where drugs can be of small avail, and mind and soul must cure themselves with aid of energy imparted by the earnest prayers of those who round him stand; but now I see he's held in grip of hormone's iron fist. Exalted by expectancy of wild success to greatest height to which emotion can aspire, the direst failure turned his ecstasy to bitter ash, an acid that corrodes the soul and locks it in a deep depressive gloom. Now we must consider how we best can help this man to save himself, to struggle back to life he used to lead, pick up the ends of broken threads, continue his career."

"What went wrong, what was it that he should have done, to bend the atoms to his will?"

"Incorrectly was the loop encoded that would stop the progress of the cells; instead, to them he freedom gave, which they abused."

Redfire's health has not improved: in sanatorium is he yet. His disposition does not yield at all to treatment or entreaty by those who daily stand around his bed and nod or shake their heads. Long has Redfire lain on bed of sickness at the clinic where the doctors all despair, for he remains in listless state: they fear his slow decline and subsequent decease, for oft he mutters to himself as if he speaks with someone else that others cannot see, who with soft persuasion, gentle words, seeks to lead him from this world to find eternal rest in nether pit.

The Boss he visits every week, the padre too. At last he turns to priest and says: "This will not do. An effort you must make anew to strengthen spirit of our ailing friend: we cannot let him win, the Atom King!"

"I have a plan," the priest replies, "which I will put in hand without delay."

In consequence of this a service is being held and prayers are being said by Abbot at the abbey by the river, pleading for his swift return from mental abyss where at present he is trapped.

The nave of abbey church is filled with scientists who've come from every part of business park; in the chancel sit the monks, their ranks opposed, ready to commence the repetition of their chant; and at the western end, just inside the door, the peasant women humbly kneeling, overawed by august assembly of academics congregated in this holy place.

The Abbot rises from his throne, and, turning face toward the gathered throng and clasping hands before his face, intones the prayer which, reinforced by concentrated thoughts of all these powerful minds, it's hoped will reach intended target and restore the broken spirit of their colleague by its combined strength.

"O Great Nature, Ruler of the Universe entire, Who spreadest out the Outer Space...."

Many are the atheists among these scientific men and women here today, drawn by sense of duty, lest it's thought they do not care enough to spare the time to help a friend, although no faith nor hope they have that it will anything avail. Also here are those who come to worship every week, finding comfort in repeated ritual, having need of some vague faith in distant deity that definition does defy.

The power of will will not go far from him from whom it emanates: forlorn indeed the prospect is that earnest prayers could travel through the air and reach the deranged mind and stem the tide of slow decline to stony hell; but lulled at first by monkish chants, and now by drone of Abbot's voice, the rise and fall of cadence of his words, into lethargy fall weary brains: they lose the thread and think instead of games of golf they're going to play at end of day; their wives, they wonder what the children do, and what they'll have for tea. Alone the ignorant peasants wrapped in worsted shawls abase their covered heads and concentrate their prayer on that poor man they hardly know. It's not enough to rouse the ginger-headed victim of atomic wrath, bring him back from edge of pit, into which by gravity he may be drawn.

Outside the sanatorium stands a figure, short and squat with brim of trilby low upon his brow. He takes a Woodbine from the packet in his pocket, lights it with a match, which, thrown upon the pavement dampened by a shower, sizzles in a puddle filled by rain. It is Death, who with endless patience awaits departure of another soul.

At last objective's been achieved, the cells line up in martial order like the soldiers on the barrack square; each rank its duties are assigned, and these they now assume.

A form is taking shape, arising from the beaker on the bench, akin to plant that grows in garden or in greenhouse: and yet not like, its flesh is of a type that's hitherto unknown. The skin is smooth to touch but with a plastic feel, inside it's like a sponge when squeezed; indigo and violet streaked with sickly pink is the colour of the twisted convoluted leaf that springs straight up from solid base, a living flame that faintly glows when darkness falls on lab at end of day and all have gone and none remains to see this incandescent light.

"Well done." So says the Boss to him to whom he gave the task of composition of the substance of the flesh, "A most unusual hue you have achieved, the texture too is strange, the prospect's bright for fabric such as this!" Each day it grows a little more, it rises from the bowl of iron in which it's now been placed; it's fed each week with distillate produced by dietician in the factory kitchen.

Nine The Day at Castle Rock

The night is spent at inn that stands beside the river bank, a furlong from the little village like the one of which the Boss has told, remote, nestling in the fold of undulating fields in which the cattle browse. By day is viewed the lawn and apple trees on which a multitude of fruitlets hang, too small as yet to pick, and on the other bank, beyond the water sliding over sloping weir, the mill-wheel and the mill; now, leaning out from window on this hot and sultry night, the darkened sky is all that can be seen, pierced by a thousand stars pulsating with the power that drives their light across both space and time, recalling summers long ago when very young, when everything was new, and every view some mystery hid. Tomorrow with the dawn Arachne comes, more lovely than the rising sun that struggles through the morning mist that hangs above the surface of the waters slowly flowing past the pastures either side; an expedition has been planned, to launch canoe by Castle Rock on lake that cascades feed, plunging through the gorges that from the mountains lead; from there to paddle down the widening river till at last is reached the great expanse of flooded valley where the massive dam the flow impedes. Long the night it seems, waiting for idyllic day that with Arachne will be spent.

Brightly dawns the day, a perfect summer day such as those on which at sunrise can be heard the pipes of Pan by children wandering through the meadows wet with dew. The sky is clear and free from cloud: this is the way that it will stay, for Arachne's coming on this outing in canoe, commencing at the rocky gorge through which headwaters flow and feed the lake that's bounded by sheer walls of stone that rise a hundred feet or more; to the east a promontory projects, and on its crown the ruin of a castle now in final stages of decay. Before embarking from the shore, having paid the woman at the cottage lower down, by the side of unfrequented lane, the winding path is followed, up the steeply sloping hill, on crown of which still stands an arch and fragment of the old fort's wall; lower down on other side, overlooking gorge and river's winding watercourse, an ivy-covered tower, the stones now held in place by creeper's leafy stems by which it's almost hid. Where once there dwelt a war-like prince who terrorised the peasants herding cattle on the plain, or was besieged by rival groups descending from the hills above, today a peace lies over all: the woman's gone inside, all that can be heard is intermittent tolling of a bell.

The boat is built of bark of birch, in style the same as those Red Indians use to shoot the rapids in fast flowing waters of the Rocky Mountains in the U.S.A. Its length is fifteen feet: it's slim in beam and light of weight for easy portage over stony stretches where insufficient water flows.

Pushing off from shingly beach and gently dipping paddles as the bottom shelves, the boat's propelled in silence to the centre of the placid lake, on which the sun, now risen high, beats down, its heat reflected from the cliffs of basalt rock.

An island's reached, and bark's drawn up on shingly beach, and here is where refreshment's taken, lazing in the heat of sun whilst in silence gazing on majestic scene. Across this stretch of water there's a narrow spit that juts from base of cliff, composed of blocks of stone, each one a ton in weight, that have been squarely split from solid rock and set in rows by Nature's giant masonic hand, their geometric shape intensified by bright intensity of light.

The solitude is not complete, for in the distance, at a cable's length, 'gainst the foot of cliff that wets its feet in water still like sheet of glass, reflecting rocks that rise above, and trees that line their tops, there has appeared an angler in a rowing boat, but motionless the man now sits, intently watching float on end of line, unaware that he's being watched.

Some saplings grow upon this little isle, providing shade against the rays of mid-day southern sun. The prow of long canoe rests on the beach, the stern lies in the shallows, ready to depart, as if it dare not come ashore too long. Arachne's lovely form lies in repose upon the sand, her eyes half closed. The great desire to stroke her hair and kiss her lips repulséd is: touched she must not be, lest her sweet simplicity be lost, and magic spell that lies upon this hallowed place should break, shattered like the globe of lamp when flame's too hot, and spoil perfection of the day.

The angler and his boat have disappeared, their going unobserved, no splash of oars was heard, silently he came and silently he's gone. The time has come to make a move, the boatman waits upon the shore of great lagoon above the dam. The winding river leaves the rocky gorge, each side the fields they flatten out, the cattle grazing in the afternoon, as sun, still hot, begins to sink; and cloudless is the sky.

Smoothly skims the craft between the reedy banks, the lofty willows overhang the water's quicker flow. Thickets line the edge, in which dead wood and branches cling, fallen there last winter when the wind with violence blew. Close in the side there suddenly appears a swirl, an eddy of some size:

"Over there, an otter there must surely be, arrest the flight of boat, heave to, that we may see this creature when it breaks the surface and its head comes into view!"

Swiftly does the birch-bark come to stop, and closer to the bank it moves, to the better see this most unusual sight.

For sure a head, it does appear, smoothly clad in black with goggles over eyes, a man it is who dives and swims along the bed among the fish with oxygen attached to back. He thrusts his mask above his face, and, smiling, asks:

"Goes it well with you today, this splendid summer day?"

Receiving answer in same vein, he disappears once more beneath the boat; of him nothing more is seen, except a bubble drifting downstream, carried by relentless tide.

The current carries craft more quickly now, and soon a narrow stretch is reached, where water's funnelled through a winding channel, tumbling in its haste to flee the pent up force of wider waters up above. Good sense suggests a portage is required, a detour through the meadow at one side, returning to the river further on: but no, decision's made too late, canoe cannot be stopped, the current is too strong. The river is the master here: taken hostage are the crew, who must onward go where led by rushing flow which now assumes canoe's command, just as chance circumstance diverts the chosen course of life and leads us where we had not thought to go.

Rapid is the passage, flying on between the muddy banks, swaying side to side, twisting round the bends, carried on by current unrelenting, the crew bereft of all control: the unseen hand of fate is deftly steering bark, ever present Providence that won't permit departure from this life until the time that's preordained. Quite unaware of threat to life posed by these waters foaming white, the danger of capsize in hungry waves that wait to pull the unintending swimmer down, who would with certainty be drowned, Arachne squeals with unrestrained delight at this exciting unexpected rolla-coasta ride.

Further on a detour's made to circle round a shallow pond that's formed where trickling brook deposits silt before it joins the mainstream's flow; here the lilies grow and crayfish can be found, and here a halt is called, disembarking on the grassy bank to sit and eat a piece of cake and drink a glass of wine. Very soon there does appear a mule, long of leg, with upright ears, and head held high with haughty stare. Slowly first he walks this way, now he trots with quickening pace.

Moody beasts they're said to be, unhappy with their hybrid ancestry, not knowing if a horse or ass they are. Is it wise to wait and see if friendly it will be, to risk again catastrophe and spoil the idyll of this perfect day? Best take brave valour's better part, discretely float out on the water where no land-borne harm can interfere with happiness and peace of mind.

At this point that now is reached, the river widens into stretch of water where the flow is slow, the tree-lined banks retreat on either hand; a house of stone three stories high stands on a spit of land on starboard side, still and silent, all its windows tightly closed. On this stretch there is espied a rowing boat, in which one might suppose some angler sits, watching bobbing float: but no, it is no ordinary craft - it's very small, with prow and poop raised up, the stern surmounted by a gilded rail; and in it sits a woman, raven-haired, and in her hands she holds short yellow-painted oars. She sculls toward canoe that's now hove to, and turning to Arachne quickly speaks seductive words that drip like honey from her full ripe lips of cherry red.

Apparent is it that attracted to this woman is Arachne from the start, in spite of aura not of mystery but of something darker, something less than good. Leaning forward over prow, Arachne greets this woman with an eager smile and likewise makes reply with sugared phrase: the other stretches out her arms with clear intent to snatch Arachne from her perch on prow and drag her onto gilded seat of her quaint craft. What then does she intend, will she carry off the fair Arachne to that sombre house that stands like fortress on the edge of marsh? Who is it dwells inside, consort of this sorceress, this witch? One does suppose some villain with moustache upturned at tips and greasy hair slicked back across his pate, and flashing eyes deep-set above the pallid cheeks.

One quick stroke of paddle blade sufficient is to separate the craft that would have a moment later been entangled in the yellow-painted oars, before the black-haired wench can seize the girl who's by enchantress held bewitched.

The blade of paddle flashes in the light of sinking sun as each swift stroke repeats, the glistening drops of water dripping from its edge when for an instant poised in air before being plunged once more beneath the surface of the viridescent stream. Far behind is left the little craft that looks from here like walnut shell, propelled by yellow oars toward the house of stone that stands alone, almost encircled by the still lagoon.

Gliding on between the overhanging trees, the willows and the alders and the larger elms whose roots protrude from bank, avoiding those now dead that gales have felled, lying half submerged, a castle's passed, rising grim and stern from water's edge without a sign of human life, until an angler is espied, standing on the shingle in the shallows. Close is the craft to fisher as it goes, the paddles held aloft lest man is struck, and yet he does not a muscle move, no sign he gives that he is conscious of the presence of the boat that he so much resents.

A house is reached, where rocks rise up again on other side, a farm with tower one end, round, with conic roof, and pressed around by thickly planted corn from which the cobs thrust out from stem. Again no sign of life, no farmer's wife who feeds the hens or threshold sweeps or dries the clothes; but not far off, beyond the cliff on further bank, the shouting of a man, his voice in anger raised, as if engaged in fierce dispute: press on before he reaches shore, and hurls abuse at those who dare intrude upon his private patch.

Again the river widens out as is approached the vast expanse of water like a sea, held in check by dam that hangs above the valley far below, controlling flow to farms whose fields are parched by summer drought. A stretch of this must now be crossed, a mile of water many fathoms deep, crossed in this frail canoe which could, it seems, succumb to gust of wind: but there is none, sea and sky remain serene; and yet Arachne grips her paddle, rows a little faster, glad when further shore approaches near.

A breeze now wafts across the lake, and almost blows the bark too soon upon the beach, for boatman stands impatient further on: an extra effort must be made at end of voyage by limbs already tired, before they can be rested, stretched out on silver sand that lines the shore.

Ten The Pyramid

The Reverend Edward has retired, weary of his work, the constant wrestle with that devil sitting on each shoulder of the members of his flock, leading every one from off the proper path.

Nothing does the Sunday service do to teach the worshippers the things they need to know: untrained voices strain to master singing of the psalms, and thus the meaning of the words is lost in vain attempt to fit the chant to unpoetic verse; prayers for persons highly placed already blessed with blessings undeserved; disconnected rambling readings from that Book supported on the eagle's outstretched wings.

His spirit's sorely tried by his unruly congregation that questions every word he speaks. He no longer has the strength of body or of mind to quell rebellious worshippers who would overturn the ways of old, introducing modern music and the speech of common herd in place of lilting language written when the Latin was replaced. Now his place in pulpit's taken by a sexless form, tall and blond, the hair curled at the nape of neck, the figure hidden 'neath the vestments' folds, the features of the face obscured by shadow in this dimly lit old church, whose builders, short of glass, reduced the windows' size. To suit both feminist and those who follow Darwin's faith the liturgy is modernised, encompassing broad band of latest modes and cultural trends.

Reason does refute the notion of paternal figure seated on a cloud, for have not space-ships sailed the heavens far beyond the planets' paths and nothing found but dust of stars? Giant 'scopes have swept the skies to further limits, listening for some message from afar that might be understood: nothing's heard but subdued wailing from a blackened hole, like the sound of dolphin or of whale.

"Let us therefore sing the praise of that that does exist and can be seen, the natural beauty all around, not created but evolved; and curse the man who would this purity besmirch: protected it must be from fumes of fossil fuels whose stench goes up to heaven, deadly incense with organo-phosphorous laced, for maybe there is nothing else, no guarantee of life on other side of great divide; every effort must be made, prolonging life on Earth, lest the curtain falls, and having fallen doesn't rise."

Because of this, fearful that oblivion lies ahead and nothing else, the rumours emanating from the labs of BioMech of new unnatural living things disturb some minds, incipient terror turning slowly into anger and inflaming anxious hearts.

Sankey Sam's imagination's caught by this new caring cult. Wearied of the past, the old traditions that appear a little bare of thread compared with this post-modern attitude, he quits the worship at the monastery and joins progressives at the other church. So keen to make his mark among the rebel crowd, he takes the lead and forms a protest group that's sworn to stop research that synthesises artificial life, creating creatures that once free could not recaptured be.

A demo's planned, it's for today, and there's the crowd assembled in the village street outside the inn, in which some lately sought to bolster courage with Dutch gin. They start to march: to keep in step a new-age hymn they start to sing, 'Beware lest comes a Silent Spring!'

The Park is reached, the mob is halted by the doors, outside the doors of BioMech, the lab that shines so white in spite of fact that lowering clouds hang overhead, matching mood of ugly crowd, presenting aspect grim. The doors are closed, the windows shut, all is quiet within. No face appears behind the glass, the light's thrown back, reflecting trees that dot the lawn, it is as if all blinds are drawn. Silently the demonstrators stand at first, thinking those inside must of their presence be aware, having heard the tramp of many feet, and the order that Sam gave to halt and stand at ease, but now they grow impatient and commence to shout abuse, demanding that the Boss come out and show his face, tell them if it's true he has inside a horse with wings.

For hour on hour the vigil's kept but none comes in nor any leaves, it is a fortress under siege, bombarded by the sound of shouts, attacked by vicious words. As the day draws to its close and darkness starts to fall, the cold and hungry demonstrators stray in ones and twos back to their village homes. Sam must abandon plan, devise another ruse to halt the work and kill the creatures that secretly are brought to life behind these whitened walls.

The Reverend Edward now is free to think and speak of what he's learnt from his research at BioMech, ousted as he is from rural church of which for long he has incumbent been, ousted by the people seeking new approach to moral matters of the spirit that will match materialistic modernity made possible by mechanical advance, led on by Atom King who tempts them with the promise that much energy they'll save when robots do the work and they can take their ease.

They say the priest's ascetic ways anachronistic are, and yet contrasting opulence of abbey church, its treasures and its works of art seem out of place beside the poverty of peasants wresting meagre living from the unproductive soil; its past association with the brutal inquisition surely must deny its faith in things divine. A middle way is what is sought, replacing bigots' narrow thought.

Mathias preaches when he has the chance, whenever he's invited, wherever he is welcome shown, to those prepared to hear his new approach, interpreting the prophets' ancient texts in scientific terms.

The Reverend Edward's going to speak tonight. Expectantly the people sit as pipes of organ cease their drone and silence spreads throughout the nave, broken only by the intermittent coughs that bark from various parts like sporadic shots still heard when battle's over, won or lost. He sips some water from a glass, he clears his throat, then starts oration with these carefully chosen words:

"Once there was a vicar, a good and saintly man and most devout, who admitted to belief that Satan did exist in quasi-human form, a spirit with an entity like you and me. Many clerics are there who like him should comprehend the other-worldly things, instead of groping in a twilight universe of things half understood. Perpetuated thus are the legends by which religion is surrounded, fruit of men's imagination, seized on by the simple minded, scoffed at by the cynics, clouding truth in mythic mists. The Church is split in many parts, which on some important points just can't agree. How to guide the faithful, when the pilots are at odds?

"How then shall wheat be sifted from the chaff, how to tell what's fact and what is fiction? How to know for sure what's right and what is wrong? While men and women live with minds confused, not knowing what is fact and what is not, sin's concept will remain both vague and undefined. Science must be brought to bear upon this subject of debate, so that it may be described, free from semantics, by numbers hard and cold, each with a single meaning and intent. Words may be spoken many ways - they may damn or faintly praise: they may frankly speak, or craftily deceive; or what they want to say may be misunderstood. All must be to scientific form transcribed, concepts expressed in formulaic shape, each individual symbol with significance unique, figures free from all ambiguity, that mystery no more shroud the Truth.

"If science is the explanation of the universe, describing laws that govern all creation, then when fully understood it must resolve all doubts, defining evil and the good. Men search the sky to find the answers to the puzzles which beset the mind, sweeping firmament with aid of powerful lens to see if they can see when did the world begin, and how it was created: and what is there to see? Naught but chaotic masses of circulating gasses, rocks, and blocks of ice, all composed of simple compounds, elemental and inorganic.

"Does not the truth lie closer to the hand, is it not that it can be discerned in the atomic structure of the organisms all around, by study of the tiny cells of living creatures, and not of mighty masses many million miles from here?

"Strangely similar are lives of little atoms to those of creatures they compose: in families they dwell, combined in molecules of various size. From reactions offspring are produced, and bitterness arises from disputes regarding properties that they possess; the unions that they make with mates of polarity opposed are reflected in the marriages that men and women undertake. The atoms of each element a separate structure have: to this they owe their character and personality, inorganic though they be. This is often manifest by colour smell or feel, even when the atom is in complex molecule combined.

"If well understood are atoms and their way and mode of life, will they not reveal the facts of this existence and how it should be lived?

"Atoms would that they could live alone in state of lethargy, with energy at lowest level, all the surplus lost to space, but they have need of mate like you and me, for fulfilment of the yearnings and desires with which they're cursed. They compromise by forming salts that constitute the stones and rocks - this is for them the Truth that constantly they seek, the worldly things, the inorganic earth and lifeless clay. This is indeed the dust from which man comes, and to which he must return, the elements in oxide form. The grass that's trodden underfoot, and other greenery that grows in soil among the stones, they are the only intermediaries between the sun and all the higher types of life: they alone can trap the energy of light and pass it on in form of food to power organic biosphere.

"Atoms find no rest in death, for they cannot die, electrons in their orbits never cease to spin, perpetual motion without end; just as the dregs are not all drained from emptied jug, some drops remaining, clinging to its side, so stays some energy in atoms that electrons cannot loose.

"On these properties of atoms does the living world depend, this green oasis in the Milky Way. Death incomplete must be, that resurrection may occur; if an atom's shattered, utterly destroyed, redeployed it cannot be in living form, reborn, rising from the dead, re-entering cyclic system that exists here on this Earth, which, once set in motion, freely runs without external aid, powered by that fiery furnace in the sky, the Sun.

"All things on Earth, in Heaven too, are hierarchically arranged (equality is not a property that in creation can be found - are not the Communists compelled to have both leaders and a rank and file? Equality's a dream that among the living isn't real: its existence is restricted to that that now is dead). From these a pyramid is formed, the Pyramid of Life and Death: all things it does embrace, but yet it has no presence in material sense, it is a concept in the mind. Composed it is of many hierarchies of lesser size, each occupying its appointed place, a little pyramid that fits within the grand design. The smallest fit inside the next size up, and stage by stage they thusly rise, until is reached the peak.

"Of organic matter is composed the covering of the surface of the Earth; it's only underneath the rocky strata lie, amalgams of the oxides of all the elements that constitute the fabric of the world, the solid base of Pyramid to which all else is fixed. The plants whose roots are bedded in this earthy matrix underneath convert solutions of these salts to living cells by means of catalysts with which they are equipped.

"Thus does commence the process of increased sophistication as all creatures of creation rise in stages through the ranks, each feeding on the lower classes that underneath them lie. The molecules of which they're made become more intricate in their design as each higher level is attained. By the nourishment they take are the creatures classified that occupy each floor.

"When first appeared on Earth the earliest organisms of them all, these had to spin the thread of nucleotides from which the webs of proteins might be weaved, sub-assemblies to be used as food to feed the carnivores, for creation's higher orders are with delicacy made, a filigree of proteins interlaced, resembling masonry and stonework of cathedral towers constructed in the gothic style and flying buttresses that bridge the air, much too refined to turn the mud to finely textured flesh, a task best left to plants and animals that eat the grass. In the nucleus of each cell there is inscribed sufficient code to guide the craftsman's hands until the members of the highest orders come alive, but potter may not mould the pot until he has some clay.

"The plants grow in the fertile soil that's fed with residues returned by rotting cells reduced to simple salts by oxidation and bacteria's work, transmuting that that's inorganic into living tissue that has life by virtue of the catalysts that they contain.

"These catalysts, they are the key to how all life began: they could never have evolved their intricate and complex shape by chance alone from amorphous masses of the salts and acids that undirected swirl through space: thermodynamic law would not permission give. If left alone all rusts and rots, chaos in the course of time's increased.

"On the lower layer of Pyramid the beasts of field, the ruminants, the goats and deer. These eat the grass that higher beings are unable to digest, transmuting plants to flesh.

"These the carnivores devour; a meaty diet gives to them agility and strength, that they may live their lives on higher plane, with chance of recreation and of sport.

"Higher in the scale there fly the birds, given freedom of the sky in which to soar, and melodious voice with which to sing and charm the other dwellers on the Earth: their diet's mixed, their food is fruit and meat.

"At the head stands Man, whose constitution needs the most sophisticated foods, which even then he cooks before he eats.

"Each individual has its proper place in Pyramid, performing that which suits it best: each has its value to the whole, what use would be the master, if no labourers did he have? Or what would the workers know to do, if Chief Executive did not exist? Man cannot feed on stones, except the plants and beasts are interposed.

"This Pyramid is represented by that Pan who's symbol of all life that here is found upon the earth and in the sky, symbolising all of nature in one creature; all creation's mystery is expressed in sound of haunting music of his pipes, heard at dawn of summer morn before the working world awakes.

"From this it can be seen the inorganic's turned to living cells, and at each upward stage more complex structures are constructed until is reached the intellect of man. From stones does man arise, by virtue of the intermediate layers of which the Pyramid's composed: analogous this is to pathways of biochemical progression by which all life proceeds in little steps, lest too much heat's released and fragile tissue's scorched: the enzymes gently introduce the atoms to their mates, and guide them through the pathways till objective is achieved, and some new structure of a higher order takes its place in the Pyramid of Life.

"All come from seed, the living things, and grow with vigour till they reach full size, then linger for a while as tissues oxidise and weaken as approaches point of death. The time of growth is full of hope, of which one speaks in middle age as 'in my time', as if declining years are not of mine, for human spirit fears the loss of strength, and only values years of youth.

The atoms seek eternal rest, the soul seeks everlasting life in scientific truth.

"The atoms drawn from soil by roots of plants are forced to form the shapes dictated by the catalysts contained in herbage and the grass. Very complex are the structures thus contrived, very great the energy imprisoned in the bonds that bind the separate parts, energy that molecules would like to loose, that elemental atoms might return to rest, partnered by the oxygen that freely fills the air.

"Intrinsically the atoms evil are, unbalanced by unfinished shells whose electrons are too many or too few: but in their hearts does goodness also dwell, for do they not attempt at every chance to remedy this hapless state, and loose or gain the particles they need to compensate for their ungainly gait?

"Atomic systems, in the way they're made, incorporate both good and bad: they influence the way it lives, this world that in entirety the countless atoms constitute.

"The atoms then are systems, made not by random chance but by great Nature's guiding hand. All systems tend to rot or rust, always they deteriorate as energy is lost to space, and never on their own acquire some more sophisticated form. Unlike the rest, atomic systems cannot die, they form a line across the world, a ridge of rock at which disintegration stops: this is the foot of Pyramid, on which stands all of Life, rising in hierarchic layers: this is the base to which all matter must return. From these idle atoms lingering on the verge of death can resurrection of all earthly creatures be achieved through action of the herbage growing in the soil. The resting atoms form the rocks, the sand and stones, and here is Hell, or Paradise if it's preferred, where can be found the Dead.

"No absolutes do time and distance have: there is no point from which they start, there is no place at which they end. But temperature, a base it has where it is nil, a point at which there's no more heat, it cannot flow. This is where the atoms cannot yield what energy to them remains: perfect crystals they become. This is the ideal state for which they yearn, the state of idleness complete in which they would they could forever sleep.

"All wastage must return via drain to soil from which it came, oxidised by ever-present air to simple salts, amalgams of the minerals mined by man, before reconstitution and commencement of another life: and with the dead it is so too, reduced to dung by carrion eaters and the worm. All creatures must return to lowest level in the ground; they cannot climb from rank to which they've been assigned to one above, for which they're not equipped.

"The human spirit, sub-atomic, wandering unattached in space, seeks living frame that will permit it to perform all things of which the mind is able to conceive, abhorring thought of union with the lifeless stones. In thought it soars to heights still out of sight, groping for perfection way beyond its ken, unimagined beauty held in edifice of infinite complexity, each part in perfect balance with its neighbour, that no stress may lie between, no strain imposed on those that coexist: this is the Truth that spirit seeks, the point when reached where randomness is nil, and satisfaction is supreme. In human terms the good can be described as that that's organised, and leads to greater order still: evil downward goes to endless chaos that exists at centre of the Earth, or in infinity of space.

"If perfect was the world, without the risk of sin and death, man would have no choice, the choice between the evil and the good: then his freedom he would loose, for he could only do that which his nature made him do - a marionette he'd be.

"Now the light begins to brighten dark recesses of the mind in which are found the misconceptions that distract men's thoughts and lead them to commit so many foolish acts, prevent them rising to the safety of the heights where gravity is less, finding freedom from the yoke of sin. Material objects, made of earthy atoms and the lifeless clay, constantly degrade as energy deserts their feeble frames which by gravity are smashed, dashed upon the ground, and ambition of the atoms is achieved as they find peace, reposing in the earth; man's immortal soul fulfilment finds in complex structures that he raises, reaching upward: restlessly is energy confined, made a prisoner in the temple that for Truth and Beauty's built, diametrically opposed to stony hell that is the atoms' goal.

"The atoms that comprise the world's material things, they all have wish for randomness, until is reached a state of sleep and endless rest, nothing left of energy but dregs they cannot loose; thus as geologic ores they form the stony ridge that runs across the natural world, preventing utter chaos, permitting grass to grow again, restarting cyclic round of life and death once more. A man can follow where these atoms call, take the easy way that downward leads: or by strength of will resist, the spirit fired by its desire for everlasting life.

"By Nature have both good and evil been devised, that man may freely make a daily choice: the system would not work if guidance always was at hand, and disaster ever turned aside. By the cunning way the atoms are constructed is Chance enabled to exist, uncertainty to dog man's every plan.

"Now the nature of the Devil is revealed: no fallen angel in the garb of man is seen, but tendency to sin in everyone, invested in the very substance of man's flesh and bone - the atoms urge to turn again to stone."

The nave is almost empty as the people file through western porch, nodding to acquaintances, and vicar wishing godspeed to them all and every one.

The Reverend Edward leaves the last, but ere he's reached the exit there, waylaid he is by farmer and the farmer's wife, who, curiosity aroused, are anxious more to hear.

Patiently the priest explains: "An outline of the basic plan you have already heard as from the pulpit I did speak; but since you ask I'll tell you more.

"Beyond the surface of the Earth, past the unseen atmosphere that clothes the world as if with cloak, a shield against excessive heat or too much cold, filtering out the violet rays that lurk beyond the spectrum's range, aimlessly the asteroids and dust of stars drift through the intervening space, blown ever onward by the solar wind. Here on the ground all things a purpose have, they must obey the orders handed down through chain from high command: and at each stage society is subdivided further still.

"Above the rocks the plants reside, their roots absorbing salt solution, inorganics ionised in rain: they have no mouths, they cannot eat more solid fare, but only drink through roots as fine as hair. They take these inorganics from the ground on which they stand, and, by virtue of the catalysts with which they are endowed, and the brilliance of the sun by which they are empowered, add carbon from the air to synthesise organics which the animals can eat.

"Within this group are many species found: lofty trees supporting birds on branches high above the ground where they in safety sleep, and saprophytic mistletoe wedged in the apple's crotch; and growing on the stones the moss on which the reindeer feed; in between a myriad mass of countless herbs make up the dwellers on this floor, each with its special duties to perform; but none may move to floor above, parity to find with creatures made with mouths.

"Very varied are the mobile mammals, birds and fish that move about the storeys higher up, although far fewer is their count - thus the pyramid is formed. Each species into tribes is split, the flocks and herds comprised of beasts, the city-states and nations of mankind, divided yet again to form the villages and towns, which are of families comprised: at the head of each its leader, its council and lord mayor.

"This edifice so vast, this pyramid inside of which is fitted biosphere entire, each habitant dependent on the one above and one below, absorbing energy to stay alive, retain its place in protocol - it's nature's cyclical, each member rising through the ranks and then returning stage by stage until once more in earth's embrace.

"Brick is placed on brick, complexity increasing as each creature is created at a higher stage. How could such a pyramid appear by chance in perfect form, blown together by the cosmic breeze?

"In the course of my research that lasted many years, seeking how to synthesise a plant without the use of sunlight or of soil, new concepts entered in my mind and there took hold, at first confusing, then with time they clarified.

"It is a fact that cannot be denied, that every system that exists, that lives or is constructed by the hand of man, will slowly rot away; rust will spread till all is turned back to the dusty clay. These atoms at the lowest stage are in a state that may be likened to the state of married man: yearning for his independence and freedom from restraint, yet overpowered by strong attraction to the other sex and great desire for little kids that bring him endless joy yet often irritate. These atoms would that they could live alone in life of laziness, but, driven on by loneliness, forced they are to find a mate. Thus are formed the salts that inactive lie as sand and stones: intact the atoms stay, disintegration's limit reached. This is the Hell, or Paradise if that's the word preferred, from which the atoms are revived. They're resurrected in ionic state, in solution sucked from soil by roving roots. Many references there are that can be found within the Book, that link the stones to underworld to which the dead have been consigned. It's not a place, it is a state in which the atoms rest when life has passed and organic structures have been decomposed. Thus the crust of Earth is formed of oxides soundly sleeping, taking rest, awaiting transformation when they're reawakened and reanimated once again.

"In this hierarchic pyramid there may be seen the steps by which creation was achieved - how grass had had to grow before the beasts could graze, providing proteins of superior sort for higher orders, carnivores and others too refined to soil their hands with menial toil."

The priest he pauses, out of breath from so much preaching, giving farmer chance to make reply:

"What purpose then is served by spreading muck or making compost at great cost, when same effect can be obtained from fertiliser in a bag? If it was cheaper so to do, or yields increased, it would be done by everyone; but as it is, the plants will always be the link between the inorganic and the animals and man. Why turn the clock back to the time when crops were light and decimated by the blight, and the poor had not enough to eat?"

Now that all is plain, enquiring minds well satisfied by cleric's lecture clear and lucidly explained, farmer and the farmer's wife they take their leave, unhitching pony harnessed to the trap.

The Reverend Edward, turning, enters in the vestry door. He falls exhausted into chair that's standing there, and fills a tumbler with communion wine and sets it down beside him on the floor.

Eleven Benedix

Each religion has its sects, which with each other disagree. How to know which one to join, which one possesses key to Truth? They come to blows, to torture and to burnings at the stake: emotive force has swept these people off their feet, forgotten is the central theme of peace, so strong their feeling for the matter to the fore at present time. Thus it is that moral code is changed, the basics of belief are overlaid with sudden passions that the mind invade, swayed by mass emotion and popular appeal. Which religion then is true, which church should one attend? None seems to be quite altogether right. The parish church has changed its stance to meet a new perception of the Truth, to suit, it's said, the style of life that most enjoy. Historic has the monastery remained, steeped in old traditions marred by brutal acts by prelates seeking earthly power, holding minds of lesser men in thrall by means of mystic rites and supernatural lore.

These thoughts pass through the mind whilst walking in the town this Sunday afternoon. The people take the air, relaxed, resting from the weekday toil, strolling at an easy pace and chatting all the while on this the holy day of rest.

The further limits of the town are reached, the streets grow meaner, shops are smaller and the paint peels from the fascias facing shabby shoppers poorly dressed. And now, these too they peter out, their place is taken by apartment blocks that once were finely built of stone four stories high, their fronts embellished with examples of the mason's art, the gables crowned with curlicues and ornamental tiles the length of ridge; the walls are made of granite setts in mortar laid by skilful hand to last a thousand years: but windows and their frames have been removed, as has the woodwork from inside; empty shells are all they are, their sightless apertures like eye-holes in a skull, corpses still arrayed in finery they wore before they lately died. But worse is yet to come.

Beyond these lifeless blocks that not long since had sheltered scores of working folk, the poor, the land is littered to the limit of the eye with the rubble left from demolition of the former homes, the slums that here had stood, now naught but granite chippings strewn on every side like sand upon the shore, washed by every tide.

The scene is what one might suppose to see in aftermath of nuclear war, a barren stony desert spread where once the people lived. Some ragged children search among the stones, crouching as they fill a pail with anything that burns, to keep alight the little fires that here and there they've lit to give a feeble warmth. They stop and stare at well-dressed passer-by, and in their eyes there can be seen the fear and enmity aroused by interloper in this hostile place. Surprise it would not be if older lad, with features gaunt and matted hair, should launch attack, attempt to wrench the signs of wealth from off the back of one who foolishly has strayed alone to this the home of terminal despair, to snatch the wallet and the watch, with which to buy some bread to share with other orphans lingering here at edge of life. He does not dare, for fear of loosing all that's left to him, his freedom and his liberty.

As is left, this dismal place, this cold and stony desert swept by wintry breeze, the plaintive voices can be heard of wretched waifs: "Remember, oh, remember us."

Beyond the town there steeply rises hill; near top of scarp an outcrop's lighted by the setting sun, a patch of brightness in late autumn's gloom. Some strollers here have stopped to stand and stare: this ray's reflected in their hearts, this sign of hope that in surrounding grey depressing scene can palely shine.

The crowded streets regained as sickly lamps begin to shed sad luminance on those below, their jaundiced glow competing with approaching night, there is espied a group who stand in circle on the pavement's edge, in animated tones they talk. Passing by this knot of men who seem as if they put the world to rights, one turns and holds a pamphlet out, as often happens in a town. He's brushed aside with wave of hand and curt "No thanks", as briskly is the crowded street traversed.

Behind, the sound of running feet is heard; he who thrusts the leaflets under noses of the passers-by does not accept to be ignored.

"Why don't you take this that I offer? 'twill be of benefit to you."

"Every day in every place someone's pushing printed papers on one's person; they are all the same, repetition of fine phrases that do nothing to explain the human state, to dispel the fog enshrouding meaning of existence and the cruel hand of fate that punishes the innocent and lets the evil man go free. No-one ever reads them: cast aside to moulder in the gutter, they finish in the bin."

"I have heard that in a quandary is your mind, confused by multiplicity of faiths: and yet there isn't one that fills for you the bill in all respects. I can tell you what you want to know. You are perplexed concerning sects, which one it's right that you pursue. Many men are puzzled by this problem, seeking answers from the mystics in the East, sitting cross-legged in the dust at the foot of temple steps, or from the cloistered monks in monasteries that cling to Himalayan heights, or else in sequestered communes in this countryside of ours.

"A consciousness has every man since time began of right and wrong, as if a guiding hand went on ahead and led the way on path of life; long before the prophets came to reinforce the natural law were men aware of how to live without the need for words engraved on stone.

"All have this sense, a sort of feel, that there must be some deity, a force by which the world's controlled and universe was set in place. In men's imagination many forms this force it takes. For some it is the conscientious sun that never fails to rise, bringing warmth that causes life to blossom on the surface of the Earth and brightens up the skies; others see it in the constellations in the sky at night, changing places in the darkened vault to indicate the passage of the seasons and tell what time of year it is; or else it's nature as a whole, self-created like a Greek or Roman god, rising like a Phoenix from the big bang's ashes, a sea of matter in chaotic state. From this singularity did all the wonders of the world unfold, it's said, self-propelled and self-controlled, evolved regardless of the atoms' wish for everlasting rest.

"Each cult worships in the mode preferred by those to whom the cult belongs; above their heads the soaring steeples upward point to place where it's supposed is source, the spring, from which an unseen force, the hand of fate, descends to bless the world and destiny decide, opposing gravitational downward thrust that would all energy release and set it free, leading to a state of anarchy.

This consciousness of some superior power, to whom most humble deference is due, with customs of the people and the culture of their fatherland becomes confused, and thus beliefs diverge and faiths that once were one become diverse.

"It matters not which church or synagogue or mosque one enters in to pray, finding there the peace and quiet for contemplation, lost in introspective thought. No ghosts remain from long ago or recent past of shameful deeds performed by men who worshiped here and may do now. No stains besmirch the lifeless stones that mason's set, reflecting only beauty sought by architect. Each soul that kneels in silent prayer does so alone, the secrets of the heart are from all others hid: freely may the individual think, speaking to a different god to those who also kneel, leaning on the pew ahead."

He turns on heel and hastens to rejoin his friends still locked in deep debate, and on the wing of wind, but barely heard, infant voices faintly call - "Remember, oh, remember us".

Who was this man, from whence was it he came? Such confidence he had that he could everything explain. Could it be that he is one of those that some suppose descend the cliff, impervious to the dangers and the risk of that dread route, bringing information from the seat of Nature to them who in their hearts have guidance sought? Unrecognised, they stand upon the street, no different to the men and women in the throng, who do not want to hear what is it that they have to say, or hearing do not wish to comprehend.

On the right, a few yards on, the open window of an inn permits the passer-by to peer inside. Level with the street, the bottom half is frosted glass, but through the upper part the public bar is easily seen, lighted as it is by oil-lamp hanging from the ceiling's beam. Dressed today in Sunday best, on the bar some workmen lean; before them stand their pints of beer, as they discuss the sports results.

At a table covered with a cloth of baize, attired in suit of yellow check with matching fleck, his sightless eyes unseen behind his shades, is seated Chance: on either side there sit the Reverend Edward and the Atom King. Chance has dealt and cut the cards, and now each man arranges hand; the parson holds his close to chest: Death lays his down before him in an overlapping fan.

They start to play, their cards they lay. First luck favours one, then goes the other way. "By Murphy's Law" the King exclaims, "if things for you can go awry they will: I cannot loose!"

But now the priest is on a winning streak, time after time he scoops the cash; the pile of coins begins to grow, all sorts of copper brass and silver, golden guineas, and a Euro.

"Blind Chance!" the King he cries, "you give this rascally priest some aid, I know not how, the cards you cannot see. Perhaps my hand reflected is on those your shades, perhaps the image of the cards is printed on their lens."

"Good Sir," replies the referee, "you know I am impartiality itself, embodiment of all that's fair. You would do well to leave me unprovoked, lest in the end I play on you an unexpected joke."

"Last orders please!" the barman cries, as Church looks sure to win. The Atom King he cons his cards and starts to grin. With care he lays them on the baize and says "Most reverend Sir, as you must surely know, 'tis I who always have the final say: 'twas I that held the winning card." With that, at last Death plays the trump!

The leaves are blown from trees and scattered on the ground. Now it starts to rain, and suddenly it stops. The clouds they fly across the sky, hurried on by autumn gale. A refuge from this blustery day is sought, by entering in the Abbey church whose open door invites the passer-by.

All is quiet inside, the wind no longer heard, but dim the day that filters through clerestory lights. When eyes become accustomed to interior gloom, two figures are espied, engaged in earnest talk. Approaching near, their lowered voices can be heard and their words discerned, whilst keeping out of sight behind the pier supporting vault.

A monk, one Brother Benedix, whilst his duties he performs, polishing the brass and placing candles in their sticks, has seized the chance to quiz sagacious priest, the reverend Edward, also sheltering from autumnal blast. He takes him by the arm and speaks as follows in a confidential tone:

"Seen from the level of the street, this mortal life seems not to offer very much: a little joy, a lot of pain. No purpose is apparent when is carefully considered the briefness of its span and completeness of its end. Its inception in a universe composed of matter in chaotic state is beyond the range of human eye, and can only be the subject of surmise, until the day some new discovery is made that sheds more light on this mystery at the present out of sight.

"That evolution played a part, and does so even now, there can surely be no doubt: the fittest will survive, the unfit perish in the fight to stay alive. Nonetheless, it could not be that salts contained in rocks and sand or heated gas should unaided form a cell, a system so sophisticated that it lives and inter-breeds: in spite of tiny size it comprises many mechanisms and a chart of every part. How could this assembly come about, how could it be that it evolved from lifeless atoms quite content to rest in peace, clasped in each others arms?

"Restricted is ability to see so very much from the surface of the Earth. The line of sight, it will not bend, it does not follow contours of the hills, it travels onward unimpeded by the gravitational pull; but soon it's brought up short by objects close around restricting field of view. The daily round of work and play keeps occupied the mind that otherwise might contemplate the things unseen whose presence is made manifest by other means. If could be climbed that lofty cliff that on horizon reaches up, its summit lost above the noctilucent clouds, maybe then would be revealed the universe entire."

"This is beyond the power of puny man," the priest explains, "but in imagination he can fly a half eternity away, navigating by such evidence as logic does supply, until he reaches point from which is seen the whole of space and all the stars with every detail clearly marked. From here he can suppose that he is ruler over all, view the world and planets too, lord of all the cosmic waste; and in this mode of mind he'll surely see the purpose of it all, and fathom out how all began and what the future's going to be."

Intrigued, the Brother Benedix now asks: "The past is easy to be seen, the evidence of what has been lies all around on every side, informing archaeologist and scholarly historian. A matter of a different sort the things as yet to come to pass, what trace can there be left by that which in the future lies?"

The priest he hesitates, how best explain such strange phenomenon in simple terms?

"When high in sky in aeroplane where air is rare and vapour trails, a new perspective meets the eye, a world proceeding at a slower pace, where clocks record a different time. Looking down one sees the Earth below spread out like large-scale map, observes the roads and rivers and the railway track. The line runs round the hills, it follows rivers, crosses bridges, guiding trains between the stations and the termini.

"One sees the train about to leave, one sees its destination where in a while it will arrive, one sees what engine driver cannot see, the place where he will later be, the people he is going to meet. Situated in the cab he cannot tell what lies beyond the buffers - all by smoke and steam is hid.

"Time and space are measurements of when and where some act takes place, measured from convenient point, an arbitrary choice. Time is not a train that runs on rails; it does not clatter by, rattling through the stations with its whistle shrill; it goes not fast or slow, in reverse it cannot go, because it's just a measure metering minutes in between, in between the happenings of the day: it's rate of change that's measured in this way.

"A metre rule is stiff and strong, and made of iron, it can be held in hand and used to beat the ground: no one would so foolish be, to suggest the distance that it measures moves along and passes by, or backwards goes the way it came. Time can't be grasped, it's insubstantial, time can't lie upon one's hands except in metaphoric terms. It represents the space between events, if nothing ever happened it wouldn't then exist.

"The measurement of time presents a problem since it's always on the move, there is no starting point that can be marked with stick stuck in the ground. The sun the only universal point of reference is, no wonder that to some a god this useful orb appears: regrettably the course it runs lasts only for a year and then repeats. One year is like another, there's no certainty which one is which. Arbitrary is choice, the choice of year from which to count; how could a Greek or Roman know when he was born, how many years B.C.?

"There was a time when sun it didn't shine; in far future it will burn away, its flames die down and light go out. How then will passing hours be gauged, how was it done before the world began, in that distant past?

"The past is not some disused piece that lies in attic of the home of Time, mysterious mansion that could perchance be reached by weird machine, product of inspired inventor's mind, the past was passing of two ships in day or night, on unruffled seas in weather calm, or tossed by waves in cyclone's storm, unpremeditated meetings by impartial fate decreed, occurrences that substance lack, existing only in man's memory or scrawled by skipper in the log.

"If from point of vantage one can see the way one's come and what there is that lies on road ahead, then if sufficient height can be attained, in an area undisturbed by gravitational force, it must be possible to see what happened in the past, and looking forward know the future yet to come.

"Each individual has a view his own, a unique aspect which he cannot share. That lies ahead for one, is in the past for those who later live: and in between a space of time.

"Time is but a measurement as is a foot, a metre, or a mile: it may be viewed from either end, its length is just the same, it is the viewer who is not. If Nature dwells in some eternal timeless place that's far removed from Earth, from there perhaps all aspects may be seen, and past and future known. This may be why prophetic texts mix future with the past, the prophets' minds confused by messages received from universe's further side."

The Brother Benedix now has his say: "Regarded from the point of human view, entangled in the daily round of tedious work necessitated by the need to feed on food produced by constant toil, no purpose can be seen, except to stay alive until the deadly hand of death no longer can be held at bay; what terrifying prospect, it does not do for mind on this to dwell. A tangled web this life appears, its thread is lost to sight in jungle of the day's affairs.

"This life here on this Earth, it is, it seems, concerned with childhood and with little else. First part is spent in growing up, and when maturity's achieved, the best of rest is spent in parenthood, until, in final stage, a second childhood ends one's days. Once weans have left the nest, what is there that remains? If this existence is complete, if there's nothing more, if beginning's all there is, what purpose does it have, this short and dreary life? How sad to think all ends in aching bones and slow decay. Would it not be better far if great crescendo marked the end, a blaze of glory preface funeral pyre? Instead it's slow decline and absence from the active list. In old age all life's lessons have been learnt, much knowledge through the years has been acquired, the well of wisdom overflows; will it vanish in a night, lost through subterranean drain, must it all be thrown away?"

"Each phase of the Creation of the universe has as a 'generation' been described, The sixth was that of Man, created when all else was well established that he might on Earth survive, fed with vitamins and proteins provided by the animals and plants.

"Now, at first Man lived alone. Did he by division reproduce, in manner of a single cell, or was he an androgyne, two sexes in a single shell? The latter view, it must be right, substantiated by the tale of how was Adam split from Eve, and thus began Man's second phase, a modern kind of man and wife. When life began, one may suppose, all creatures led hermaphroditic style of life, a style still evident among some species of a lesser sort, a few of which display ability to propagate both on their own or with a mate.

"The myth tells of a passion so extreme that Hermaphroditus and the Nymph became as one, their limbs entwined until a single entity they were, bisexual yet inseparable, a single pair. However, if the story is believed that out of Adam there came Eve, it was in fact the other way about - precursor of the human race was hermaphroditic from the start, and only when it was complete, the human form, were they by Nature prised apart.

"Hermaphroditic offspring must surely be a clone, clone after clone, the only variation that produced by evolution as the population was dispersed and experienced varying circumstance, and after many years slight differences appeared between the separated tribes. Now if the purpose of this whole great project is production of a race of individuals, every one unlike the rest, each with an independent mind and way of life, capable of thoughts unshared, expressing views of which few others may approve, then reproduction must be by some means that eliminates all similarity of traits. To this end, in the day of Adam, did the two parts separate, to be re-shuffled like a pack of cards, so that in the future all would have a partner new. At night they recombine that population may increase, but at the dawn each half goes his or her own way to lead an independent life until, enveloped in the darkness once again, an existence hermaphroditic does resume.

"Mankind's second scene is in this manner acted out, a halfway house to follow on initial phase. Logic does demand a third, the final act in which all is complete, each individual independent on his own, revealing then the plot and purpose of the play, on which the curtain has no need to fall - no more procreation is required, since the population's now sufficient, like the evil for the day. The caterpillar and the pupa are an ugly pair, how could reason at this point call for a halt, does it not demand that transcending beauty be the end? Another generation there must be, fulfilling promises inherent at the start.

"On this journey through construction's phases are some sort of vague and undefined emotions or ghostly memories incorporated in the genes, that on rare occasion surface in the conscious mind, which give explanation to a sense of reincarnation sometimes felt by those more sensitive to esoteric things, the 'dreamtime' as by Abbo's it's been aptly named."

Benedix: "Long I've wondered why should Nature choose to have man breed like this, and not in some much simpler way; but now I see why it must be - to guarantee that things on Earth will be diverse and spontaneity display."

The priest returns to theme with which he seems obsessed, a view of life that might be seen from distant place, maybe beyond the universe's bounds, freed from earthly time because of motion at a different speed to that at which the Earth proceeds. "If man will in imagination flee this Earth and fly at speed of light up into space, to point of vantage whence whole world at once is seen, between the poles a panorama of the lands and seas, and eye can follow tracks of asteroids and comets as they pass along predestined paths, if he can visualise what it is like to live in this exalted place, to think as Nature does, and not as man, compelled to dwell close to the dust from which he sprang, his view restricted by the struggle to survive and stay alive, then he may come to understand the reason and the rationale that lies behind construction of the living World.

"The apex of the Pyramid of Life and Death is very far from Earth, very great its height above the base: the view from here is panoramic, all the world it can be seen at once, moving at a different pace - the past and future too: a changed perspective from the one below.

"No man can reach this point although he often tries: once more imagination must be used, the sum of knowledge brought to bear to plot the scene that might be viewed from point of observation located on galactic rim. The present mingled with the future and the past appears no more a point of culmination in development of man, but just another epoch in the long procession peopled by, it seems, the same old faces in a slightly different guise.

"The Pyramid of Life and Death, its peak must be a single point: one alone can occupy this lonely throne, endowed with total power, to which all creatures in subservience bow. There are none with whom to disagree and start debate, arousing wrath till reconciled by joint consent; no peer with whom to chat on equal terms, discuss the day's affairs, reflecting on the state of play.

"Consider then the solitude of this exalted seat, the loneliness of living at this dizzy height, whilst all below, descending in hierarchal chain, obey the orders passed on down from overhead. With fear are filled the hearts of subjects of a Universal king; the common soldier dares not disobey the officer who's charged with his command."

Benedix now asks: "If all creation's perfect made, how to banish boredom when the future's sure, and everything with certainty's foretold?"

"By raising up a race of men with mind their own and will to discipline themselves and live within the bounds of natural law" the priest replies. "How is this done? 'Tis Chance that's introduced, all decisions made by roll of dice; and men and women, made from stones that litter shore, are from the Truth at present hid, that they may freely choose, decide what they should do, without external aid. Opinions form inside their heads, their conversation shines, illumined by the bright ideas conceived by fertile brains: and all the time they're tossed on waves of treacherous seas and driven by the fickle winds that back and veer, lacking reason it appears, vicissitudes of Life that is by Chance controlled, crushing seeds of self-conceit.

"These men and women then, they are the salt that shall to Earth its savour give, a piquancy that in the unexpected lies: uncertainty the only certain thing, round every bend a big surprise.

"Given that this which I have said is true, could you think that Nature's self would act in manner unconforming to the law? It must therefore follow that the way the world was made, and the many forms of life that cover all its face, can from the Handbook be found out, if comprehended it can be and the meaning of its content properly construed (I trust you're with me still, not lost in web of logic that I weave).

"Since I have started study of the way the biosphere was made, how all the creatures were created, not from metal, wood or stone, but from those elements of which the ancients of the classic times were wont to speak, of water, air, and earth, and fire, a different view I see, perspective changed from one below to one above.

"The earth, of salts it is comprised, on which the plants may feed when ionised; hydrogen from water is obtained, and from the atmosphere the carbon is derived, as is the oxygen that carbohydrates need. Ah yes, and then the fire! From sun the photons come, the energy to give the impetus and drive! From these has Nature fashioned all that walk on Earth or spring from bosom of the soil."

"How then shall this conundrum be resolved?" the monk enquires, "How should creation of companions be achieved, without the desecration of the holy pyramid, the consecrated mount?"

"The answer lies in generation of a race of men, a little lower in hierarchal rank, but given freedom, liberty to choose between the good and bad, a property no others in the pyramid possess. Those that choose the downward path that leads to Hell have damned themselves; they who elect the other way and natural order to obey, do so without duress."

"If blest with power to all things do, to all things perfect make, how then to introduce the element of chance lest all be preordained?"

"If man can freely choose, all must by chance be ruled, that no one else should know how each is going to move. For man to live this way provision must be made, an Earth set spinning in the sky, on which no certainty exists. In space the bodies astral swirl about, but bleak and bare it would appear are surfaces of moon and stars; small in size the world may be, where else is there that can compare with Earth for fecund life and scenery? Everything upon the Earth organic is, composed of living cells; there's nothing Nature's made that is inanimate, except the rocks that form the base on which all else may live. All artefacts are made by men, they cannot make themselves, but are conceived by human mind and shaped by human hand. Nature's children act as agents for the force that gave them life.

"Chaotic is the rest of universe, no galaxy or single star can be described as central part. Nature has devised the laws which govern all the things which are by Universe embraced, circumscribing all their actions, what they do and how exist. If Nature did construct the sun and stars and lonely world, put them in their place and set them spinning at colossal pace, it must surely be that it was done according to those laws and not by supernatural power.

"There is no magic wand to wave, that in an instant may the world be filled with men and women ready made; the mode of manufacture may be seen as by evolution does the population of the Earth increase, guided by the unseen hand that put the catalysts in place.

"This life is but a stage upon the journey up from simple cell, prokaryon to perfect form. From shiny ovum, small and round, comes the larva, ugly bug. As it grows in size it sheds its several skins before it falls asleep in pupa's shroud, and lies as if it's dead for many days; when time is ripe it once again becomes alive. Emerging from its living grave it spreads its iridescent wings that free it from the earth and lift it in the air. It was not dead, it only slept.

"Is not this the course pursued by all the natural world, small beginnings at the start, atoms laid like brick on brick as aeons pass, and then the final rest before the dawn when rises sun that never sets."

Moving softly from the door at which he's also entered to escape the wind rampaging through the trees outside, the Atom King he too stands unobserved behind the pillar, listening with attention to all that's being discussed between the ancient priest and novice monk, the both quite unaware their words are heard: and now Death mutters to himself beneath his breath, his words can hardly be discerned - "Oh! Come this happy day, my work will be complete, no more the need for man to be seduced, induced by me to take the road that's paved with gold and leads on down to Hell below, lest he his worth he proves by choosing steep and rock-strewn route that upward leads, beyond the gravitational pull."

The cleric clears his throat, returns to theme he used to preach from pulpit in his little church before being ousted by the followers of a less ascetic sect.

"On the mind two forces act, sometimes in unison, at other times opposed. One is inherent in the human frame, a system of control that gives protection to the body (not the soul) and guides it through the day, providing supervision for the metabolic function. The second is the will, which to the anima pertains. The power it has to override instinctive acts, to bring to bear considered thought, and quench the burning passion's flames, or sometimes fill with fear the minds of others standing near, without the need for show of might."

The Atom King, impelled to state his point of view, no longer shows restraint. Leaving shadow of the lofty pier he joins the other two, and this is what he has to say:

"There is another force that bears on all the creatures of the world, be they inanimate or live, as very well I know. It's that exerted by the atoms, by the way that they are structured, and the natural laws that they obey.

"Energy's the mortar binding bricks with which each creature's built: each does require of power a great amount to hold the structures in their place, resisting gravitational drag. The latter causes flow of water, fallen on the hills as rain, which rushes down the beds of streams, and, reaching river, flows on down until it joins the sea that rests on rocky crust, the surface of the Earth.

"In like manner does all energy behave, seeking equilibrium with environs that surround, always flowing downward from the atoms highly energised to the cooler regions occupied by those less well supplied, until a balance is achieved. If this flow was not contained, all warmth would seep out to the void and atoms go to rest, perfect crystals forming grains of sand.

"This need for energy's potential to equate, to atoms gives appearance that they live, that they have animation too, like the creatures whose beings they compose: but this is not the case. They are systems mechanical in form, but unlike systems made by man they cannot be of all their energy bereft, but will continue ceaselessly to spin; so they seem to be alive, forming friendships with others that they meet, then growing tired and seeking sleep.

"In me you see this concept symbolised, incarnation of the natural force which drives the atoms on their course, made manifest in minds of men by Nature, so to offer unto man alternate choice, thus his freedom to ensure."

These are the words he speaks, the Atom King, in explanation of his role: what is to men the downward path to death, to him is route to rest, purification, and point from which the resurrection can commence.

Now Benedix again he speaks: "You ever talk of up and down, whatever is it that you mean, when you use these common terms with reference to the abstract things, when judging what to you is good and what is not?"

Pensively the priest he pauses, pondering on reply he'll give to this peculiar point that has by Benedix been raised.

At last he lifts his head and slowly starts to speak, he chooses words with care: "The ancient sages held the view that Earth is flat, and none there were that disagreed. If Earth was spherical, they said, when kicked with foot a ball would ceaselessly rotate, and man on bike would freewheel round for ever more: and yet, they must have often seen, like you and me, a ship rise up on edge of sea. Perhaps they wiser were, in fact, than we. Consider now, if cubic were the shape of Earth, appearing flat on every side, would not the waters gather in the centre of each face? Would not to walk toward one edge feel like as if one climbed a hill? The eyes deceive, that which we see is not quite real. 'Upward' means away from Earth and into space, where there's no longer east and west, and gravity grows less and less. It is gravity that dictates rise and fall, drawing all things to the centre of the Earth, where everything's bereft of life and turned to molten ore. That is why the will of man must this force oppose, and try to rise to where exists a life that is from this oppression free."

A further point there is that comes to mind of novice monk, a puzzlement that troubles many minds, which he now puts in words:

"Are all living things confined to Earth, is it only here that life can spring from stones, substances of which the underworld's comprised, whose representative is Death who stands beside me even now? The sky's replete with stony spheres, some flaming hot like shining sun, others hardened by a cold intense, but none it seems is home to those who live and breathe, as is this world of fields and trees."

On hearing this the King he whispers to himself, "My only task is tempting man, to offer choice of right or wrong, that every man may tested be. I wot not of these other things that are at present hid from men and also me."

"Other worlds there well may be," replies the priest, "places that you cannot see, for unseen forces fill the void that is the atmosphere and space beyond. Much from the Handbook have I learnt, much more is hidden yet in metaphor, or by the lack of light to lighten dark recesses of the human mind which cannot comprehend as yet the whole of chemistry of life. All the answers are contained in Book, but I know not what the questions are that I should ask: and so I cannot tell to what it is that they refer. Some solutions are quite simple, such as every man can understand, but most concern philosophies beyond the ken of ordinary men - how can I understand those things of which I can't conceive? Wait I must until the study of the atoms shall reveal these concepts hanging on the Tree of

Knowledge out of reach; persistent effort is required to snatch them from the lofty branch on which they are ensconced."

Benedix now has the final word: "Each man a prisoner is of Chance, incarcerated as he is in mortal form from which there's no escape but death, restricted by the limitations inherent in the body which is the spirit's home, driven by emotions deep inside the psyche, which on impulse uninvited fill his frame and try to take control. Man cannot do what he would wish to do, Chance will snatch the cup before it reaches lips. His freedom's circumscribed by circumstance that changes all the time; and at the end, when he meets Death, who really knows if he finds perfect peace, eternal rest?"

Twelve Intermission

The monks at monastery a tedious life do lead. Rising early in the morn, in the cold and misty dawn, as the sun creeps over yonder hill, its rays reflected off the frosty fields, and waters of the river darkly flow down to the weir, turning as they go the wheel of water-mill, the monks they start the day with prayer, kneeling on the cold unyielding flags in the church's chilly air.

Divided is their day between chanting in the choir or lonely meditation in their cells, and working in the mill, grinding corn to make the flour they sell, and so support themselves and aid the poor of parish who are always here. A small diversion is enough to cheer them up, to break the monochrome monotony, the sameness of each day as dawn and dusk relentlessly repeat.

Thus it is one day a cry is raised, and sound of running men along the stone-paved passage that of custom only hears the muffled shuffle of the sandaled feet.

"Arachne's fallen in the water, she's fallen from the weir!" The Brothers rush to windows of the cells, the ones on western side that overlook the slowly flowing waters coming from the dam.

She clings to parapet and pulls herself to safety on the wall beside the water-wheel, beneath whose rim the mill-race runs, which might have dragged her down and drowned her, crushed against the metal mesh. Beside her stands her duffle-bag, which by good chance did not get wet; from it now she pulls dry gear. Behind, there rises up the edifice, its walls are lined with windows of the cells. In her bedraggled state she gives no thought to what's above, she sheds her jumper and her skirt, and wrings the water from the saturated clothes.

"Arachne's standing there, nothing on but underwear!" exclaim the monks who press against the window pane to catch a glimpse of this forbidden fruit of which they must not even think.

"What is this rumpus that I hear?" It is the Abbot, wrenched from prayer by this unusual noise that interferes with concentration on affairs concerning management of monastery, the profit and the loss of milling oats, and adding up donations from those who thus would save their souls.

"Most unseemly does your action seem. Go back to work, return to cells you wretched men, unworthy infidels!"

Thirteen The Wingéd Horse

The janitor at BioMech a young man is, who something lacks in intellect, of manner mild and keen to please. His hobby is to gaze at stars, he knows them all by name, what their brightness is and magnitude, and their refractive hues.

The Boss he is a kindly man, he's bought a powerful lens and mounted it upon the roof, and there the boy spends every night when sky is clear, searching for some form of life, a flash of light, a signal from afar. If some other race can cruise the skies, swiftly passing through the space that separates the planets and the stars, why should their ships be made of tin, he asks, resembling rockets powered by kerosene? Does not the Boss in factory underneath intend to shape new forms of life more suited to the needs of man, composed of tissues of organic origin? Why shouldn't men from inner space come riding on some reptile specially made, like Jonah crossing seas in belly of his whale?

Tonight, as usual, as his custom is, he sits on roof, awaiting for the mist to clear, that hangs above the higher ground behind the Business Park, at rear.

Suddenly he gives a shout: "The Horse, the Flying Horse, I see it through the haze, its wings raised up above its head!"

He tumbles down the ladder from his point of vantage up above, and madly runs up village street, waving arms in terror of the sight he thought he saw, crying all the while: "Pegasus, the Wingéd Horse, it flies above the Business Park this night!"

The sleeping citizens awake, disturbed by sound of running feet and frightened cries that rise from street. Leaping from their beds they fling their windows wide, leaning out to see what is amiss.

When morning comes the Abbot sends for boy and has him fetched, for surely happenings supernatural fall within the jurisdiction of ecclesiastic law. The lad he closely questions, but no account coherent can he elicit from the boy, who's now more frightened than before in daunting presence of this stern inquisitor.

"Too little sense, too much imagination," this is what the Abbot says. "Too many nights spent staring into space, seeking non-existent men who fly through air like witches on their sticks."

He calls two monks and has them take the boy to dungeon down below and flog him with the cat, to teach him not untruths to tell, and frighten honest burghers in the night, causing breach of peace.

When the young man's been released, and sent back to his duties in the Park, the Abbot feels some slight regret, he's overstepped the mark, over-zealous in his aim to scotch all witchcraft, and belief in evil forces extant in the dark. A hypocrite he'll be declared by some, preaching peace and gentleness to fellow men, and forgiveness of sin; but yet in church each day the peasant women shrouded in a shawl of black will come to pray, to marvel at the dark magnificence of massive pillars that support the arches of the vaulted roof, the masons' sculpted scrolls and grinning faces cut from stone that stare down on the worshippers below, twisted in grotesque grimace; the only light the stately candles standing on the sanctuary steps, and those each side of altar shining on the ornaments of polished brass, and on the brazen beak of lectern's golden bird, whose outspread wings support the open book for all to read the words that few can understand. Comfort they derive from constant drone of mumbled prayers, the words as meaningless in mother tongue as when they're spoke in speech of Rome. Each day the lesson's read, but no instruction does it give. Alone the words carved on the stone by Moses on the mount give all the guidance that they need to steer them through the stormy seas of war and peace. Their simple faith is all their own: the certainty of mercy at their Maker's hand, and at the last eternal life. Nothing do they know or care of rivalry between the clerics, the arguments about the Articles of Faith, or interpretation of the Canon Law.

A feeling of disquiet remains among the village folk; had the apparition really risen from the lab below? Many rumours circulate about unnatural nature of the work that's carried on, wild speculation based on information leaked through keyholes of locked doors. This latent fear has raised the ire of Sankey Sam, leader of the action group of what has now been named the Independent Church of Human Rights, dedicated to the fight for peace and personal protection, no matter what the cost in human lives. He plans to raid the works again, lest some new creature of a type not seen before escapes into the wild and interbreeds with animals already there, giving rise perhaps to plagues of lethal snakes or vicious rats that lie unseen among the bracken on the heath.

The self-styled Atom King is told, well pleased is he, to free the atoms trapped by man's device, imprisoned in a structure given life and power to procreate, and all for self-aggrandisement and incremental wealth.

These two collude to find a plan, to kill the horse and shoot it dead. It still must be corralled within; somewhere inside a stable there must be, adjoining lab where cellulose by process is produced, with which to feed the beast - synthetic hay! The other night, a little canter, trial flight.

If entry could be made tonight when all is quiet, the stable could be found before the break of day, and horse despatched before the doctors came to work. The janitor he has the keys, they hang from belt around his waist. They dare not attempt to overpower the boy, for as is the way with those who have more brawn than brain, he is most muscular and very strong. A subterfuge must be employed, a trick to make him think they have the right to enter block at dead of night.

The twilight dies behind the hill, the pinkish tinge that touched the tips of snow-capped peaks as last light fled has gone; the mountain range is left a line of black against a sky of midnight blue. The lad is seated in his usual place with face beneath the eye-piece of the powerful lens. Orion stands astride the southern sky, his dagger dangles from his belt; low in the west the Square of Pegasus, the sign of wingéd horse, looks down and watches with a stony gaze.

The desperadoes climb the ladder, rifles slung across their backs, until they reach the level of the roof. They feign a great desire to scan the stars and plumb the depths of space, and see what lies beyond the Milky Way. The boy gives up his seat, flattered by the others' interest, as each takes turn to press his eye against the glass.

As he rises from the seat, Sam slips the bunch of keys from off the young man's belt. They quiz him with regard to lay-out of the labs, and if they're locked at night.

"Professor Yorke is last to leave and lock the outer door, but not before he has released the dog, Cerberus the canine cur, companion and protector of the Flying Horse, whose eyes like saucers are. This is what he told me, lest I peeked inside when all is quiet at dead of night."

They drop down to the ground again, and easily they enter in the armoured doors that in the day were folded back right out of sight, giving access to reception desk. Inside the darkness is complete, except for diode's liquid light, greenly gleaming as electronic clock ticks off the hours before the dawn. No dog appears, its eyes two orbs with hatred filled, its hackles rising on its back, bared fangs revealed between its lips.

By light of darkened torch the two search every room, passing through the labyrinth of passages and corridors that twist and turn, but no stable do they find, no scent of hay hangs on the filtered air. Labs there are for every use: spectroscopy, and synthesis of haem and chlorophyll, and that in which assembly of the cells is carried out.

At last they reach a little room, unfurnished but for metal stand on which is stood the convoluted tongue whose tissue's not herbaceous nor of flesh, its iridescent shades invisible at night: instead a pale aurora at the spectrum's lower end surrounds the twisted leaf, vibrant with the power of life.

They stand and stare, astonished at this living flame that is in fact the grail for which they've searched. Diminutive, hardly seen by feeble glow that from itself does emanate, it holds them in its power more than would have done a stamping horse that frothed at mouth.

Their eyes begin to prick and itch, and of a sudden Sam gives out a strangled cry: "My eyes! I cannot see, I've lost my sight!" Thus it is the Boss's creature keeps its enemies at bay: although it cannot move it is the first to strike, emitting UV ray.

The King he takes Sam by the hand, and drags him through the rows of rooms, down parqueted passages and corridors, until at last the icy air outside is reached and iron doors locked shut; he drops the keys at ladder's foot, as if they fell by chance from young star-gazer's leather belt.

A call has come from ancient Angstrom, to come at once to room in which he works: adjustment's needed to his hearing aid. His room is not like those of others working here at BioMech, more comfort does it have, in keeping with consideration for the old man's age. Before an open fire he sits in easy chair, his pipe and baccy by his side, and many pictures on the wall, Nordic scenes of snowy wastes and frozen lakes. Each day he comes at ten and leaves at four.

Adjustment's made to hearing aid and sound restored inside professor's head, no longer need to shout for all to hear the platitudes with which one greets one's colleagues and one's friends, that sound so silly when repeated several times in rising pitch. Irascible with age, irritated by the aches and pains that accompany advancing years, he now makes hurtful, though deserved, remarks:

"To university you have not been, no training have you had in scientific methods and researchers' ways, yet you think that you can mix on equal terms with those who have, proposing theories quite absurd, based on ignorance on its own - no wonder that that other night you left like dog with tail between its legs, ashamed to show your face again amongst (I quote your phrase) those intellectual snobs.

"How is it then you dare pay court to daughter of that senior man, Professor Yorke? Is he aware of your affaire, does he know that every night you stand without, or thinks he that you're studying stars or gazing at the crescent moon? When he hears that you to her attention pay, he'll not be over pleased I'll swear."

"It's no affaire, a friendship of the purest sort, although it's true, for her I deeply care.

"The Boss, he's kind to me, he treats me as one would a friend, gives ear to weird ideas that I to him do sometimes tell; 'twas he who got for me the invitation for that night that went not well. He'll take my side if anyone should interfere with my career, but cease to see Arachne, to that I never will agree."

"It is a different world to yours in which they live, where cash is never short, in fact it is a word that's never heard. Polo is the game they play, and bridge at night for serious stakes; the talk is all of horses, and the hats they'll wear on Ladies' Day."

"Like all else on Earth or in the firmament above, the social scene is cyclical as well: some gentlefolk become distressed, some common men rise to the top."

"For you this won't be true, to you Dame Fate will not be kind, I see it in your eyes, I hear it when you speak: you do not have what it requires, however long you strive."

"Are all my theories rubbish, is my time all wasted, searching for the truth about creation, how it works, and why? I read how men of old in times historic had ideas that now seem quaint, believing Earth to be quite flat (if space is curved this could be true); in their time held they were in great esteem: if they were wrong how do we know that we are right?

"Fogwatt says that time does not exist, it merely measures intervals between events, it's not a road on which men tread. Are we no further forward than the people of the past?"

"Life starts afresh each time a man or woman's born, their mind a canvas bare as virgin snow on which experience makes its mark: a unique picture's drawn, that nothing owes to those long gone, long since passed on. Man's span is brief, a hundred years at most and usually less. This is all that each man knows of second phase, the one that with Adam did begin, when Adam split with Eve.

"Each man and woman is complete. By Pauli's principle no two can share the view, standing on each other's feet, sharing point in space and time: perspective of the universe is never quite the same that others see as that that's seen by you.

"Because of this the second phase is seen by each as lasting but a life-time's length, too short a time for intellectual gain and consequential evolution of the brain: he who lives at end of epoch will no wiser be than Able and his brother Cain.

"Corollary to this is that the first men of the second age they were as wise as we are now and as the fellows who will follow us in future years. Advance is in technique alone, passed on to 'prentice by the master of his craft. Thus are new inventions handed down, forming steps on which succeeding generations tread to raise them up that they may higher reach to add a few more bricks to tower of knowledge and technique until all learning is complete: and then, when unified is physics in one theory into which all fits, Nature's self shall be revealed to everyone who would it know.

"I can't conceive a time when men and women in a cavern dwelt, though beavers could build dams and birds wove nests from mud and twigs. The paintings in the caves have been preserved, graffiti on the rock that cannot rot, drawn by hunters sheltering from the storm, waiting for the rain to cease, whilst all else has disappeared, destroyed by wind and water and the flames of forest fire."

"In the future humble I will be: no more foolish schemes or propositions misconceived, bred in my untutored head, treading where the wise men hesitate to go, leaving safety of the well-trod road that signposts clearly demarcate. I will to uniformity conform; but abandon courtship of Arachne is a thing I'll never do."

Leaving Angstrom's office in a humble chastened state, outside it's found that night has fallen, and the air is cold and clear. There is need for time to think, so feet are turned toward the ladder leading up to roof-top perch where sits the youth who scans the sky each evening at this time, searching for a Nova or White Dwarf. Few words he has, his simple mind dwells not on social scandal and intrigue, it's just the wonder and the beauty of the nebulae dispersed across the darkened dome, the mystery of the distant galaxies and the people who perhaps are sheltered there, that occupy his mind: in his company disturbed emotions may relax, finding rest just staring into starry void. No haughty glance here meets the gaze, no need to duel with rapier repartee, or thrust and parry with a sharp-edged tongue.

"It's kind of you to come up here and sit awhile, and watch the constellations as they wheel across the heaven's arch. I cannot comprehend the talk in which astronomers indulge, their perehelions and their apogees. Suffice it does to seek the comets as they weave their way around the sky and watch the shooting stars."

"What was it made you study space, sit here hours and hours in spite of frost and bitter cold? It is in winter that they burn most bright, celestial lights, on nights when canopy is free of cloud and warmth is drained from Earth."

"It was the priest, the Reverend Edward, that I heard one Sunday morning as at matins he did preach. He spoke of end of world and how dread Nemesis would come from out the east, to strike like lightning from a thunder cloud that covers all the sky; he said one should remain on roof and not descend. They filled my heart with fear, these words I hear, and so each night when clear are skies I sit and watch lest unawares I'm taken by surprise."

The stars progress across the darkened sky, surprising is their speed, as if they dared not linger longer lest they're overtaken by the rising sun before they've reached their bed, the bed in which, like owls, they pass the daylight hours.

Stirred by this moving sight, imagination's not for long content to idle be. Inspired once more by awesome sight of sweep of constellations from the left toward the right, good intentions are forgot, new theories crowd the mind. What really is it that the eye can see, what is it lies beyond the ken of men, what is this Outer Space? The Universe is how it's named. This would imply the set encircling everything, the world, the stars, the roving comets, all of cosmic dust, the total of all matter that by mathematical expression is defined. If indeed the Universe expands, growing larger by the hour, then it is misnamed, for it then could not encompass all, for nowhere else there'd be for it to go. It is restricted to the stars and stellar dust and other objects floating in the sky, all that part that's from the atoms made, excluding all that endless space that lies beyond, in existence when the atoms had no form, before they had been shaped.

All of Earth and all those things that on its surface move, the air that fills each aperture and everything surrounds, the sun and moon and stars, all are atoms, nothing else. The atoms are not solid blocks like bricks with which to build the artefacts that fill the universe's empty space: each is a system carefully structured that its destiny it will fulfil. Living systems are these atoms, not mere crumbs of lifeless dirt, but limitations do they have: they cannot die or multiply.

Electrons have their fields in which to play, held in place by mutual forces, some attractive, some repellent, forming web in which each particle is caught. In its natural form with outer shell unfilled, unbalanced will an atom be, electrons' flight elliptical as atom sways from side to side, in hope that in this way its orbit may another atom overlap, and a marriage be arranged. The inert atoms, finely balanced, in their symmetry can smoothly run, ignoring those more highly sexed who proximately pass their way.

In space there's no fixed place where can be said it all began. A gravitational force each body has that bends its course, be still it never can. Rotate it must, it cannot stop, for if it did, who with certainty could say: "It does not move, but only me"?

The Universe is not a football or balloon to be inflated till it bursts, just a concept that best by mathematics is explained. Free from all constraint, it has no size or weight, nothing but an algebraic sign.

Fourteen Return to Sacred Peak

The lab is entered at the start of day, another like all others. Cool grey dawn small welcome gives to workers filing through the door and punching card. Where can Arachne be, her desk is unattended, she is not here today.

"Arachne has not this morning come to work, is she ill or indisposed, does she have a flexy-day?"

"How is it you've not heard? She's gone away, I thought you must have known, for in her company you always seem to be. It's said she's gone to northern coast, there a new life she intends to lead. An address she's left, her destination's Culdene Hall."

What sudden whim has seized her mind, persuaded her to leave without a word? Life would be bleak without her happy face to lift the heart, how can she be let go? Time it is to take the road again, to search her out and bring her back. Great the distance she has gone, short the winter day: darkness will have fallen long before the journey's done.

At first the route leads to the east. The sun with brilliance shines, not rising far but skimming hills as it its journey makes toward the west, reflecting off the frozen fields and snowy wastes that are the countryside this time of year. Gathering speed along this road that heads straight at the rising sun, the eyes are dazzled by this blinding light, and screen is smeared with salt and mud thrown up from gritted road: constantly the wiper's used, until all water in the washer's bottle's gone: now not only sun but salt upon the screen blots out the view, soon something must be done. A watch is kept for source of water, surely streams there'll be, passing under bridges on the way.

The first is rushing through a gorge, its channel cut between the rocks that rear up sheer on either side, the next the banks are overgrown, undergrowth of brambles and barbed briars beneath the sapling trees. The third a better prospect is, the water can be reached by squelching through the bed of rushes and the slimy silt: a can is filled with water, carried back with care to car; both feet are soaking wet and icy cold, but screen is clean and route begins to turn toward the north. Flat fields give way to mountainous terrain; the towns are left behind, they dwindle into distance as their place is taken by the trees, and people are outnumbered by the sheep.

A halt is called and car is briefly left to snatch a moment's rest. There is a silence settled on the scene that's seen by man who stands alone upon the heath surrounded by the sitka spruce, the space between their topmost tips filled by the sky of pure azure. When all distraction absent is, this is when there can be felt the spirit of the forests and the hills.

In the city and the town one is surrounded by the buildings and the artefacts of man, it is man's spirit that's reflected from these things inanimate; no spirit have they that is their's: but craftsman and designer leave their mark indelibly imprinted on their work.

The mountains, rivers, forests, they do not have a spirit of their own although the grass and trees are animate and overflow with life. What spirit is it then that seems to speak when all is quiet? Perhaps it's that of Pan.

The sun has slipped beneath the line of hills and darkness spreads its wings across the vale through which the road now twists. Lights are dipped when meeting travellers southward bound, though few they are, gathered up in little groups, slowest at the front and fastest in the rear.

It starts to snow, flurries in the front of screen, throwing back the headlights' beam so that the road ahead cannot with ease be seen. Colder is the climate in this province of the North: the snow already heaped at edge of road is slowly spreading like a veil of white across the tarmac's face: the verge is now completely covered, merged with boggy marsh that lies to left and right. A bend is reached, and, hidden heretofore by rising ground, a moving wall of light comes into sight, the headlights of a cavalcade of cars, confusing mind and blinding eyes. On the right the dazzling light, on the left the verge is hid beneath the deepening snow: too late to brake, impossible to stop, carried forward by momentum's force. Beyond the road a gully there must be to drain the rain that floods this wet terrain, this damp and soggy land; to finish there would end the journey prematurely. The brain bemused, the eye confused, the narrow gap is not discerned, and yet unerring is the path of car, as if an unseen hand the wheel it grips, safely steering past the hazards either side.

Danger past and on the straight, the traffic's gone and so has snow, once more can headlights bore a hole through which to pass unhindered by the blackness all around. It is as if an unheard voice speaks in the head, and speaking says "Your time has not yet come, in safety you will pass this way tonight." For sure it was the hand of Fate.

At times a turning does appear, signalled by seductive signs glimpsed for an instant in the passing light, a fork perhaps or roundabout, that beckons to unwary man unsure of route that he should take. Do not wander from the way, straight ahead it lies, at either side the lanes a maze.

Journey's end is reached, near here stands Culdene Hall, along that lane and in the trees. The hour is late (or early really, if you will), midnight's past an hour ago, nothing else there is to do but wait for dawn and start afresh tomorrow morn. For now, to sleep, warmly wrapped in winter coat, the car parked under trees, the firs that line the lane. White the frost that settles on the roof, and covers fir-trees' boughs, stardust scattered by a liberal hand that glistens even in the dead of night, for winter days are short, but winter nights aren't dark. The Moon peers down through scudding clouds, or rises from behind the trees, lighting up the mountain peaks. When the Moon is on its holiday and does not come to work, lighting up the snowy scene, then the Merry Dancers do appear in this the northern hemisphere: their eerie luminescent light spreads out across the Arctic sky, the fingers of their rays reach up till almost overhead, and touch the twinkling stars. And so for hours they come and go, these Northern Lights that brighten nights with iridescence cold and cosmic, emanating from the Snow Queen's polar palace carved from ice.

The dawn of winter's day's a sight to see, sun rising red and gold, shining on the sheet of snow it tinges pink: but no heat is given by its rays, cold as steel the iron grip of frost on fields of stubble and the furrows left by plough.

A little later in the day, when sounds of voices can be heard, carried from afar on still and brittle air, as is the bark of dog on distant farm, the way to Culdene Hall is sought, the house to which in haste was journey made. First encountered is a little church behind a wall that hides the burial ground in which great slabs of stone, supported at each corner by a granite block, protect the graves of those who dwelt here in the heretofore. Steps lead up to door in side of tower, and from this vantage point the house itself can be surveyed, set amongst its lawns and elms and noble oaks, imposing pile four storeys high, each fenestered with windows row on row, the sashes fashioned from the native stone. Descending steps and passing through an iron gate, approach is made to massive door of solid wood that to this mansion entrance gives. To one side a signboard stands, and on it is inscribed: "Convent of the Blessed Sisters of the Holy Cross".

The heart it sinks, what can this mean, what can have brought Arachne here? The answer will be found by knocking on this door, by pulling on this handle hanging from the porch's roof, that rings some bell hid deep within this hallowed Hall.

A pause there is, and then at last the sound of footsteps that approach on flag-paved floor. Set in the old oak door there is a grill: the shutter's slid to side, and, peering out, the face of nun. It is the Abbess who, seeing stranger wandering in the grounds, comes to see what it might be this unexpected visitor desires.

"It is my wish to speak with Miss Arachne Yorke, who's lately come to this your House, so I've been told. If this is true I beg of you to take me to her, for I would dearly like to see her face and talk, persuade her to return with me to bosom of her family and that of all her friends."

"This cannot be, already she has sworn to life withdrawn from world" replies the Abbess with forbidding frown. "Converse with her I have for many weeks upon the internet; her mind's made up, her will is set to do this thing, to flee the company she used to keep, the men (and women too) who would monsters make, creatures by the devil spawned. Are you also one of those?"

"Lady Abbess, with respect, I must confess I work at BioMech, but they aren't monsters that we make. Conform to Laws of Nature do the creatures that we bring to life in lab, that they may lighten human load. Constructed in like manner to the natural objects in the universe, they are more natural than the tools men use, lifeless artefacts hewn out of wood or cast in steel."

"Young man, it is of no account, your loss is Convent's gain; girls obedient to my orders I can train, and wash their brains with my ideals and concept of the Truth, unsullied by your science which would everything describe in terms that chemists use, life's great mysteries simplified in algebraic form and formulaic code."

Nothing more can here be gained; no argument will change this bigot's mind who thinks to save young women's souls from all the wickedness of world outside these walls; she'll fill their heads with images of feathered angels seated on the clouds, creatures with a woman's figure and the wings of dove, a hybrid species somehow mixed, one half man, the other bird: is this not a concept more absurd than that of Pegasus, the horse with wings? In the heart the image of this lovely girl will always stay, chaste and pure she will remain, till, old and wrinkled, by the sisters she'll be borne to final rest beneath those slabs of stone that shield the graves from sun and rain.

The day is nearly done as homeward run's begun; the sunset's rosy red fades in the south-by-west, and darkness spreads its wings across the northern sky. Great haste is made on dual carriage-way, the roundabouts loom up with suddenness and heavy foot applies the brakes; when the open country's reached and far behind is town, the route is not so wide, and as it narrows starts to twist and turn: the countryside's by darkness hid as if it were a shroud.

Heavy is the heart within the breast, it is a leaden weight. No more will be Arachne seen, her beauty brightening every day; no more be heard her voice like song of tiny bird: instead will all be dull and grey. And yet she is not dead, she can't be mourned: in that great hallowed house she'll flit about, as full of life as ever was, and make the dourest Sister smile.

Perhaps one day, the aeons past, when souls are reassembled, clothed in bodies incorruptible, in that new world where oxidation's held at bay, preventing death and slow decay, where marriages are not arranged and no-one lives in married bliss but in a child-like innocence, perhaps she'll reappear to grace eternal life, but still beyond a lover's reach.

Encouraged by these sentiments, this thought that all's not lost, a little faster do the miles go past, although the night is still as dark, no gleam of light on any side except the strip that slips beneath the car, tarmac that's by tireless tyres devoured and swallowed by the blackness that follows close behind.

With suddenness the bends appear, leaping into view, requiring wrench at wheel to keep on course, and pass between the columns of the railway bridge that's built obliquely to the traffic stream; the motors move in single file, controlled by amber, red and green. By nine the flow of traffic's almost nil, no need to dip the beam, but road's still serpentine, and now ahead a tractor blocks the way, its trailer piled with bales of straw or hay so high the topmost can't be seen, lost in opacity of winter sky. Impossible it is to pass the farmer by, who has no wish to waste his evening hours in idleness or sleep. The forest firs encroach on either verge.

Many miles and minutes have elapsed, straight the stretch that's reached and speed increased to leave the farmer far behind, proceeding on his dogged way to barnyard where impatiently his cattle wait for feed.

A town now comes in sight, the rows of amber lamps delineate the pattern of the streets and shine on ruined towers and crumbling arches of cathedral church let fall in disrepair when pomp gave way to form of worship more austere. On the outskirts, as the twin-track road gives way to urban thoroughfare, there's a filling station on the left; and on its forecourt rests a 'plane, a bomber painted black. It will not take the air again in soaring flight, striking terror in those people crouching in their bomb-proof shelters down below, an eviscerated hulk is all it is, a cadaver on show.

By day a busy town, its streets with traffic choked, an unusual aspect it assumes when hour is late: deserted roundabouts have eerie look akin to those ecclesiastic ruins on the right dimly lit from overhead. A slow progression during day, tonight it takes not long the streets to thread.

The houses fall behind, the upper windows now illumined as the burghers go to bed, their cares forgotten while they sleep, returning in the morning when they reawake. Gently bends the highway in a sweeping curve, once more the forest closes in: above the road the beeches' branches meet. In front an 'artic' loaded high with logs is travelling fast, no need to overtake.

The sadness and despair give way to bitterness, acidic is the feeling filling body and the mind: why did she never give the chance to be persuaded by a silver tongue? Instead she kept it to herself, what she thought that she must do, dedicate her life to constant prayer and caring for the poor. The work at BioMech the aspect had for her assumed of being that more suited for the Devil's hands than those of gentle maid. No opportunity did she present for presentation of the project in the light of great advance in betterment of life and freedom from the serfdom of the manufactory belching smoke.

Across the fields, along the coast close to the sea, a string of lights marks site of airfield where the pilots ever watch, on alert for rescue call from seamen stranded on a sinking ship. Few the miles from here to home, and comfort of a bed, but sleep likes not to be denied, its hands it stretches out and tries to close the eyes. A constant fight ensues between the will to stay awake and almost overwhelming yearning for a snatch of snooze. The chilly wind through open window blows to cool the brow, but nothing does to rouse the senses from the hideous wish for rest; the motor's drone and brush of tyres induce a heaviness of lids that feign would shut.

A mile the village is from here, so near it pointless is to stop and rest, perchance to sleep. The will is strong, but stronger still the natural law by which the body is controlled. No one knows they are asleep until they wake, oblivious to the moment when oblivion seizes senses 'til consciousness returns. Thus it is tonight, as car it follows curve of road, an interval of unknown length is interspersed as if it never did exist. It can't have been so very long for no great distance has been gone before awareness has returned, but once again the Hand of Providence, of Fate, has held the wheel when else disaster would have intervened.

The news has filtered out again, no secret can be kept for long; it is a human trait, to tell the world of all one's triumphs and one's woes. Since information's lacking, only rumours spread about, the detail is imagined and invented as the stories pass around.

Up in arms the brethren are, the members of the Independent Church of Human Rights. What right, this man, the Boss of BioMech, has he to interfere, to tamper with the natural things of which environment's composed? New species will emerge from through those doors, or seed will blow from ventilation vents and breed amongst the weeds that border roads, or infest crops and cause a famine of the food that to survive the population needs. No army on the march could do the damage that these scientists could do (albeit that they're very few) by inadvertent loss of breeding pair, or worse, a viviparous clone. A final onslaught must be made, to rid the Earth forever of these misguided men who by their dabbling in their bio-engineering will unleash the pent up force of all the evil extant in this world. Already Sam is blinded by this deadly fungal growth that greeted him the night he entered in its lair by stealth, repelling him with ultra-violet ray: next time the factory must be set on fire and everything therein destroyed by heat of flames. It must be done at night, when there's none inside, lest anyone is hurt: it is the creepy creatures that must burn, synthetic devil's spawn, no harm there is intended to the scientific staff. The janitor is warned, "Do not sit on roof this week, gazing through your telescope, but take it home and keep it safe; this is the time the little men from outer space will strike. The Abbot has agreed, if aught that's untoward should damage fabric of the factory, a roost he'll find for you between the towers surmounting mill where corn is ground." So the rumour gets around that mischief is afoot: the Abbot tells the monks, "Prepare the fire appliance, for I fear it may be needed all too soon, we cannot let the business park burn down."

This village so remote does not an engine own with which to fight a conflagration, should it so occur, and that is why the monastery has trailer pump retrieved from army surplus sale. This pump is towed by touring car, bequeathed by previous prelate, abbot of this monastery some fifty years before who used it on his visits to the Vatican in Rome; now it carries ladders, branches, hose, and from a bracket by the side of screen depends a brightly polished bell of brass.

A plan has been prepared for launching an attack on labs of BioMech: the Brethren from the church are now assembling in the road outside the inn, drawn up in line in order of the march, armed with baseball bats to keep at bay any who would bar their way. To penetrate the science block and kill the creatures that in the lab are said to dwell, two grenadiers they've hired to fire grenades that rockets will propel.

The sun has set on frosty fields and woods and hedges bare of leaves, gaunt branches blackly silhouetted 'gainst the sky, the sky that's streaked with cirrus, all inflamed an angry red and orange hue, presaging the storm that's going to break on BioMech when labs deserted lie and working day is through. Darkness now enshrouds the countryside, and village lights appear, the while the cotters close the shutters, leaving little group illumined only by the light of lanterns that they carry in their hands. Sankey Sam is led by new-age priest to column's head: he will lead although he cannot see, holding high the crooked cross, standard of this new-age band. It is some way they have to go, beyond the shoulder of yon hill. Those in front commence to sing 'The grass is green, your blood is red, don't hurt the Earth, don't kill it dead' - the newest of the new-age hymns. At the rear the armourers bear the rockets that they'll fire through windows of the labs to set aflame all that's inside till naught remains but gutted shell.

The Abbot's been informed by runners sprinting through the village street, turning down the path that leads to river's bank where monastery is perched on brink; faint glow of light seeps out from windows of the church where vespers are being said. On hearing that the party's on the move, armed with missiles with incendiary heads, he mobilises fire brigade composed of monks trained in the art of fighting flames. The trailer pump is hitched to car, the one in which the previous priestly prince was wont to visit Rome. Six monks in habits with their hoods pulled over heads, protecting them from bitter cold, climb on the old machine, which promptly takes the road with janitorial youth afoot the running board from which to reach to ring the bell, the brazen bell beside the screen.

The business park at night's protected by a watch, employees of the firms on site, taking turn by turn to guard against industrial spies, or saboteurs from rival works.

On this portentous night the turn has come around to lie in wait, hidden by the branches of the firs that hem the site of BioMech. Rarely is there anything to see or hear when standing guard on business park: who would dare intrude when well aware that sentinels are posted in the trees, keeping vigil in the dark? Now crouching under cypresses that line the service road by which are brought supplies, approach of raiders can be heard, sound of singing growing clearer, ever nearer. The Boss must be averted, alerted to the danger threatening all his work, and that of all his staff.

The Boss, he reaches site coincidentally with the march, he stands before them, raises arms in air: he remonstrates, then pleads with them, in desperation states his case, his voice filled with emotion, a feeling of despair.

"You know not what you do, the harm you're going to cause, the knowledge that'll be destroyed if all my books you burn. No monster dwells within these walls, there are no viral cells that will spontaneously divide and multiply, escaping through the ventilation ducts, contaminating earth and sky; there's nothing here that you may fear. That which we have achieved, it has been done adhering to the natural law, and by interpretation of the cryptic verses that within the covers of the Maker's Handbook are confined. If we had followed evil ways the project would have failed: when errors are compounded the edifice that one would build will ultimately fall.

"You have no wings, and yet, unafraid, you fly beyond the bounds that Nature's set, restricting height of avian flight; you have no fear of Earth's recall in spite of fact that natural order you defy; but G M crops and artefacts that live, existing only if the laws of chemistry are well applied, these are the things you daren't, you can't abide."

This oration's heard in silence by the crowd, but a murmur rises at completion of the speech, dissenting from the sentiments implied, the heresy that's spoken by this scientific man. Sam alone is moved, a chord is struck within his breast, now he knows he's been deceived: the old traditions are the best, for all the faults and misconceptions gathered over time like dust and cobwebs in some neglected garret or a lumber room. Is it now too late, can he yet, blinded as he is, break away and turn his back on these misdeeds they are about to perpetrate?

The armourers impatient stand, their only interest in the pyrotechnics they release; arsonists they are by trade, they care not what the cause, so long as they get paid. No more time they have to waste, striking match they light the fuse and missile rockets through the air, a stream of sparks lights up the night, the demonstrators and the Boss. With crash of glass the firebrand flies through front of factory, starts a fire in labs inside.

At this point the monks arrive with threatening shouts and waving staves, clinging to the ladder overhead; behind, the trailer pump is snatching at the hook attached to bumper at the rear of car.

Two more rockets are released, they follow where the other went, passing through the shattered glass: the flames increase, and smoke begins to billow out through hole where missiles entered in.

A cheer arises from the mob as flames take hold, and all the time the monks are flailing with their sticks as they attempt to beat the miscreants on the head. The priest is caught up in this fight, and hatred flares against this man who has opposed advancement in ideas, and would remain, as Abbot does, clinging to the ideals of the past, still thinking that the Earth is flat.

The Atom King is thrilled to see destruction on this scale, his heart ecstaticly pulsates and sets electrons racing through his inorganic veins; with childish joy he jumps like little boy to see the Reverend Edward felled by blows rained down by three or four who hate him most, who fear persuasive power of logic that he preaches when he's called upon to speak: motionless he lies now on the ground, no longer conscious of the conflict unresolved.

Poor old Sam, blinded by synthetic flower, now hears the cries of combatants as battle's joined, he hears the roar of flames that follows whistle of the missiles hurtling through the air, exploding with a bang. Terror fills his heart and mind, he cannot see the havoc that he's caused, and suddenly he knows he has done wrong, seduced by wily words of anarchist, by Death the Atom King. Regret now wrenches at his soul, how can he put things right? An awful cry he gives, terrified to die caught in an act of anarchy when what he thought to do, what he did intend, was not to cause this chaos but complete reverse; in attempt to stop the manufacture and escape of monstrous creature from this biotechnic works, he had only made the matter worse. The scientists had aimed at organism more refined, complex and sophisticate, of benefit, they hoped, to all mankind, enhancing style of life. The rebels, on the other hand, fearful of those things they could not understand, had brought but ruin and destruction to the delicate and elegant construction now reduced to ashes, nothing left but smoke and soot.

Sam wrenches free from grasp of those who guide him in his blindness, now no more than mascot for the milling crowd, the Church of Human Rights, seeking to impose their sort of peace upon the populace by age-old way of bloodshed and of force. He runs with stumbling steps he knows not where, but by good chance his flight is halted by the bushes lining road at point where watch is kept: he's snatched to safety, swift escape being made across the fields and open ground until the road is reached, fearing some may follow in pursuit lest Sam turn traitor if the case should come to court. This is the road that leads to barren rock-strewn land beneath that mighty cliff and path that leads to Nature's home. If perchance those heights they can be scaled, it's said there can be found eternal life and everlasting end to trouble and to strife; but many miles it is to go, too far to go on foot, to reach the base of cliff and start the climb.

Although it's dark it isn't late, for sure some vehicle will pass this way, and seeing Sam, disconsolate, who sits on ground with head in hands, the driver will relent and proffer ride to end of road, by Tourist Centre and the Gifty Shop.

A covered truck comes rumbling by, and seeing Sam now lying prone upon the ground at side of road the driver slows, and comes to stop. A market gardener coming back from nearby town, his van is travelling light, but still it strongly smells of odours of the onions and the greens with which it recently was filled. A surly man, embittered by low prices for his crop and escalating costs, he hardly speaks but mostly grunts, a habit gained from daily contact with his pigs. Accustomed to the weight of fertiliser sacks and bags of feed for swine, he lifts the semi-conscious Sam with ease and puts him in the cab.

On reaching rock-strewn dried up desert close to where the cliff rears up, unseen in blackness of the night, the road veers off to left to take the gardener to more fertile fields, where his holding and his cottage lie. A rough unmetalled track leads on to foot of cliff: down this the driver will not go, the surface is not good this time of year, and light that glows in cottage window beckons from afar with promise of his supper on the table and a warming fire. The final mile, it must be traversed on the hoof.

At last the Gifty Shop is reached; a frosty moon begins to rise, the creamy colour of a cheese, illuminating rocks and wooden shed; round its eaves the prayer wheels spin in evening breeze, and little flags and pennons fly, left from the previous summer's season, made ragged by the winter's nagging wind and constant drenching rain. Though locked and barred is shop, the Tourist Centre too, veranda gives some shelter and a chance to rest before commencement of ascent.

The Boss looks on as fire takes hold: all his work will soon be lost, the secret files containing knowledge gleaned world-wide from esoteric texts or forced from lips of holy men and seers in distant lands; briefly for a moment there's a tongue of purple flame that leaps from seat of fire, it is the living artificial leaf that in this instant shrivels up and dies, those precious cells that took so long to bring to life now turned to nothingness, as if they never did exist.

The demonstrators and protestors have in the darkness disappeared, fleeing 'cross the fields to their homes on village street, lest they're caught by abbot's men and then arraigned at County Court for arson and possession of offensive arms: but the monks are totally absorbed in fighting back the flames and damping down the sparks before the danger spreads to other buildings in the Park, they too falling victim to the hungry tongues of fire.

The Boss he turns away, no reason here to stay, all his hopes have been destroyed: his hair is turning white and suddenly he's aged beyond his years, exhausted by the effort of achieving his ambition, then see his dreams all come to naught, consumed by conflagration in a single hour.

In spite of Spirit's aim to do what's right, to make a better life by acting in accordance with the wish of Nature and its great ineffable design, so often failure has occurred although the faults had lacked intent. It is the intervention of some force, it seems, that forces faults to be committed, seducing honest men with siren song, a force imposed by idle atoms seeking rest, the origin of sin.

Regret now weighs on soul, a burden hard to bear; all efforts turned to ashes, the heart now in despair. If in this final hour an extra effort's made, if another being can be dragged from jaws of Hell and aided in ascent to land where life's eternal, will then entry be refused, will this insufficient be as remedy for all the former failures of this life? To take just one, a single soul, on upward climb to justify a life of limited success, this surely must be counted as a plus. To save another's life, will this not save one's own?

The face of cliff is dimly lit by rising moon, the clefts and corries in the shadow stay, black as black can be. A hundred yards behind the sheds is start of path that leads, they say, to summit of this towering rock and commencement of the road that leads to everlasting peace. Rough and steep at start, it narrows further still, almost sheer in places, testing strength of will. With weight of Sam upon the back it is a Herculean task, but now that hand is put to plough there's no return to plain below except by suicidal fall from ledge above abyss. Icy waters lie in pools where rocks are flat, spilling over edge and moistening hand and footholds, causing feet to slip. All sense of time is lost in pain of aching muscles and a bitter cold that cuts like knife through skin and bone: and then at last the gradient eases and the wind is not so chill; the force of gravity is less, the weight of burden is reduced; the air, though rarefied, possesses quality it did not have in world below, refreshing weary flesh.

Fifteen Envoi

The plateau at the top is bathed in light. It comes from all around, it's bright but does not glare: it has a softness, yet all things with clarity are seen, both far away and near.

No hosts of singers dressed in white, no harpists plucking chords are heard. Instead a landscape fertile and fructiferous is now observed. The fields are watered by a brook, the hills are crowned with cedar trees, the vines climb up the slopes, their leaves a green of lighter shade. Here and there a husbandman leans on his hoe, and cattle fat and sleek go down to drink from stream. Contented farmers care for kine and cultivate the rich red loam, they know that they will reap their full reward and not be robbed by middlemen or overlord.

Far in the distance can be seen a city, glowing in this bright ethereal light with all the colours of the semi-precious stones from which it has been built - amethyst and chalcedony, quartz and chrysolyte. Here in this land where gravitational forces cancel out it's truly flat: unimpeded by horizon's edge the eye can spy remotest parts, as on Earth it did when looking up, observing stars.

A few yards on there stands a man upon the path. Tall and straight, he's silhouetted 'gainst the cloudless sky. Raising hand he beckons: now he leads the way.

BOOK THREE

THE GARDEN OF INNOCENCE

EPILOGUE

Shall the Earth be made to bring forth in one day?

Sixteen Epilogue

I the Abbot was a novice when first I met the priest, a man well versed in science in addition to his calling of the cloth. The priest had sought to find the meaning of the Book, to break the seal that hid from Man the truth contained therein, hidden in the words the prophets heard, spoken in the visions that were vouchsafed to them to see. "All creation's secrets may from science be retrieved," he said, "revealed by way the atoms have been made, and how the rays of light impinge on electrons as on their course they race, and drive them on in frenzied haste; or bitter cold of outer space takes back this energy as artefacts that men construct decay, becoming heaps of rubble and of rust, and they themselves are laid to rest amongst the dust."

He told me then that from the Earth the Earth could not be seen, that I should in imagination fly to Universe's furthest side and see creation's whole expanse laid out before my eyes, freed from time, the future mingled with the present and the past, see how the world began and what is going to be, and know at last the purpose of this life.

But ambition seized me, drove me on, of the Church a prince was what I aimed to be. The old priest's words were soon forgot: ordination set my feet upon the rung of ladder which I wished to climb, leading to the post that now I hold, successor to the man who was Abbot here when first I took my vows. Alas, the priest he has passed on, and only now do I recall what he then said, that earthly power and pomp are naught compared with comprehension of the Universe, what it is and how it works. Now at last I make the voyage on this mid-summer night from vantage point betwixt the towers that rise above the roof, projecting eye of mind between the twinkling stars that swarm across black velvet sky; far below the subdued roar of river falling over weir to stony bed beneath excludes extraneous earthly sounds and merges with ethereal music of the cosmic wind that plays upon Aeolius' pipes. Imagination reaches out to Universe's edge: beyond this point one dare not go, for in the void devoid of matter does the radiation freely roam, energy so strong the atoms can't survive: and in this space do power and glory have their source.

The Universe, what does it mean? At first assumption's made it's what it says, the set of everything that in existence is, all that fills the endless space; but then a doubt creeps in when talk is heard of time before it was, and how it still expands. Expansion predicates a space unfilled: if Universe is everything there'd be no room to spare; a different definition there must be to make some sense. The Universe it seems is all that part of boundless space wherein high frequency is held in check, made up of all the atoms in their varying elemental shapes, existing at the start in state of chaos and confusion unrelieved. By the unseen power that had devised the complex systems that the atoms are they were released, to freely roam the empty void. Free from fear of death or loss of potency that is for others linked to age, their natures made them shun a life of solitude and seek a partner each with whom they might co-habitate in stable and lethargic state; inert elements alone required no mate, in themselves complete and free from stress, electrons balanced, shells all filled, for passion do they have no need.

Everything that can be seen or felt or touched, it is of atoms that it is composed, including water and the air that infiltrates all nooks and every space. All the wonders of the Universe depend upon these tiny mites, how they congregate and, joining hands, create the many forms of plants and beasts and even Man, because of special way that they've been forged in furnaces of stellar fire, the balance of their longings and desires not quite in line but on the skew, so that the balance is redressed by union with another, sharing nuclear power. The structure of the atom in itself is evidence that there exists a plan of life devised by reasoned thought, the property by which the intellect's defined. Has not the atom been in manner so designed, its forces some in equilibrium and some eccentrically inclined, that it acts so that its Master's wishes it fulfils? In order are the elements arranged in manner that permits them to combine and form the things to which life appertains, and separate again in death, becoming dung on which the growing crops may feed. Electrons too their place they have from which they dare not move, unless displaced by sudden wave, or else by stealth they're robbed of warmth, and even then they must, like chessmen on a chequered board, obey convention and the rules by which the game is played.

The heart of atom's in its core, it is unchanging nucleus that decides what element it is: electrons come and go, fortune's footballs kicked about, engulfed in waves of force that lift them up and cast them down and knock them into touch. Strict the rules in this the game they play, by logic written in the book of natural law. Precise positions they must occupy where plus and minus cancel out and equilibrium is maintained; and yet stability is never quite achieved, for if it was the world a block of rock it would for ever stay. When the atom's on its own, electrons' outer shell is overfilled, or else is incomplete. When speed picks up as energy's increased, eccentricity makes atoms sway, causing orbits to assume elliptic shape and overlap a neighbouring atom's private space, thus filling mutual shells when lying side by side, restoring harmony of motion that is of stress relieved: in co-valency are atoms held, fearful lest they fall apart and start again to violently vibrate; when energy's reduced their orbits shrink, releasing grip, and atoms sink to lowest state and lazily rotate.

All the matter that in this universe exists is of these elements composed and nothing else, be it woven into cells that throb with life, or inorganic like the water and the other vapours in the atmosphere. On every side they press about, intricate and with precision made: was it just by chance they came to be, produced by magic though no magician did exist that I can see?

So were formed the rocks, the water, and the air, uncomplicated compounds, their atoms quite content to rest, if undisturbed, for ever more, with energy the least that they're allowed, the stones and sand amalgams of these ores. How then was introduced into this bleak and inorganic scene abundant life, springing from inactive rocks, briefly blooming then returning to the earth, lifeless dust becoming soil? How could a single cell be sire of many species, each so unalike? Could they come from common source, growing larger every day, changing form and shape at whim of chance and circumstance, evolving into separate species in unordered way? Such a process would proceed, aimlessly, without a goal, for if purposeless such creatures would not have ability to see beyond today, existing in a life that from the start is doomed, the future nought but death, oblivion, and decay. Why should the good be sought, why is it thought that it is right that nature should evolve this way? Do not the atoms seek simplicity, what benefit do they obtain, the mighty atoms incapable of death? If no spirit nor no soul the microbes can possess, and no emotion show, why should they wish to live and to survive, when without effort they could at rest remain? An external force there has to be to drive them on and show the way.

No system can be made unless there's first conceived a plan, a detailed drawing from which the craftsman can the measurements obtain and how they are arranged, the parts that must be made to fit together, forming one harmonious whole; each organism has its DNA that shows the way it should be made. The nucleic acid must have been before the first of protozoa could have come alive.

From the fluids of the atmosphere alone are made amino acids, the air and water that came first, when rest of elements were locked in rock in solid form, simple compounds that may well have on occasion formed by chance as wind and rain stirred up the sky. No structure can be built except some intellect a notion has to meet some need or ambition to fulfil. By taking thought an image forms within the mind, and from this image can a plan be drawn to show the shape and measurements of size: without its guidance how would parts know where to go or how it is they're meant to fit? They would remain chaotic heap. The plan precursor is of all that's made. In imagination first conceived, an insubstantial form of energy alone it is, that then is drawn in DNA, the bases synthesised from vapours freely floating on the wind, blown about above the ground. A detailed copy of the thought that occupied the mind, it can for frequent use be copied many times in RNA, but does not itself react, being rendered impotent by hydrogen that guards its active site and blocks the ingress of those atoms that would its virtue violate. When dies the organism that's its host, the DNA thus stays intact, for is it not comprised of atoms that by their nature cannot die? It must remain amongst the dust until in aqueous solution it's to life recalled by energy that's sent from source beyond the confines of this Earth.

Hydrogen has but a single one, a lone electron on its own, it wishes that it had one more; quite unbalanced, highly charged, by Nature is this useful atom used as plug to fill a gap in atom's shell when further action's not desired, and molecule is kept intact.

Without genetic guiding hand, heat randomly applied would merely raise electrons' speed and aid the atoms mate with any others that stood near at hand, ever-present oxygen most likely candidate, and thus in sunlight does the surface of a fabric fade, a film of oxide forming as degradation starts upon destructive path. As if the rust and oxidation weren't enough, gravity will play its part: any structure that is built or system put in place, be it by intent or just by chance, it is upward that it grows, the pieces bound against their will, and all the while will gravity its force employ to try to downward drag the artefact and fragment by force its form that atoms may be freed to find the rest they always seek; constantly are caused to fall from workman's hand his tools, and minute parts fall to the floor and roll until they find a nook in which to hide as downward do they work their way. Against such odds could never chance, unaided by the DNA, construct a creature capable of life and ability to reproduce before befalling prey to one or more of these destructive powers.

Suppose that chance had overcome the odds, and that it was by chance that atoms met and proteins formed and living tissue thus ensued, still unanswered the question would remain: whence came the atoms in their ordered ranks, performing their precision drill? Were they also forged by chance? The iron requires a smith to beat it into shape; left in the fire it merely melts. Essential is the intellect to give the product form and shape: undirected energy alone will only increase heat. All hinges then on DNA, and on the atoms too, the pair that must precursors be of all creation, well before the Earth should flower and burgeon with the fruit that feeds the beasts and birds and fishes too. There the secret lies, hidden in the haze where microwaves hold sway, and where the Tree of Life its boughs it spreads, which bear the fruit of certain knowledge of the Truth: it is not meet that Man should eat of this and know the origin of life and how the world was made, lest he his life may loose and find instead in entropy his final fate.

"These are the generations of the heavens and of the Earth when they were created, in the day that the Lord God made the Earth and the heavens, and every plant of the field before it was in the earth, and every herb of the field before it grew:" so speaks the Book. Plainly does it state, before creation of the world commenced, designs of all the creatures were complete, ready for the sowing of the seed from which would spring, each in its turn, the living creatures from the soil when watered by the gentle rain from clouds brought by the zephyr breeze.

No system can itself construct, because it cannot function till complete. Close at hand must lie materials, pre-formed enzymes too to join the parts. The labourer, he cannot dig the trench 'til he a shovel has: the maker of the tools must come before construction can commence, before the founds are dug. That is why each level in the hierarchy of hierarchies must feed on levels lower down; the products of these lower ranks they cannot use themselves, but from their flesh those higher up obtain the enzymes that they need to flourish and to grow. The DNA of each new species that's scattered in the earth must wait until there's nourishment enough of sort that it requires, dissolved in moisture of the soil. Bountiful is Nature: much more seed is sown than is needed each species to maintain, the surplus feeds the orders higher up; to feed upon one's own is not allowed.

Most simple were the creatures when at first the world was made, inside was little room to hide the nucleotide. Some of the first, they died, and from the protein residue the next in line could larger frames construct.

This process was repeated, up and up, until the series was completed: but the one above must still feed on the ones below, the hierarchy remains in place, apart from predators become redundant who are now extinct.

Perhaps the creatures of the Earth had best be classified by what they eat: it will have been observed, it will by now be seen, the higher is the intellect more varied is the diet that's required.

At commencement of creation, when were few the species started into growth, those that in the future would the staple diet be for them that occupy a higher place upon life's tree, proliferated much too fast; a check was needed till such time as higher orders settled in and took control of increase in the crops and herbivorous herds: to this end some predators were introduced, but not too many, for they are not food except for scavengers, hyenas and the vulture birds. The lions and wolves and bears that kept in bounds the populations of savannahs and the grassy pastures are they themselves in number much reduced, their place being taken by the rancher and the farmer who now control the quantity of cattle, and spray insecticides upon their crops that formerly the pests reduced; wild beasts that used to roam the lonely hills are rarely seen as cultivation spreads, their services no longer are required. This surely was the fate that did befall the dinosaurs and others of that ilk. Thus do some extinct become when redundant rendered by some species higher in that Pyramid of Life extending up until its peak is reached among the crags where eagles fly. Only meat these predators do eat, it gives them strength and a ferocious mien, but not much brain, lacking diet that the intellect requires. Look at that cat, see how it blankly stares, unflinchingly it meets one's gaze: behind those amber orbs there nothing lies, no hint of feeling in its eyes.

The living creatures thus a stairway form, each flight supported by the floor beneath: to reach the top the treads must each be trod, crushed beneath the weight of those who climb, its strength imparted to the one who would a little higher go: itself it cannot lift. Each step is bruised by climber's weight, its strength imparted to the one who climbs. The creatures of a baser sort must die to feed more complex ones, though nonetheless their numbers by prolific reproduction are maintained; abundance of their offspring's far in excess of that required for species to survive.

The first to be created of the creatures swarming over face of Earth, they are no more than air, fabricated from the gases and the water vapour that compose the atmosphere: very small they seem to be, but there's a limit to their smallness, because all atoms have a certain size; thus there is restriction of amount of mechanisms for the maintenance of life that in a cell may be contained - complexity must wait until sufficient size has been achieved, and many varied proteins produced by those that go before. It has been observed, it is the highest intellect that of most varied diet has the need, of which a goodly part should be of meat: it would appear the herbivores, although they have the size, are not given overmuch to contemplation, to ruminative thought.

Clearly now it surely can be seen, there's nothing made that isn't planned, conceived in its creator's mind before it is of substance made. Things organic, having been conceived, are then produced as plan drawn with assemblies of amino-acids, the nucleic acid code. It does not physically participate, this code, in assembling that of which it is the plan (he who builds with bricks does not cement his plan within the wall), being prevented by the presence of an atom, that of hydrogen (and hence 'de-oxy' designation) but is the template for a copy which then acts as catalyst, the labourer laying bricks; the code remains, its basic state unchanged, for ever and a day, unless on purpose it's destroyed by hand of Fate in those eternal fires that light the sky by day and night.

Before creation had begun the plans had taken shape; air and water first appeared, from which fluids can organics be prepared: the inert rocks as yet too hard, unable to react. The plan could not proceed until sufficient was the product of the corpses of primeval creatures, enzymes and co-enzymes to catalyse more complex cells. Thus stage by stage were made the living things to fill the Earth, each level gaining compounds, feeding on the one below. When plants appeared, their roots grew down into the soil, the debris from the rocks that frost had split and acid from the atmosphere had decomposed, sucking up solutions of the elements that were thus released. Then a greater range of creatures came to be, their DNA supplied with enzymes that they'd lacked before. This is how the hierarchy has grown, location in the pyramid of life decided by the type of food a creature needs if it's to live and thrive. This is why it seems that Nature is so cruel, why those above must kill and eat the ones below, but never those of equal rank: if the latter were consumed no profit would accrue. So it is that creatures cannot change their status, move up or down the scale, because their DNA, by which their identity's defined, could not cope with different food. A sideways move is all that they can make, facilitated by alleles, the better that they may survive: but this assumes they want to live, that they have a fear of death. This is the level where they will evolve, making variations that appear as species new.

The question next most vexed, it is of course the one of sex. It is a fact that androgines remain today among some lowly creatures of small size, and plants their dual sex do flaunt within their flowers, displaying organs brightly coloured of surpassing beauty in their form: all modesty they put aside. In this way is shown the method that's employed, hidden in hermaphrodites that have of animals the form, how it is that they can reproduce: it is the obvious way that they should replicate, but they are clones that are produced, identical to those from whom they come, and not some species new, which it seems is what by Nature is desired. Separation of the sexes surely comes at early stage, before the nucleus in a membrane is enclosed, so that parts can be exchanged between the cells. What then of Adam, did such man exist, or is he just a myth, a means of telling how life came to be to men and women still unversed in chemist's lore, lacking those long names that stem from greek in which professors seem to take perverse delight? The organs now are split, external where they once were hid, and this is why they must be kept from sight, as are all other parts that lie inside. Did not male and female live their separate lives from long before establishment of Homo S, although in potency he did exist?

No individual can there be until parental chromosomes have in the zygote paired, producing being quite unique that fills the cell, a creature whole and totally complete: no addition can be made, added on at later date.

The DNA its alleles has, that gives to each a character that's all its own by giving body and the mind an individual twist, an altered shape or colour or a way of thought, perception of the world about that is not with others shared: and yet the purpose of the gene's not changed, the organism's basically the same, but uniquely it's adapted to environment and circumstance, subjected to combined external force. If in creation all the organisms had evolved from one, each would self-sufficient be, and in itself produce the enzymes it required; all its need would then be energy, life sustained by power supplied from source outside; the less successful species then could fade away, their absence unobserved.

Well known it is in fact, that those most primitive, the single cells, still prosper and survive and play their part, participating in the lives of all the complex creatures which in more recent times have come the Earth to colonise, their enzymes still essential to the health of intellects and brains so far above their humble selves.

In the Introns does the spirit lie, the intellect that as it grows in substance gains the power to think and speak and dream of things it has not seen and comprehend the universals if to Man it does pertain; for lesser creatures it is instinct it supplies. In this intellect is also found the way that one should live, what are the things it is not good to do, and some slight consciousness of a creator and a grand design, and like a distant beacon barely seen, the knowledge of a resurrection leading to eternal life: impossible it seems these latter should exist, and yet this light impinges on the mind and does not go away, although at times obscured as if by mist.

One speaks of speaking from the heart when revealing feelings most sincere that seem as if they rose from somewhere deep inside; what is this heart that is the central part, that with emotion frankly speaks, and does not dare dissimulate but tells it as it is? It cannot be that heart that beats within the breast, that is but peristaltic pump that circulates the blood, that is itself affected by emotions emanating from elsewhere that set it racing, causing palpitation, or slow the beat when in despair. So what heart is it then that knows what's right and what is wrong, conscious of the way a man's supposed to live if he would the vicissitudes of life survive? No individual organ can be said to have such attributes, but is not each cell itself complete, with power to replicate, its image to repeat? And at its heart is found the nucleic code, in which is writ instructions that in life one may succeed. A heart in every part of human form, giving guidance through the day, and watching over hours of sleep. This is indeed the heart of which I speak.

Moses brought the Law engraved in stone, but from the start men should have known, the natural law was graven in the human heart. From those traces of the ancient races that remain in crumbling ruins of the long deserted cities it is plain that right and wrong were understood, long before were sent the prophets to remind of what is written on the soul in print too small to read.

From each zygote comes a creature new, ready to be moulded by the hardships and disasters of which this life's composed; this is how proceeds creation, construction of the parts that will comprise that perfect world that in far future lies. Death is not complete, the DNA remains from which will come the resurrection in its time, when undying atoms will their previous shape resume.

In every race on this Earth's face there will be found an inequality in level of the intellect, dependent on the genes most dominant in each. In every population, therefore, some there are who might as 'primitive' be classed, were it not the community at large lives in a manner more 'advanced', led on by intellectuals blessed with better brain. Those who have ability and will to learn can build on that which they've been taught or gleaned from study of the written word and observation of the world around; impression thus is given of a culture of a higher class, although the average brain remains the same: it is only tools that are improved, passed from hand to hand, and not the character of Man. With great regret it must be said, those lacking will or weak in head, inevitable it is that these are left behind in race for wealth, compelled to eke out life on margins of the less productive land: in time may new communities be formed, consisting in entirety of those possessed of low intelligence and lack of skills, existing in infertile lands as best they can. Lacking leadership and learning and knowledge of the finer points of farming, unaware of mineral riches lying deep beneath their feet, they soon become a primitive and backward race, as if they never had progressed from that primeval state existing at the founding of the world, when first did man emerge to take his place in biosphere among the beasts already there.

Varied diet does the human need, including meat of cattle and of sheep, if intellect its full potential shall achieve. When contact is renewed with people from more favoured areas of the world, colonists who come to seek the undeveloped wealth that lies beneath the feet, the precious stones, the lodes of gold, the waving wheat and runs for sheep, people of ability emerge among the backward tribes as do they share the better fare that adventurers from distant parts provide, seeking fortune from new lands not previously explored.

At the resurrection there will rise again the phenotype of each etched on the DNA just as it was at time of death: no need to start afresh, as was the case when first conceived in previous life, construction's now complete. How is it then that nucleic acid has survived when all around has rotted, returning to the inorganic state from which originally it came? In the thymine does the answer lie, whence comes the reason why 'deoxy' is included in the name: for this compound is securely tied, with not one but three of hydrogens and an extra one of carbon too; no space is left unoccupied in which a molecule could infiltrate and cause disintegration and subsequent decay.

Thus through life the DNA it does remain, alleles alone absorbing all the changes forced by circumstance and fickle chance, and most importantly by will of individual to which it does belong, who seeks to rise toward perfection, goal that's ever out of reach, or else goes with the flow, drawn down by gravity to regions subterranean down below. Untouched by death this is the phenotype that will inviolate remain.

The sexes kept apart ensures that chromosomes are stirred to make a mix that always is unique. Evolution's done its job, and here now stand the men and women who must seek a partner new if they would the race perpetuate. An androgine or two may have escaped the net and live here yet in regions far remote where rarely are they seen, but most must do the best they can by sharing life with whom they best relate: so mating is a matter of the intellect, a place where hearts and minds can meet, and briefly every night find hermaphroditic harmony again the whilst they soundly sleep.

Since the partners cannot match so very well, some make-believe is added to the mix: it is imagined that one's mate is more perfect than is really so, attached to dream of boy or girl for which is wished, a dream cemented by the passing years: reality is brushed aside, in marriage is life lived in an imagined bliss, becoming fact one would not wish to change, fulfilling that that has by Nature been designed, satisfying bonds of those atoms of which the hormones are composed, until severed at life's end when phenotypes are ready, each prepared to go its separate way when in eternity it is reborn.

Creation did not happen once, long ago in distant past: it happens all the time. Each day new people join the earthly throng who were not here the day before, and so it is with all the swarms of organisms everywhere. Each species breeds its like, and not one of another, and perhaps superior, sort; the genera are not related, connected only by the fact that some are food for others of a higher rank because they can supply the enzymes that the latter need, essential if they're going to thrive.

All of the most primeval living things, the unicells and even those that have no cell at all, remain alive and prosper still: among this crowd there must be found, if only one could see such objects tiny wee and very small, the very first, and then observe the means by which it is it comes to be.

In this way creation goes on all the time until there is enough, stored in immortal DNA, to furnish that new perfect world where life's eternal, the goal that's sought by one and all.

So much for past and present; what of the future, of the things to come? Not a lot there is that can be seen; what there is does not appear so very different from the present - this should not surprise, for basically the system must always be the same: ingestion of a fuel providing power, combustion to release the ATP, exhaustion of degraded products from the rear, a system of three cycles, not the usual four. The ground shall still be tilled, but in that future time by men and women of good will; the chosen few who have achieved a childlike innocence shall cultivate their plot, and world at last will peace enjoy. This at least is known, for reference has been made to drinking of the wine, the slopes of hills will still be covered by the vine for all to share who don't like beer.

In two dimensions do electronic systems deal, composed of printed circuits and transistors, passing news by radio waves or text that travels down a wire, or solving calculations too complex for one human brain, memorising all the things it's done today; information by the yard, scrolled on screen or printed out on paper ream by ream; but no substance is produced, just words and constant speech. Electronic systems only deal in objects insubstantial, words and sounds of other sorts, ideas and imagery that occupy the mind but cannot on their own cause motion of more solid sort: to take effect a human hand is interposed by means of touch or through mechanical device used as a tool.

To bring to life the living world all three dimensions must be used, not by some supernatural power (that would indeed be quite absurd) but by means of bio-chemistry, words written in the way the atoms coalesce, forming compounds of material mass in accordance with the natural laws of logic, animate, and possessed of power to self-perpetuate. By catalysis the elements of air and water that abound on every side combine, breathing life into an inorganic world composed of inert stone. Subtle is this DNA, acting in material way, words written in the nucleic bases that speak not to the immaterial soul but have themselves material presence, participating in creation of a product that is animate, possessed of life and ability itself to replicate.

The third and final phase. The first had seen the coming into being of the creatures of the biosphere, all in their ordered hierachal ranks in pyramidal shape, most stable form in which to build, in equilibrium is the weight of each. In second phase they multiply, enough to fill new Heaven and new Earth, and all the while they're hammered as it were by hardships at the hand of Fate, wrought as is the iron in smithy's forge until demands of specified design are met.

The third and lastly phase is quiet and peace: the hammer and the saw are put to rest, driven home are all the nails, the timbers have long since been cut to length: the pain and weariness, the loss of strength, all these are in the past. What then is there to come, what will the future be? It seems as if its manner will be much the same: the house and garden, field and forest, these are the things that shall remain, but in the absence of disaster, sadness and despair, and freedom from the yoke of guilt, reminder of those foolish acts and thoughtless words that formerly one spoke, the guilelessness of childhood now master of the mind. No detail can there yet be seen, all surmise is in vain; such things would not be good to know, but in this life of second phase are glimpses given of perfection, peerless days, enchanted nights, which are the good that should be sought in face of evil that's by atoms wrought.

Many mysteries hid in Handbook did the Reverend Edward bring to light as he aided Boss of BioMech to comprehend the content of the sacred text. The meaning of that creature Pan that Ezekial does describe in detail from his opening verse is now revealed, model of the system in which have been arranged the airborne avians and the earth-bound beasts of field.

Ezekiel's Book, it opens not with threats against a stubborn and rebellious race; instead it is a vision strange of satyrs flying back and forth through space, composites made up of all the types of beast, commencing at the feet with cloven hoof, and at the head the face of Man. In between, the ox and then predacious lion, and eagle representing realm of birds. Who are they, then, these compound creatures seen by seer? It seems they represent the classes that in the pyramid of life exist, sorted by the food they eat; and are they not the mythic Pan who on his pipes plays haunting tune at break of day for those who have the ear to hear at sunrise his unearthly air?

Pan a satyr is. No one now has seen the like, and yet it seems that in the past the satyrs weren't so rare; without comment does Isaiah write of scenes of desolation, tracts of land that briars overrun and thorns and thistles join with drought, a desert where dwell doleful creatures, owls and moles and bats, and the satyrs dance. Did the latter in their lives a purpose serve for which no longer is there need, did they become redundant like the dodo and the dinosaur and disappear like them and many more who ceased to be of further use? But Pan was not of these, a mythic creature giving clue to structure of the hierarchy of life seen only in his vision by the seer and in the minds of unsophisticated folk or those who on occasion may the voice of Nature hear.

The Reverend Edward and the Boss had gone too far, they'd tampered with the Tree of Life, not thinking what they did: forbidden fruit indeed it was that they had picked, although it was with good intent; therefore with their lives they did not have to pay, permitted to attain old age, and Redfire too recovered from despondent depths to which he had been dragged. He has in holy orders been ordained, a monk in monastry he's now become. By prayer and fasting he has conquered lasting dread and fear he had of atoms rampant in his head that if they could would drive him mad; but reduced to rubble was the lab, and thorns and thistles thrive where once professors toiled, and cockatrice the only sign of moving life. Was it justified, the act of Church of Human Rights, were they the tool the Fates employed to end the work on Babel's Tower? Poor Sam, he did not know which way to go, pulled apart by faiths on contrary courses: should increased knowledge always be one's aim, or are there things that should be left alone, lest atoms be disturbed, given freedom to perform the evil that in their nature dwells, creating proteins whose malignant motives aren't benign?

The Handbook is intended as a guide for all who traverse on this earthly road, the way that leads from childhood to old age and ultimate demise. Alas, so much is hid in unintelligibility of phrase, the odd distorted sentences of which the verses are comprised - nor sage nor common man the signpost can decode, decipher name of avenue or road on which he should proceed: how can a man the proper route decide? Almost it seems as if it were intended to mislead, some times I wonder why.

www.ingramcontent.com/pod-product-compliance
Ingram Content Group UK Ltd.
Pitfield, Milton Keynes, MK11 3LW, UK
UKHW041946190726
13854UKWH00004B/1825

9 781409 201670